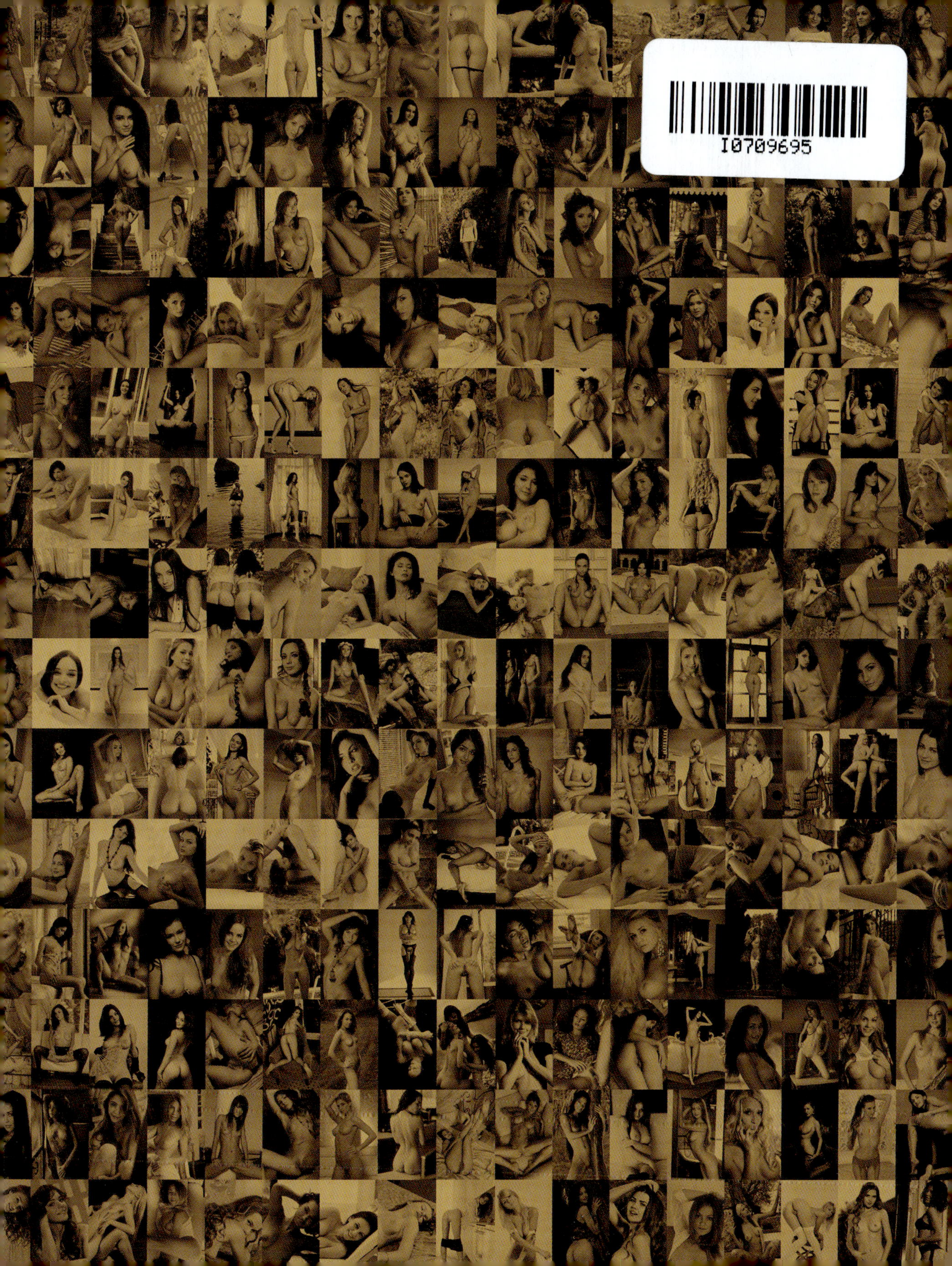

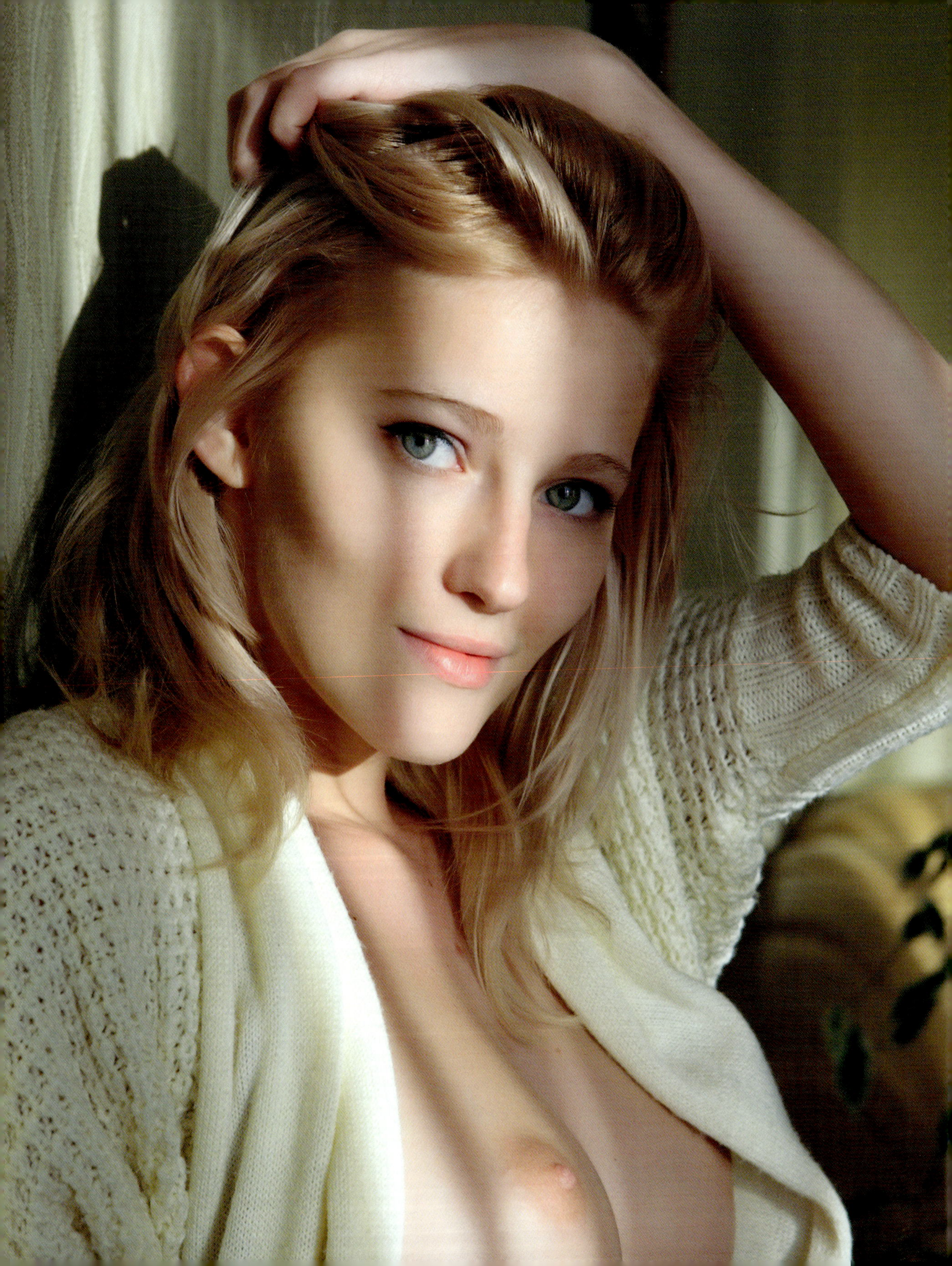

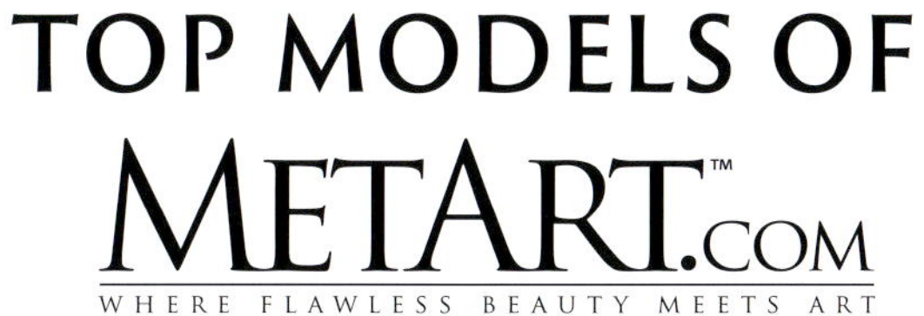

MILA I

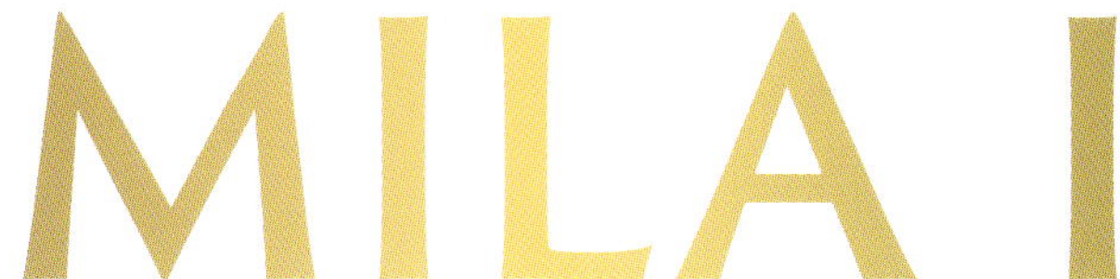

COLLECTED AND EDITED BY ISABELLA CATALINA

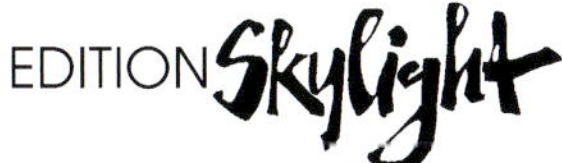

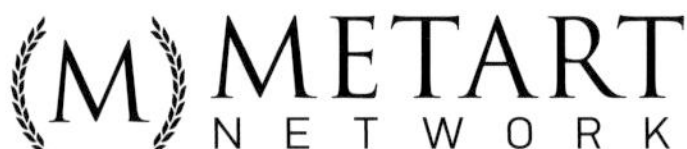

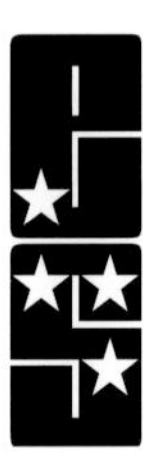

First edition 2024
Copyright © 2024 by Edition Skylight

EDITION SKYLIGHT
Rosengartenstrasse 13B
CH-8608 Bubikon / Zürich
Switzerland
info@edition-skylight.com
www.edition-skylight.com

ISBN 978-3-03766-703-3

Bibliographic information published by Die Deutsche Bibliothek
Die Deutsche Bibliothek lists this publication in the
Deutsche Nationalbibliografie; detailed bibliographic data
are available in the Internet at http://dnb.ddb.de.

Printed in Bosnia and Herzogovina

Mila attends a medical college and wants to be a nurse

Charming, quirky and effortlessly sexy, Ukrainian blonde Mila I would just be the ideal night nurse for all of us. The tall, slender sweetheart is on many members' all-time favorites list, and it's easy to see why. Blue-eyed beauty Mila made her debut at the age of 18 in "Atenian" by Goncharov. She has appeared on several other sites in the MetArt Network: Erotic Beauty, Errotica Archives, Rylsky Art, Eternal Desire, and Domai and Goddess Nudes (as Kissa). Mila's appeal can be attributed not just to her athletic good looks – long legs, incredible breasts, butterfly-winged pussy, peachy ass, and pretty face – but also to the vibrant personality that radiates out from her pictures. She is 170 cm tall with just 52 kg. From the cute sun tattoo around her navel to the many candid shots of her playing the fool, everything about this irresistible girl suggests she is a whole lot of fun to be around. No wonder the many adoring epithets bestowed upon her by members include not just "goddess" but "to marry immediately." Mila is eye candy and just pure perfection. Discover the essence of beauty through the lens of Metart, an innovator in artistic nude photography and film for over two decades. With a passion for showcasing the world's most beautiful women, Metart presents a collection of enchanting erotic models who radiate natural allure. Witness the unveiling of their beauty as they bare their souls before the camera. Immerse yourself in the world's premier destination for erotic photography and film at www.Metart.com.

Charmant, eigenwillig und mühelos sexy, die ukrainische Blondine Mila wäre einfach die ideale Nachtschwester für uns alle. Sie besucht nämlich ein medizinisches College und möchte Krankenschwester werden. Die große, schlanke Schönheit steht auf der Liste der Allzeit-Favoriten vieler Metart-Mitglieder, und es ist leicht zu verstehen, warum. Die blauäugige Schönheit Mila debütierte im Alter von 18 Jahren in "Atenian" von Goncharov. Sie ist auf mehreren anderen Seiten des MetArt-Netzwerks erschienen: Erotic Beauty, Errotica Archives, Rylsky Art, Eternal Desire, und Domai und Goddess Nudes (als Kissa). Mila's Anziehungskraft ist nicht nur auf ihr athletisches gutes Aussehen zurückzuführen – lange Beine, unglaubliche, vorwitzige Brüste, eine appetitliche Schmetterlingsflügel-Vagina, pfirsichfarbener Po und hübsches Gesicht – sondern auch auf die lebhafte Persönlichkeit, die sie in ihren Bildern ausstrahlt. Sie ist 170 cm groß und wiegt nur 52 kg. Vom niedlichen Sonnentattoo um ihren Nabel bis zu den vielen ungezwungenen Aufnahmen, in denen sie den Clown spielt, alles an diesem unwiderstehlichen Mädchen lässt vermuten, dass sie eine Menge Spaß macht. Kein Wunder, dass die vielen Kommentare, die ihr von Mitgliedern verliehen werden, nicht nur „Göttin", sondern auch „sofort heiraten" umfassen. Mila ist Augenweide und pure Perfektion. Wie definieren Sie Schönheit? Mit dieser Frage beschäftigt sich Metart seit zwanzig Jahren. Als weltweit führendes Unternehmen im Bereich der künstlerischen Aktfotografie und des Films hat es sich Metart zur Aufgabe gemacht, die bezauberndsten Mädchen zu präsentieren, die unseren Planeten zieren, wobei viele von ihnen sich zum ersten Mal vor der Kamera ausziehen. Besuchen Sie noch heute www.Metart.com und erlangen Sie Zutritt zum grössten Erotik-Portal der Welt.

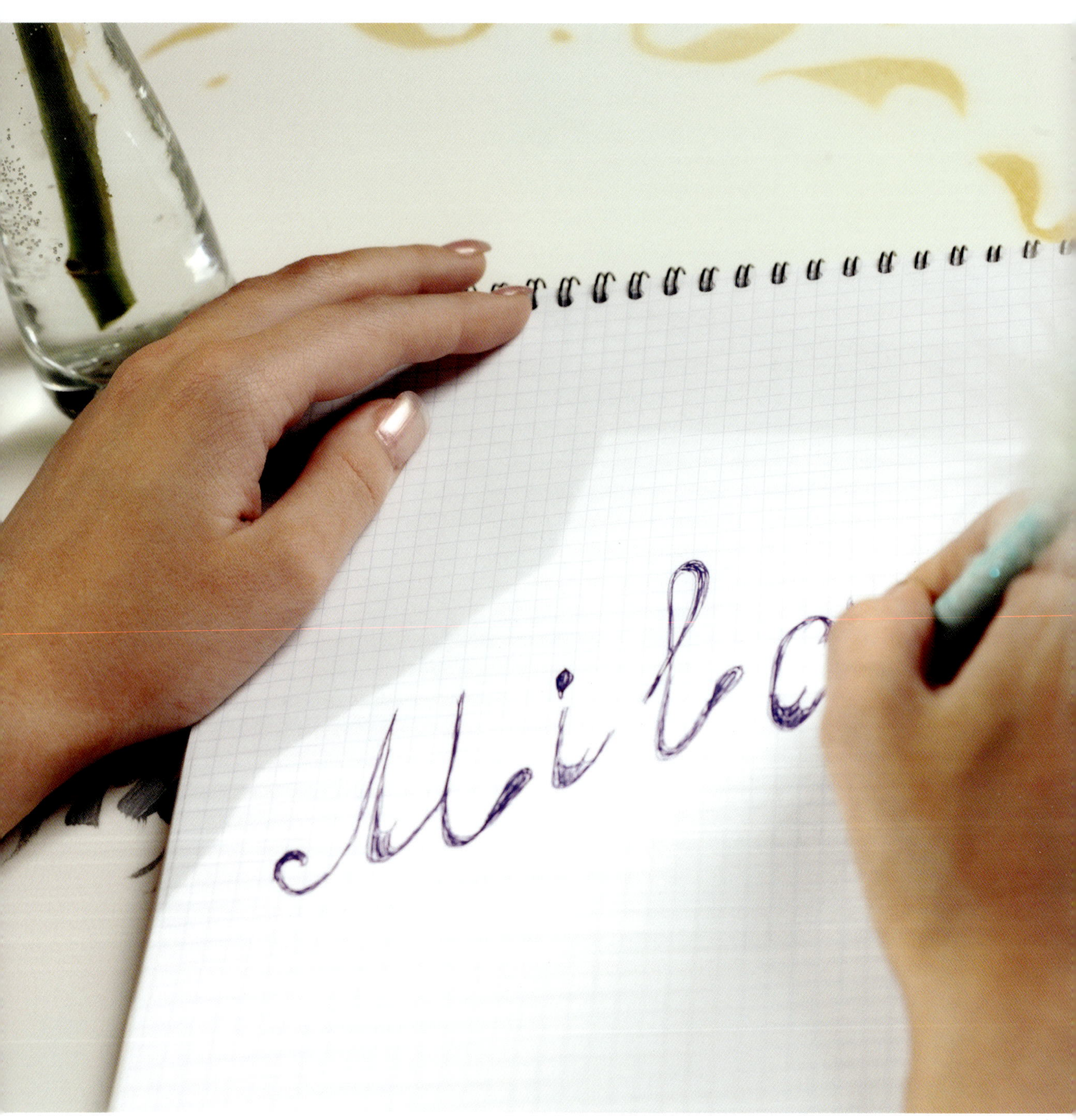

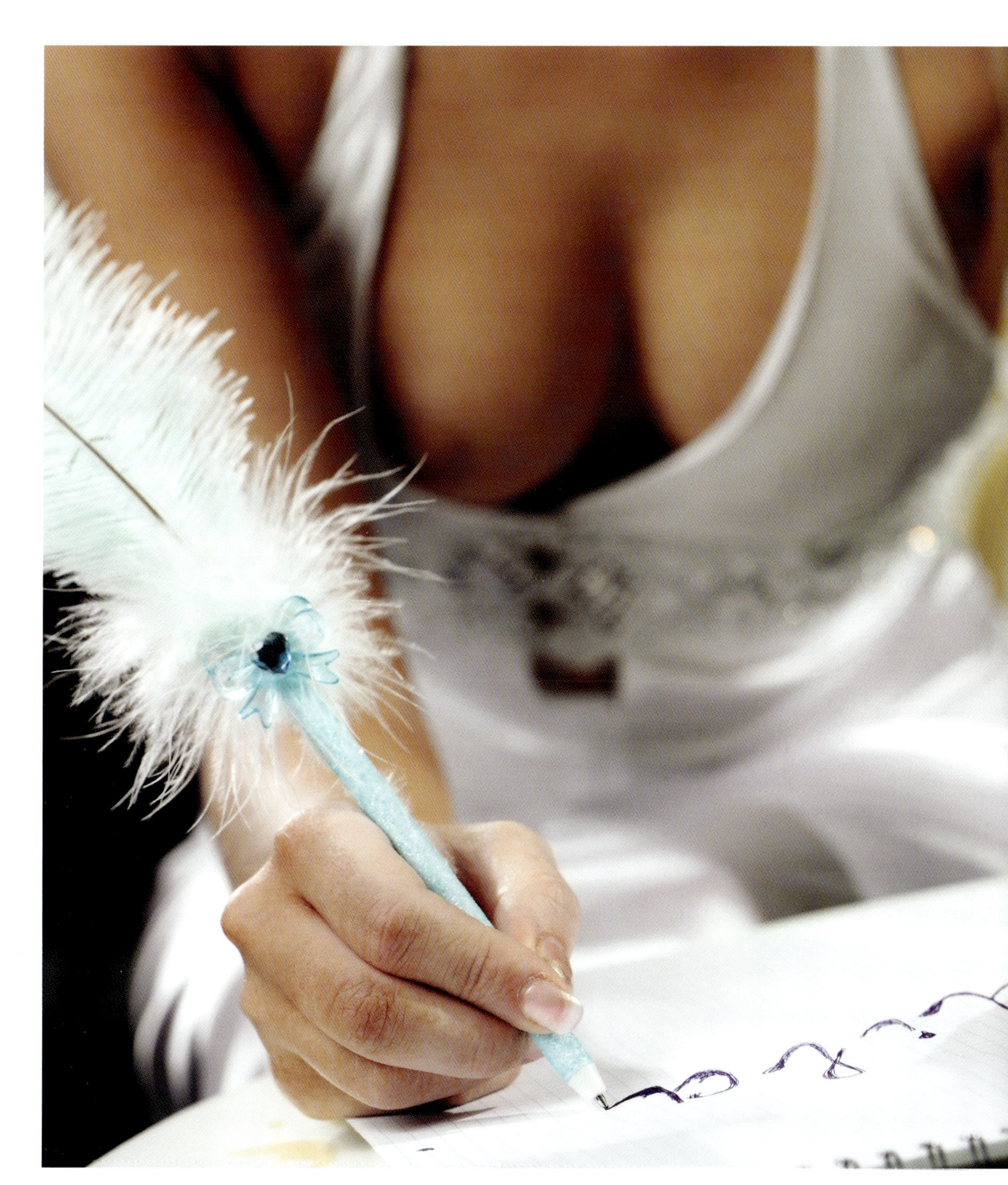

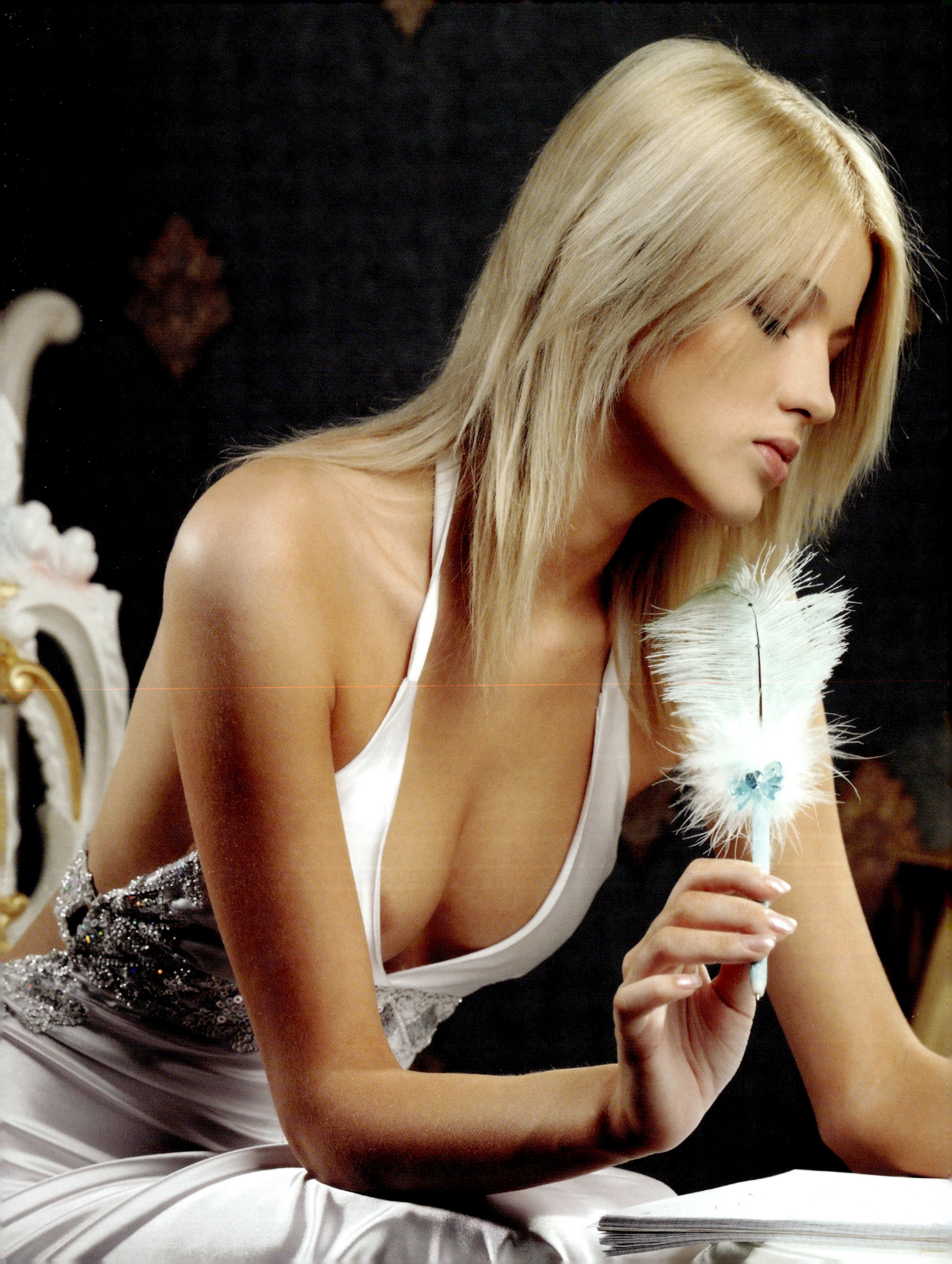

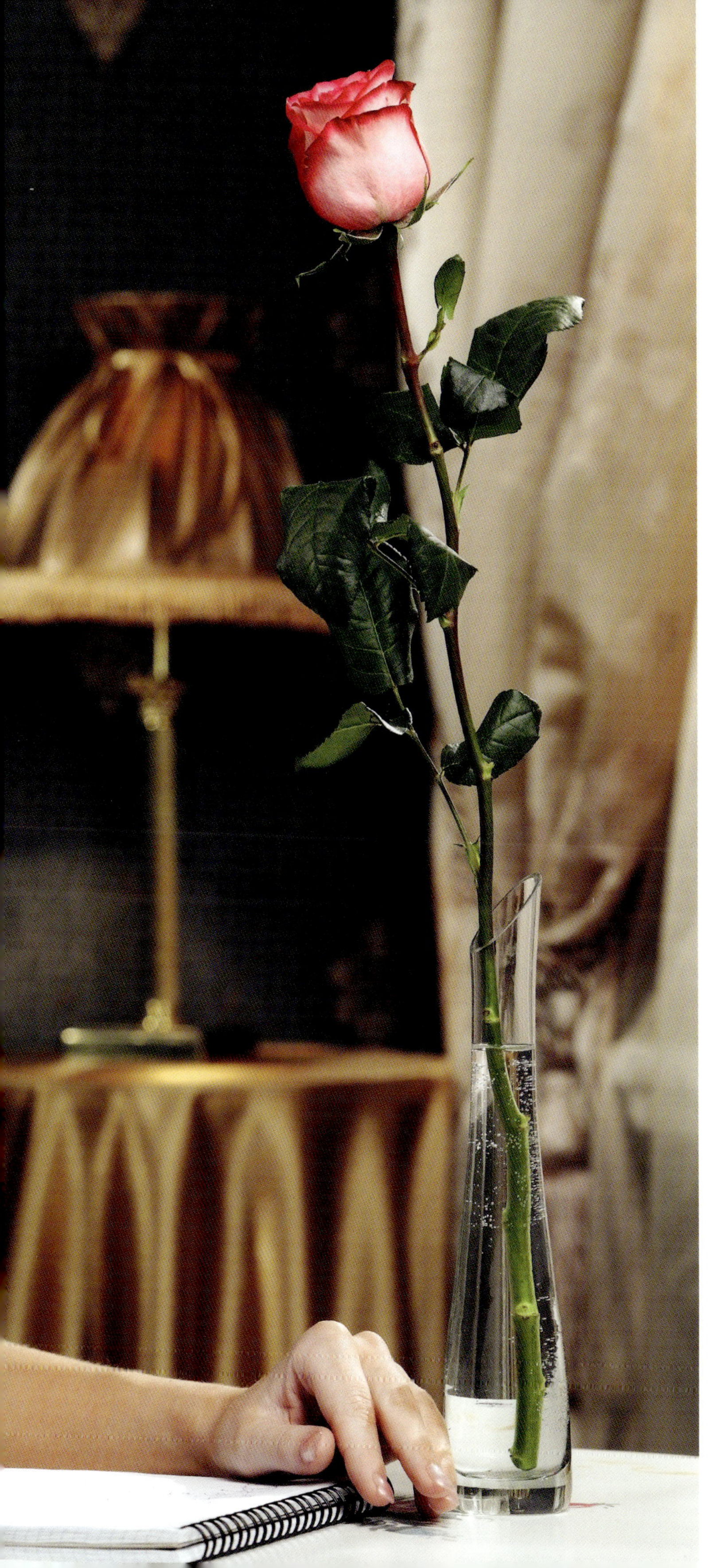

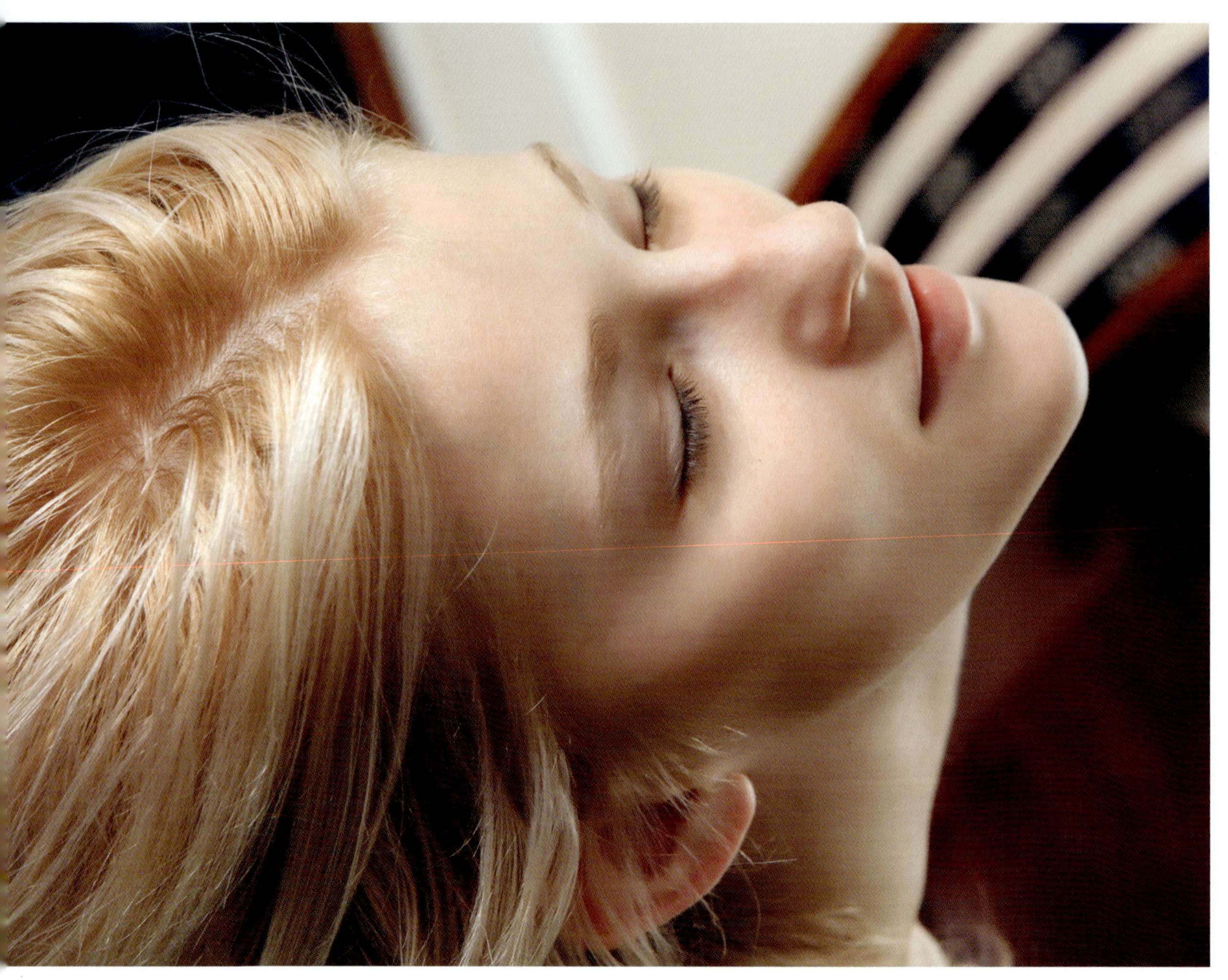

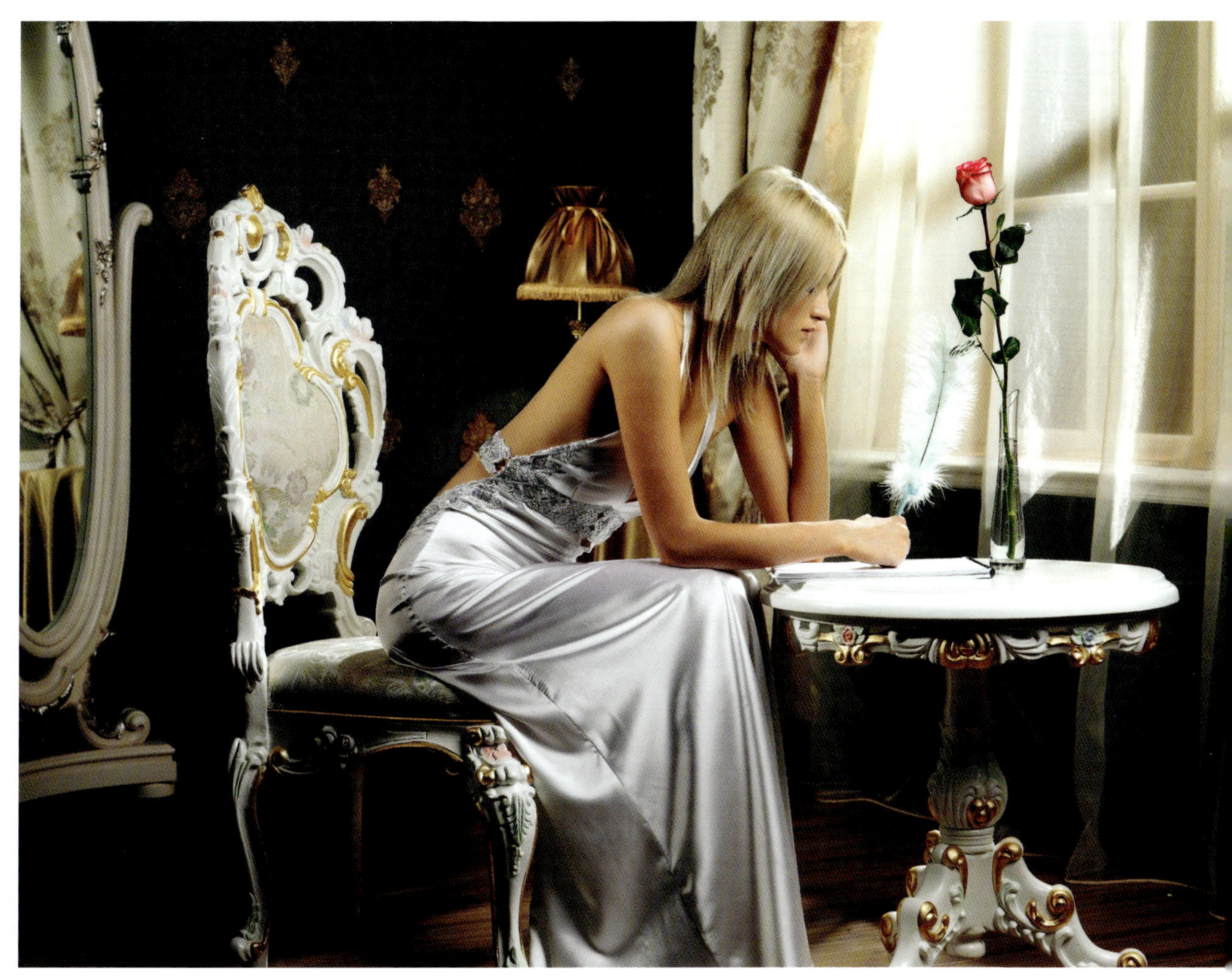

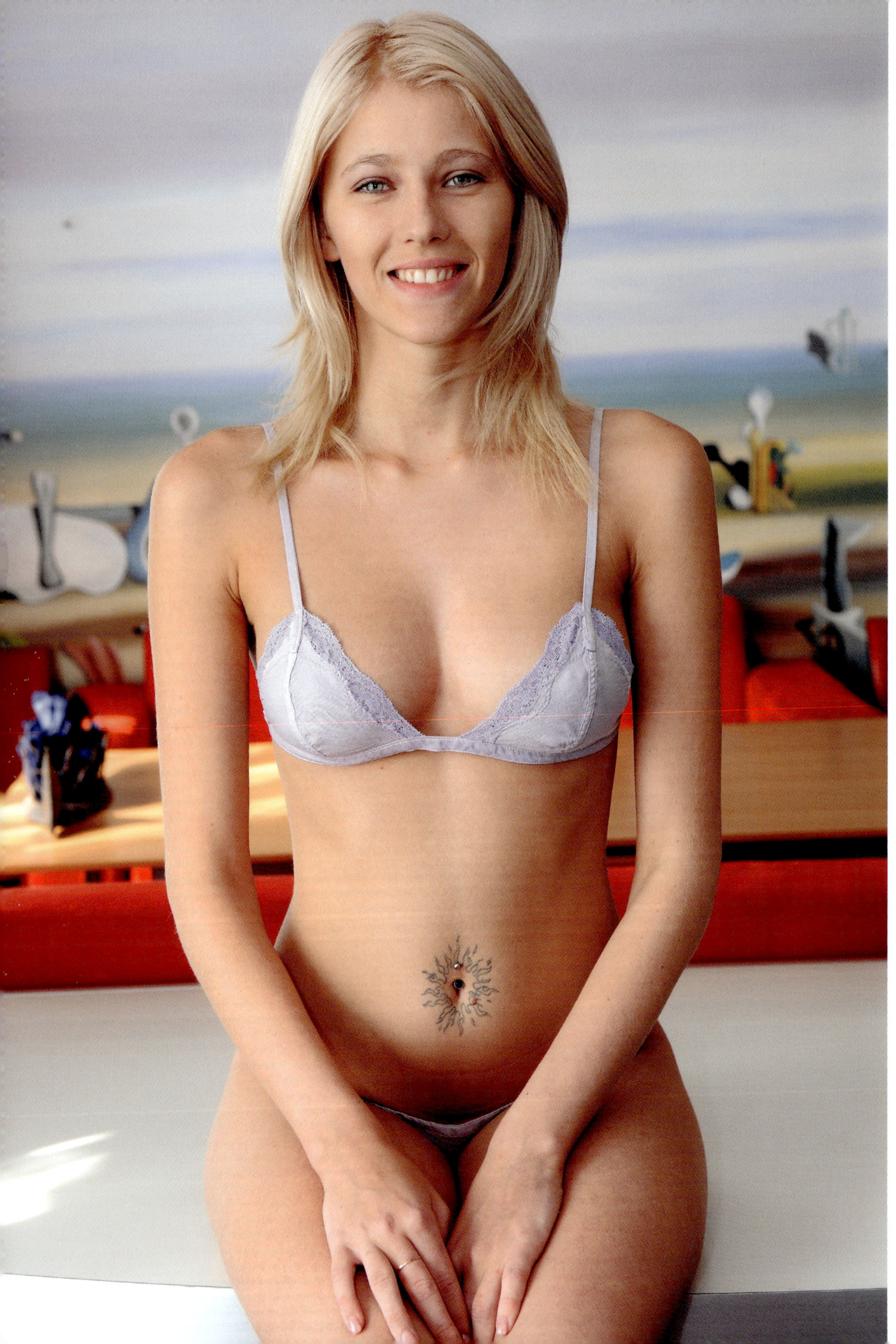

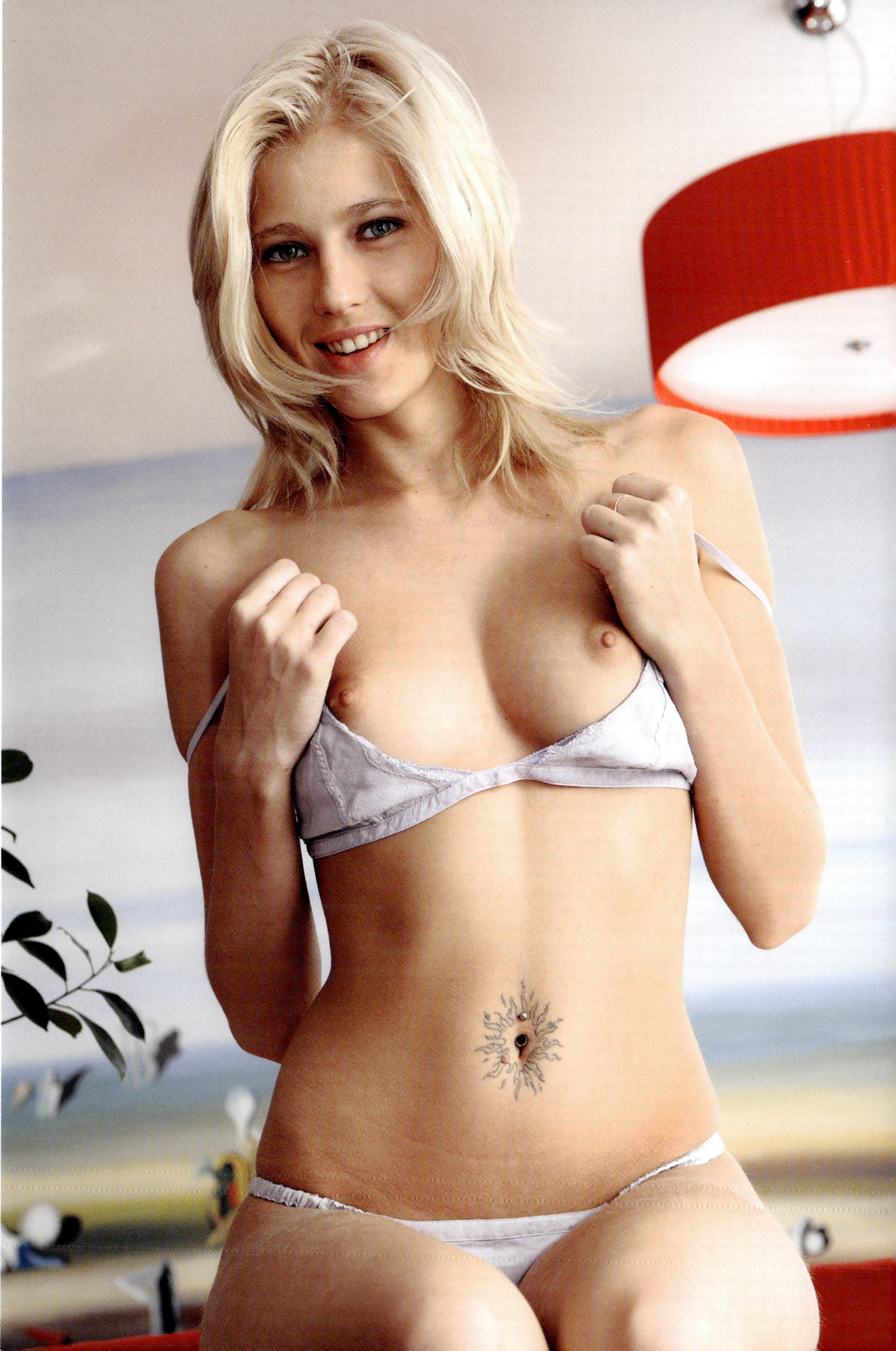

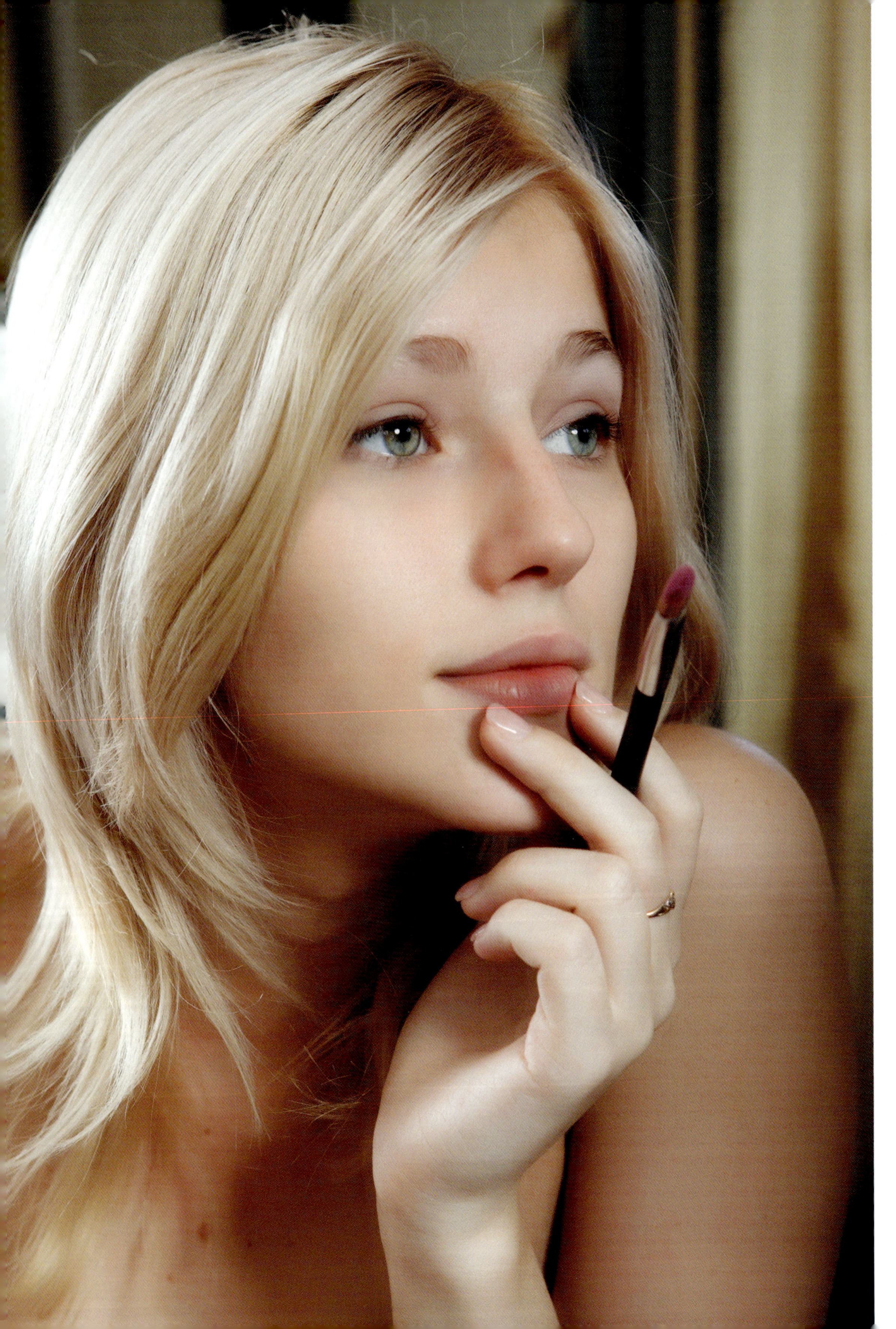

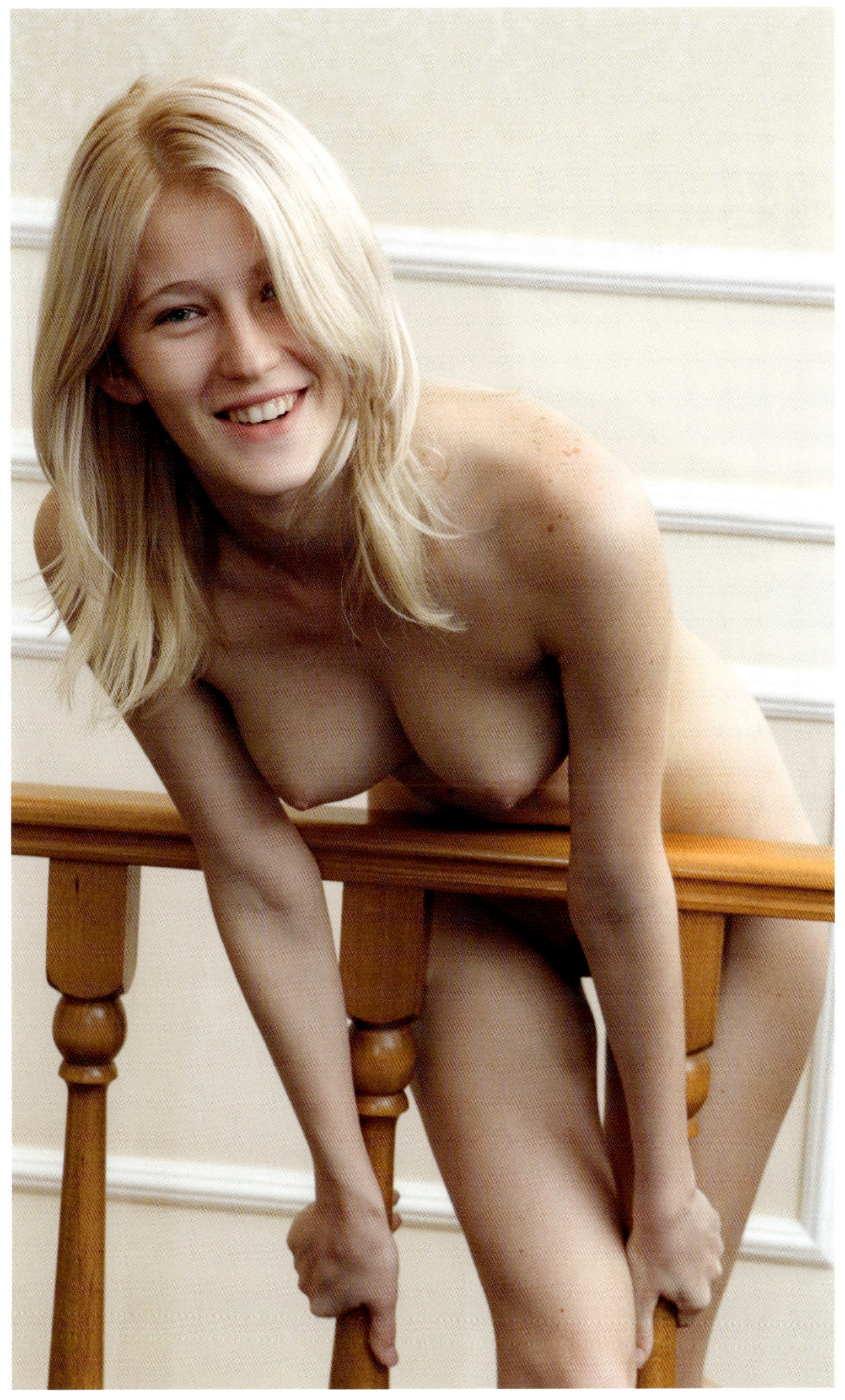

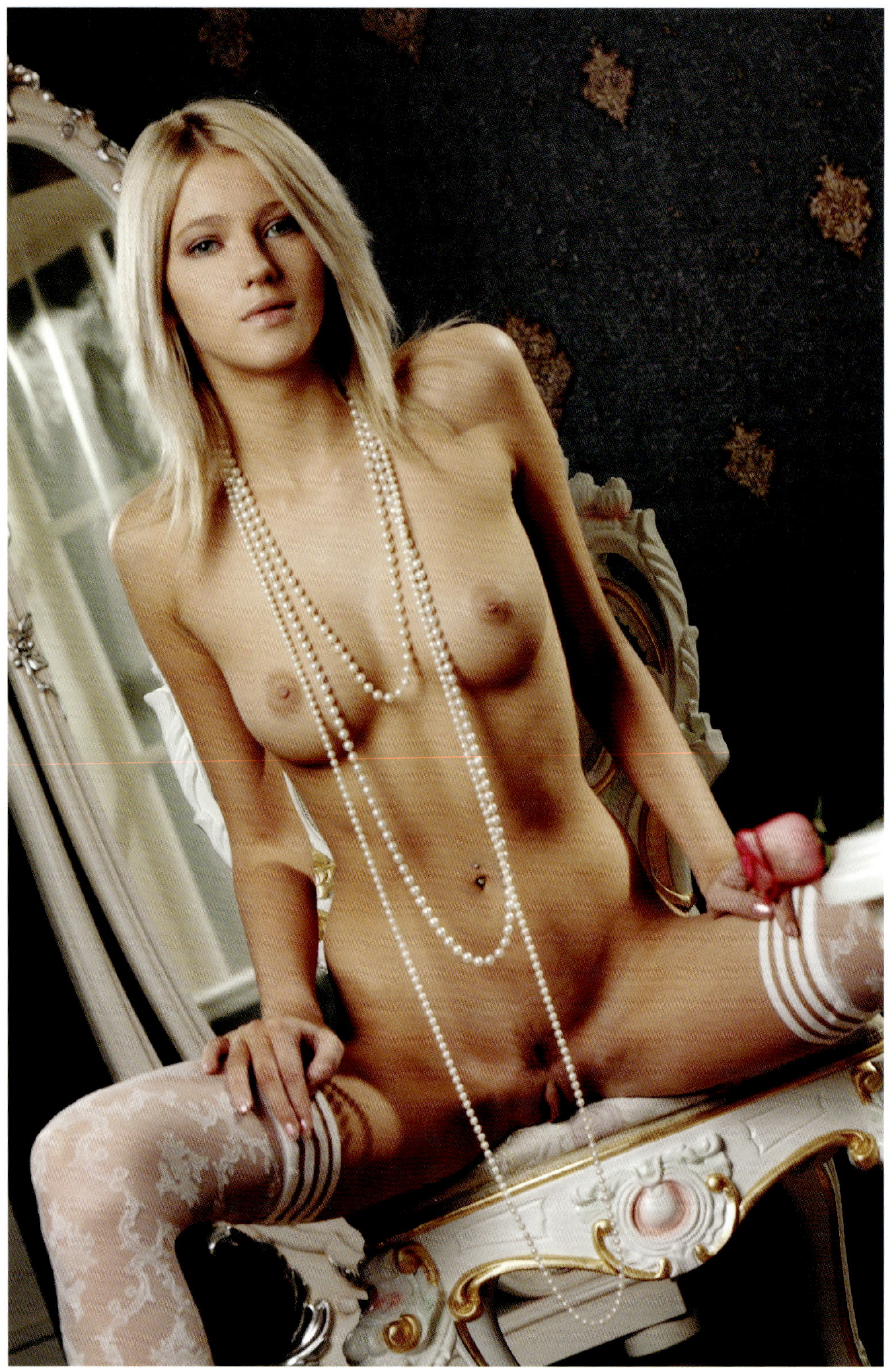

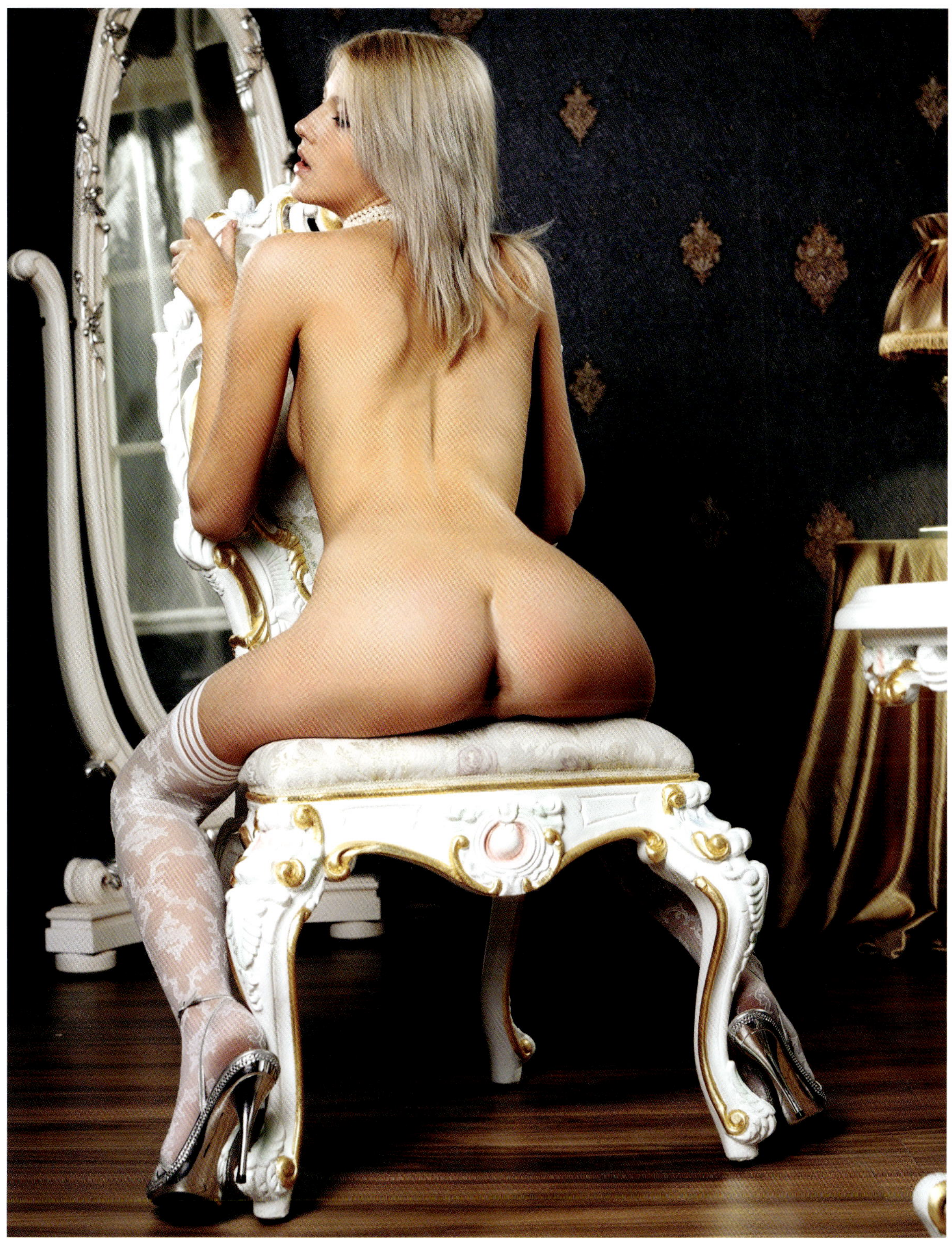

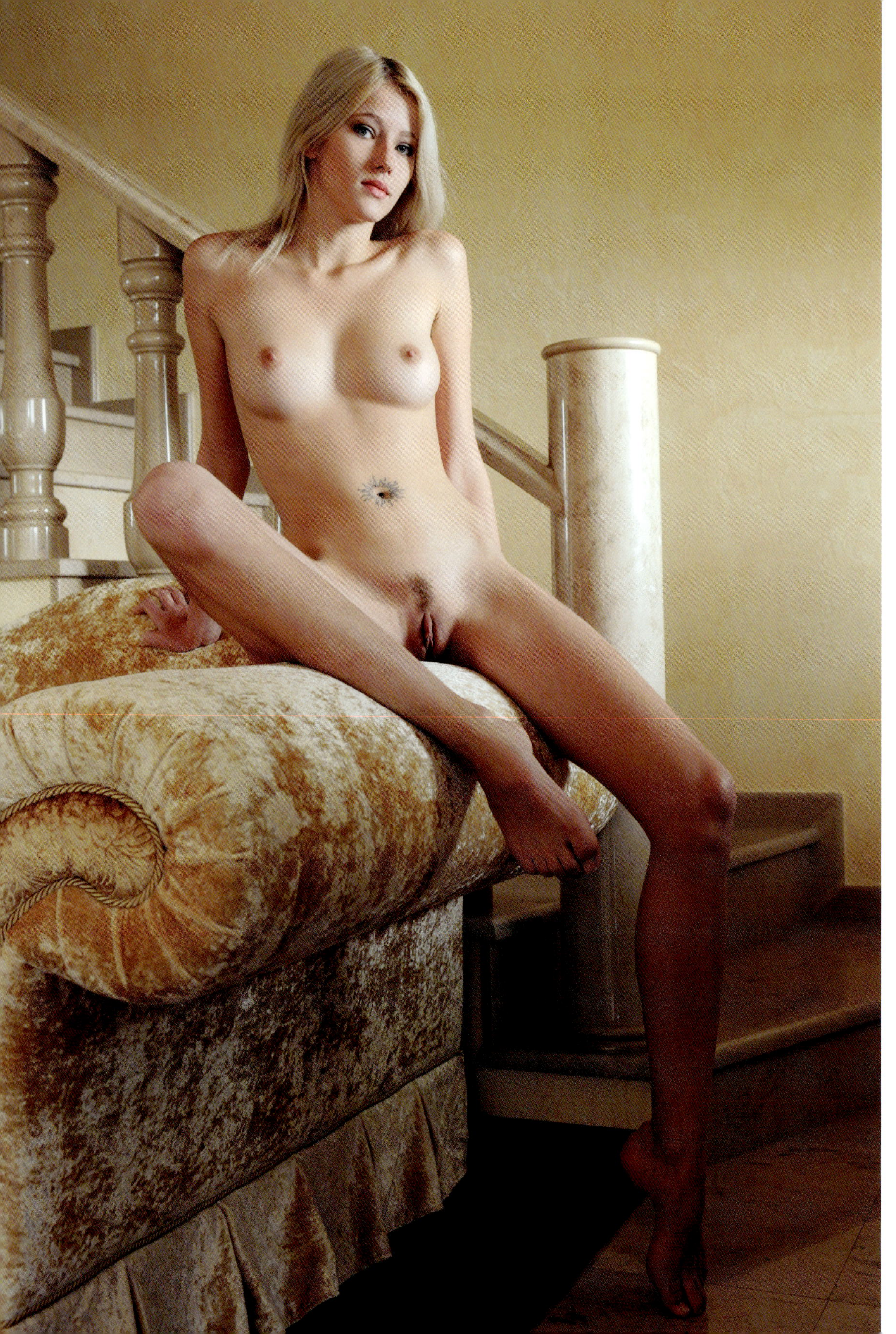

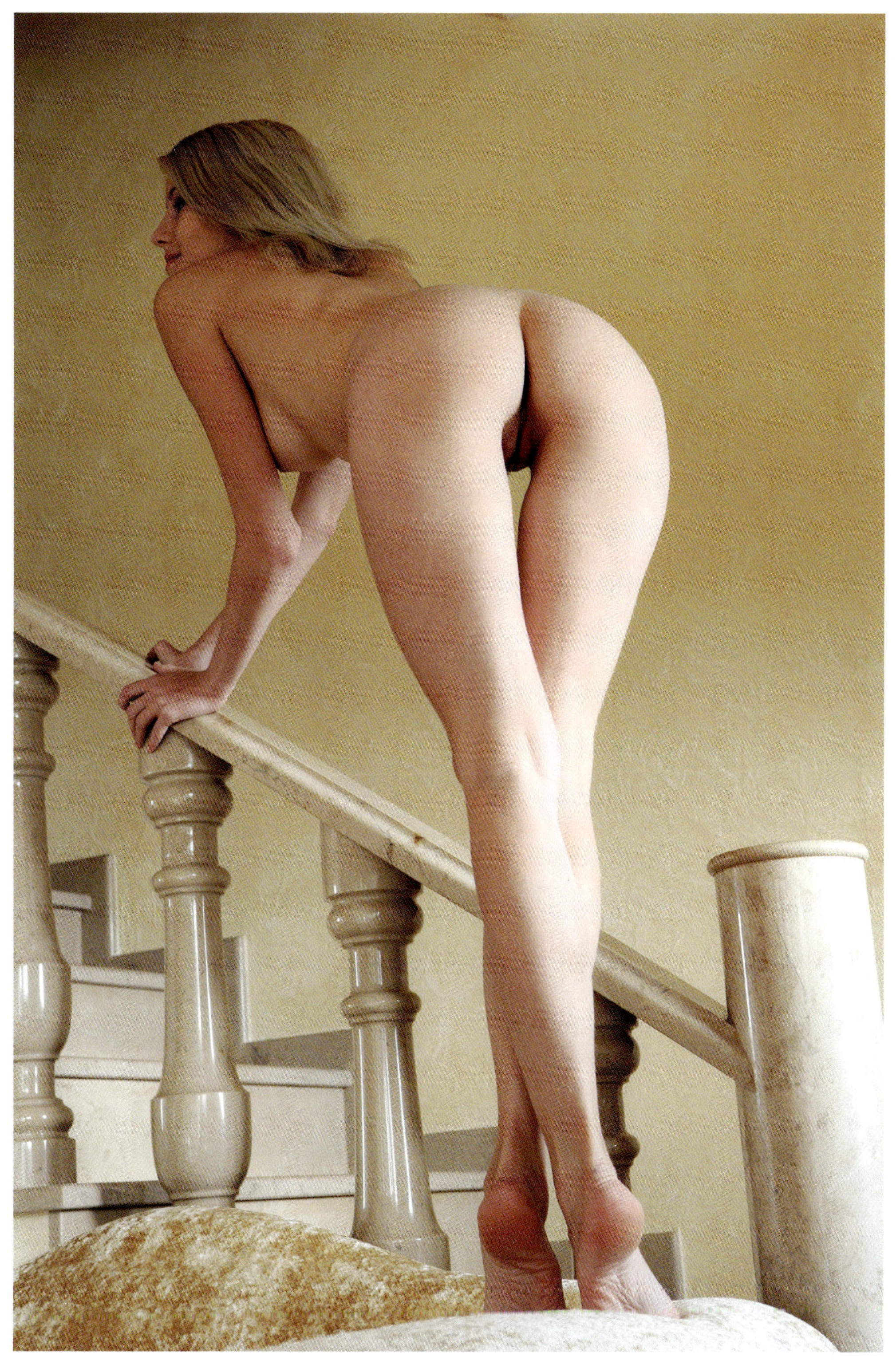

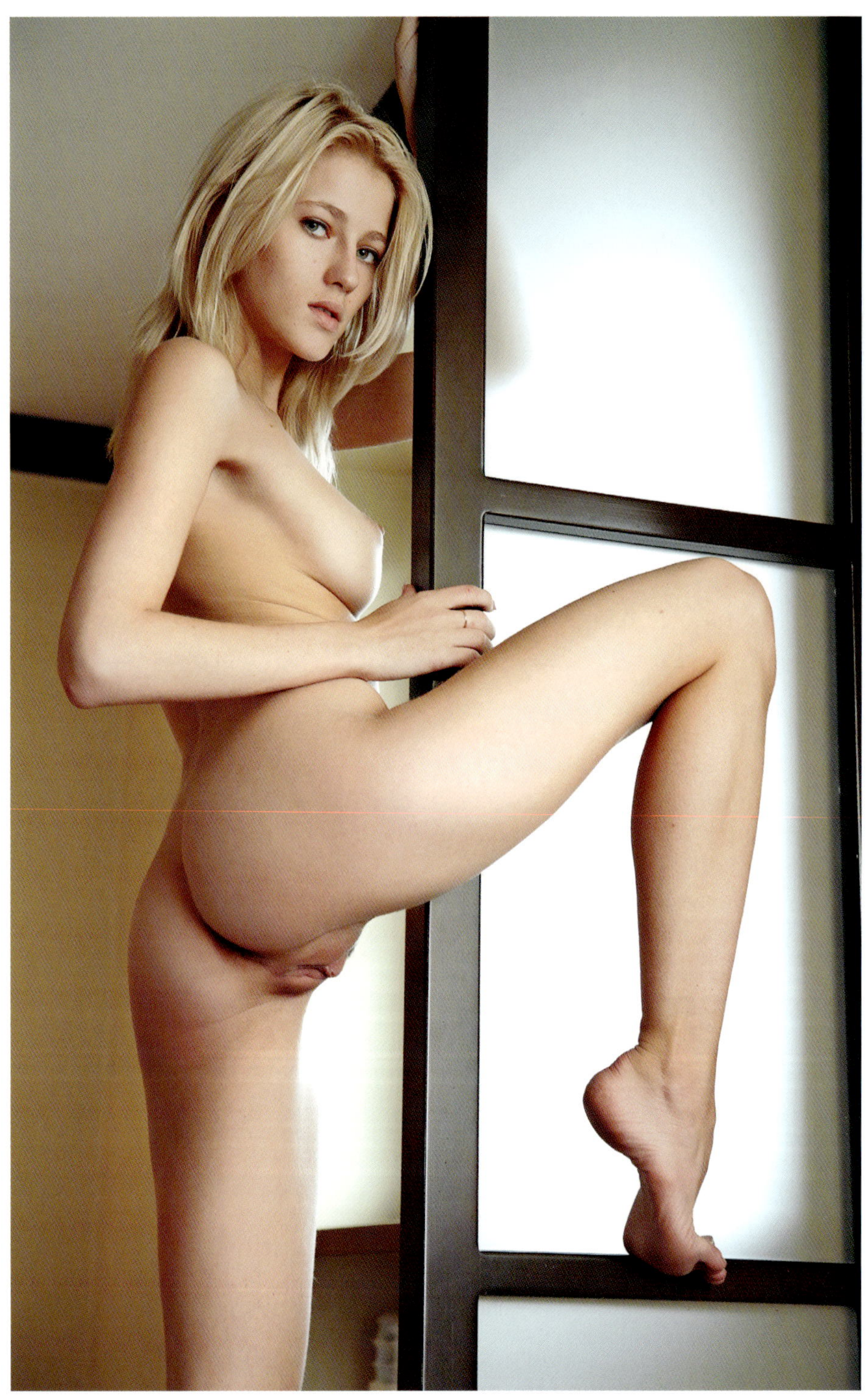

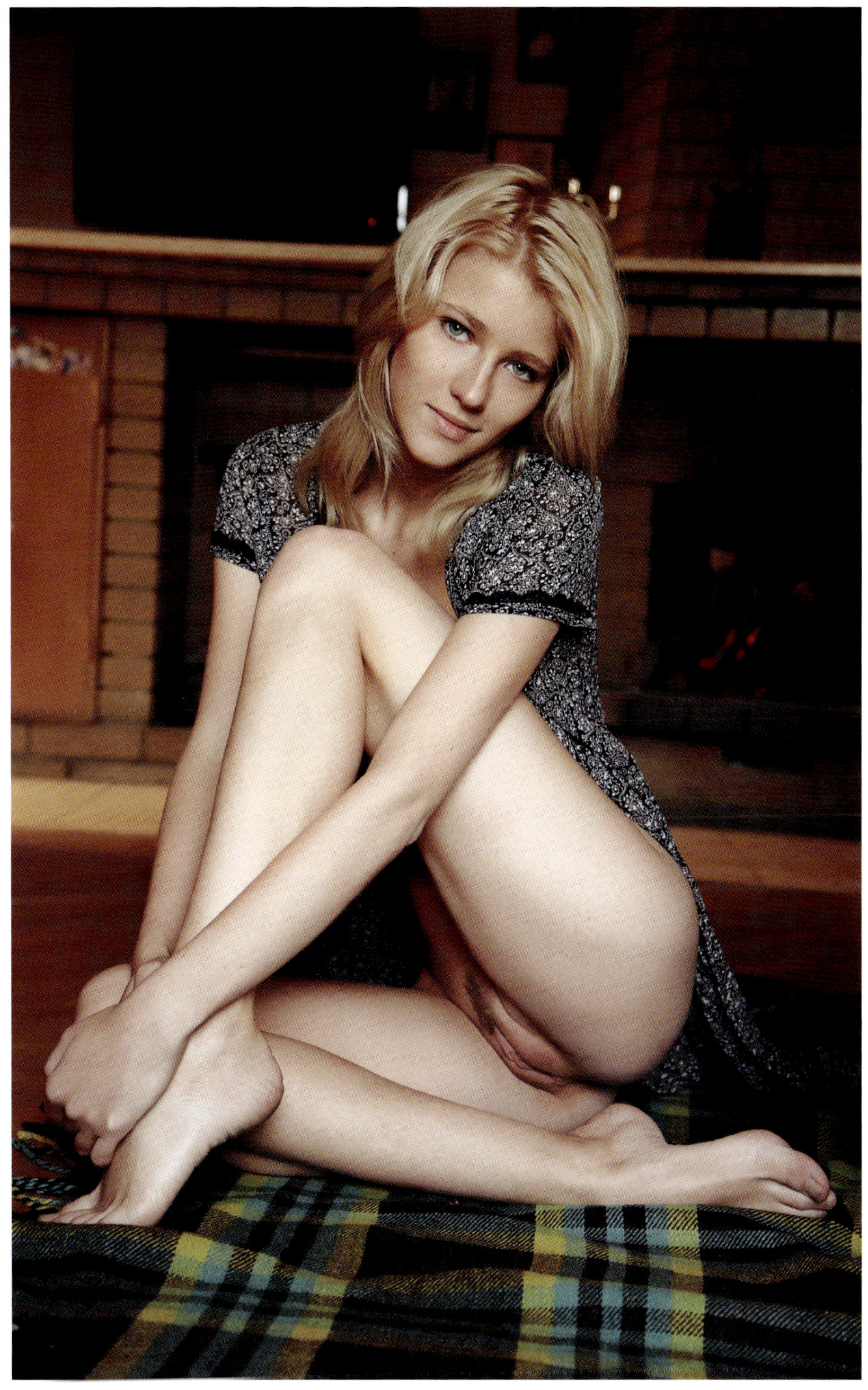

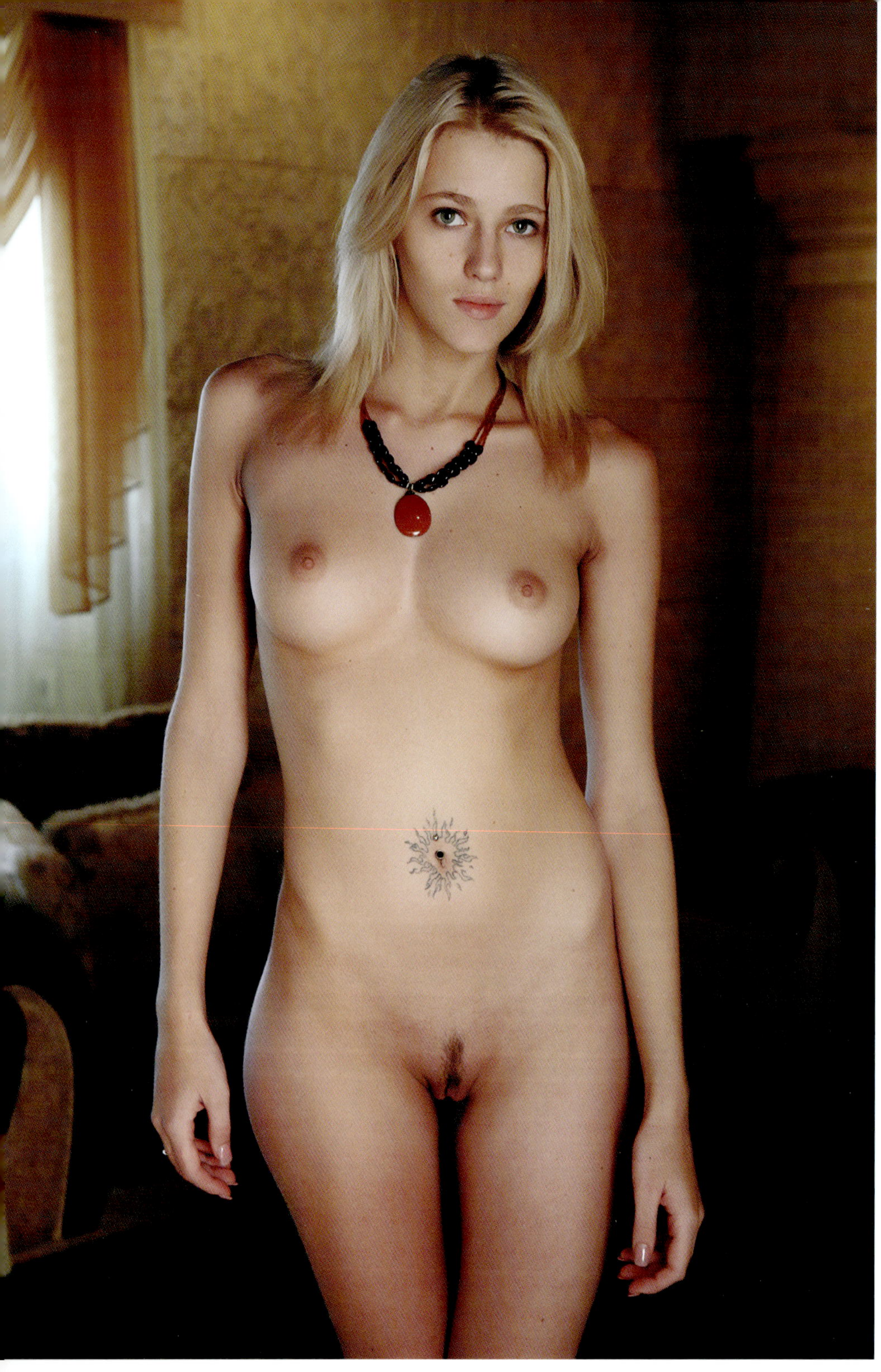

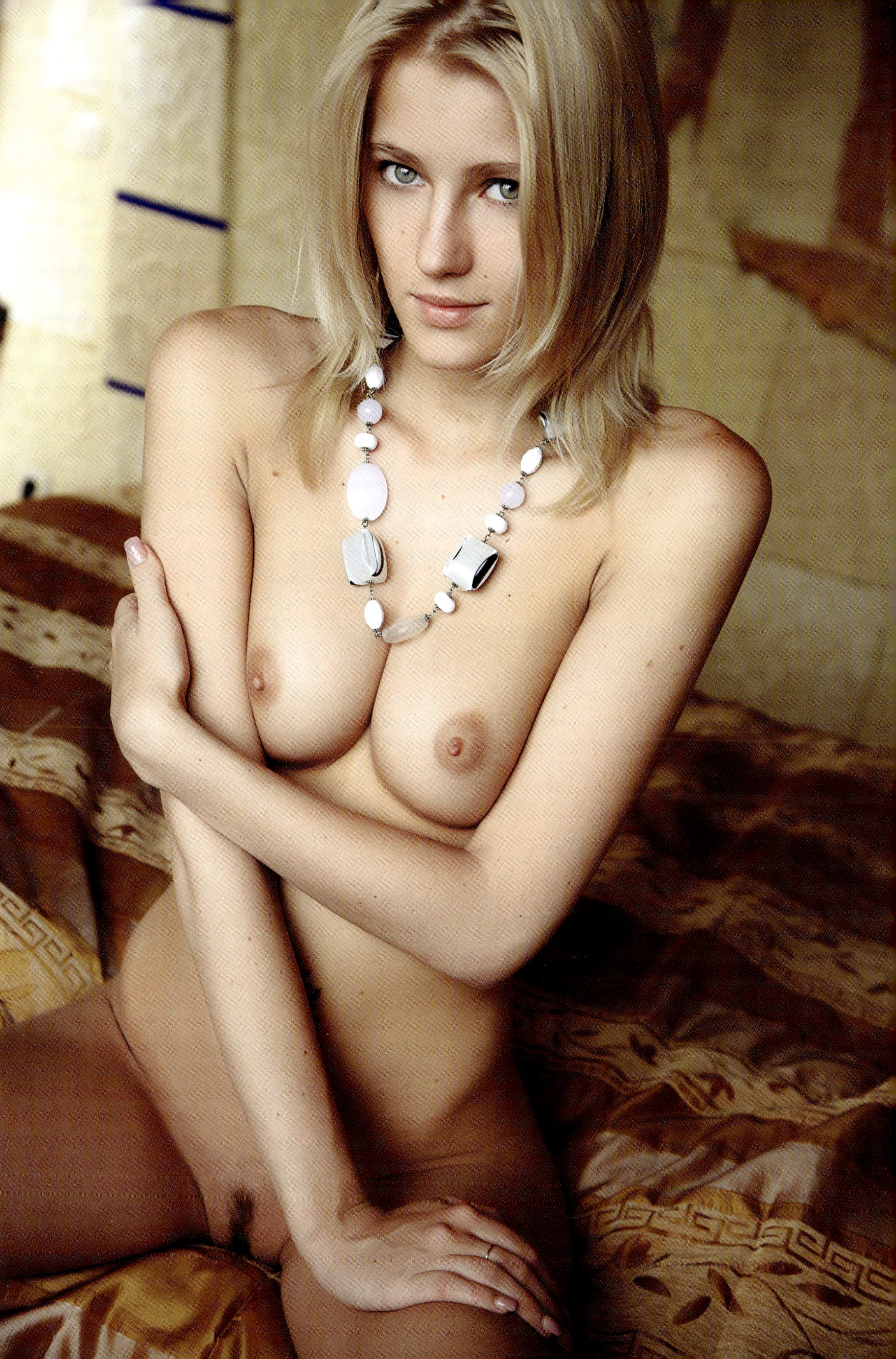

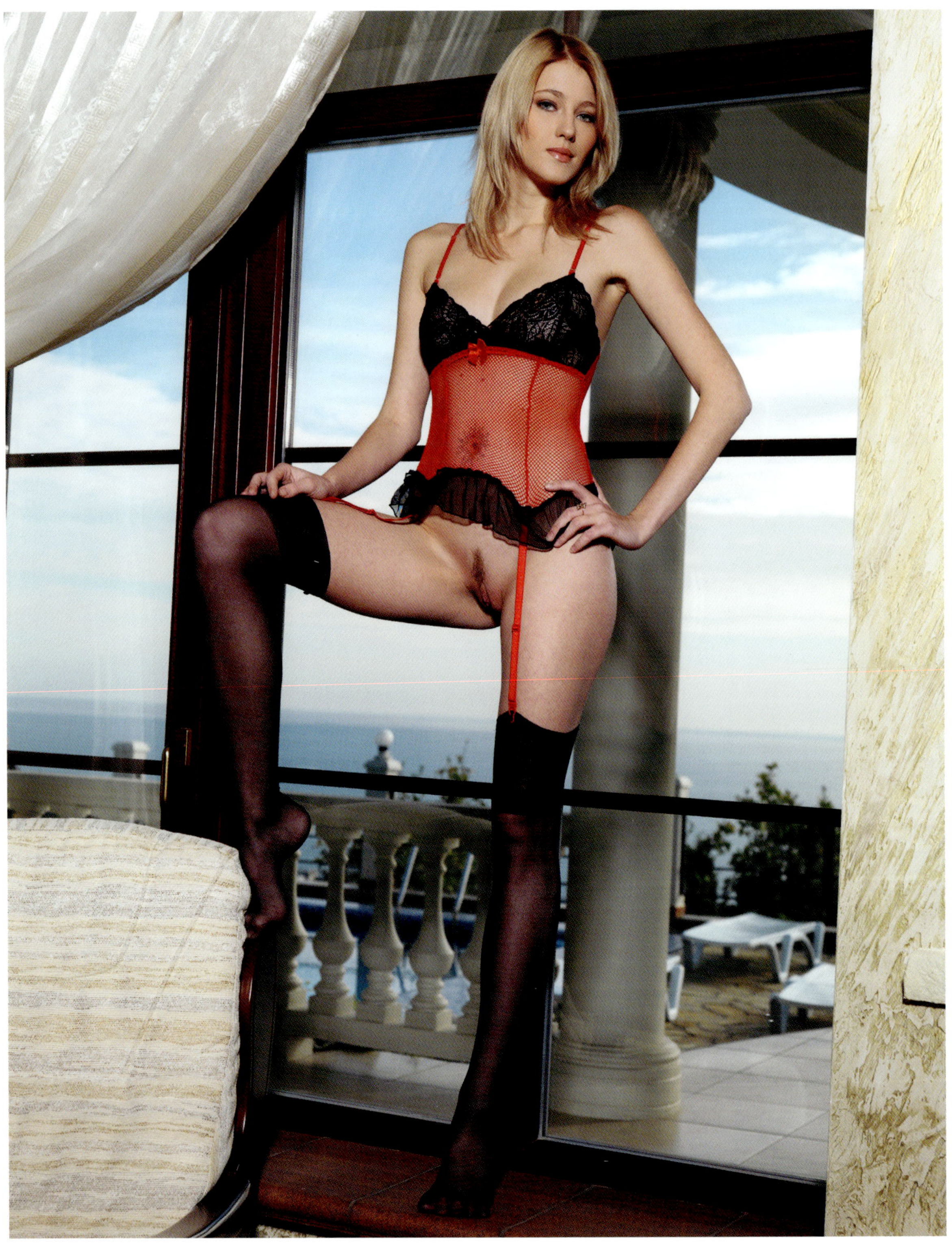

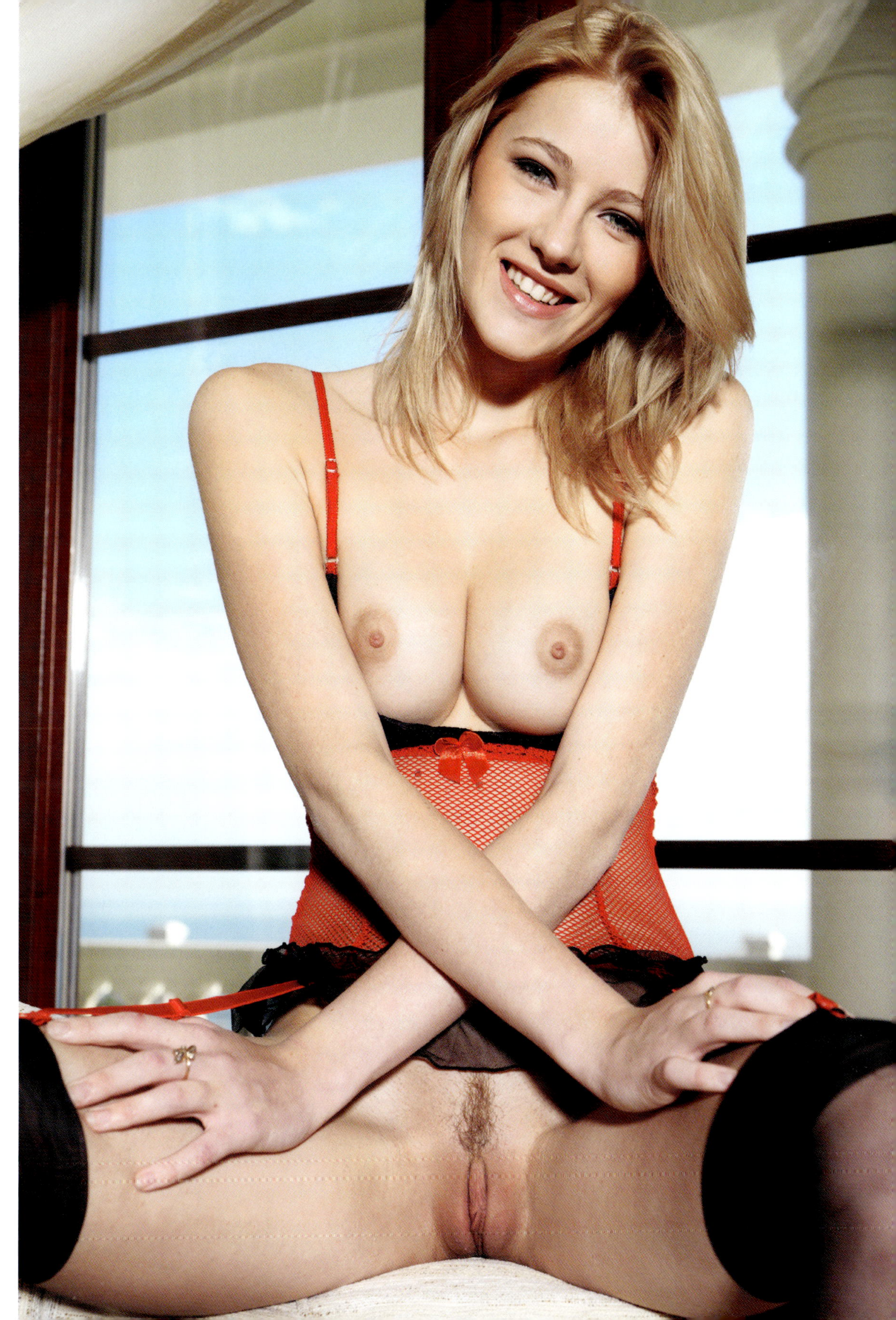

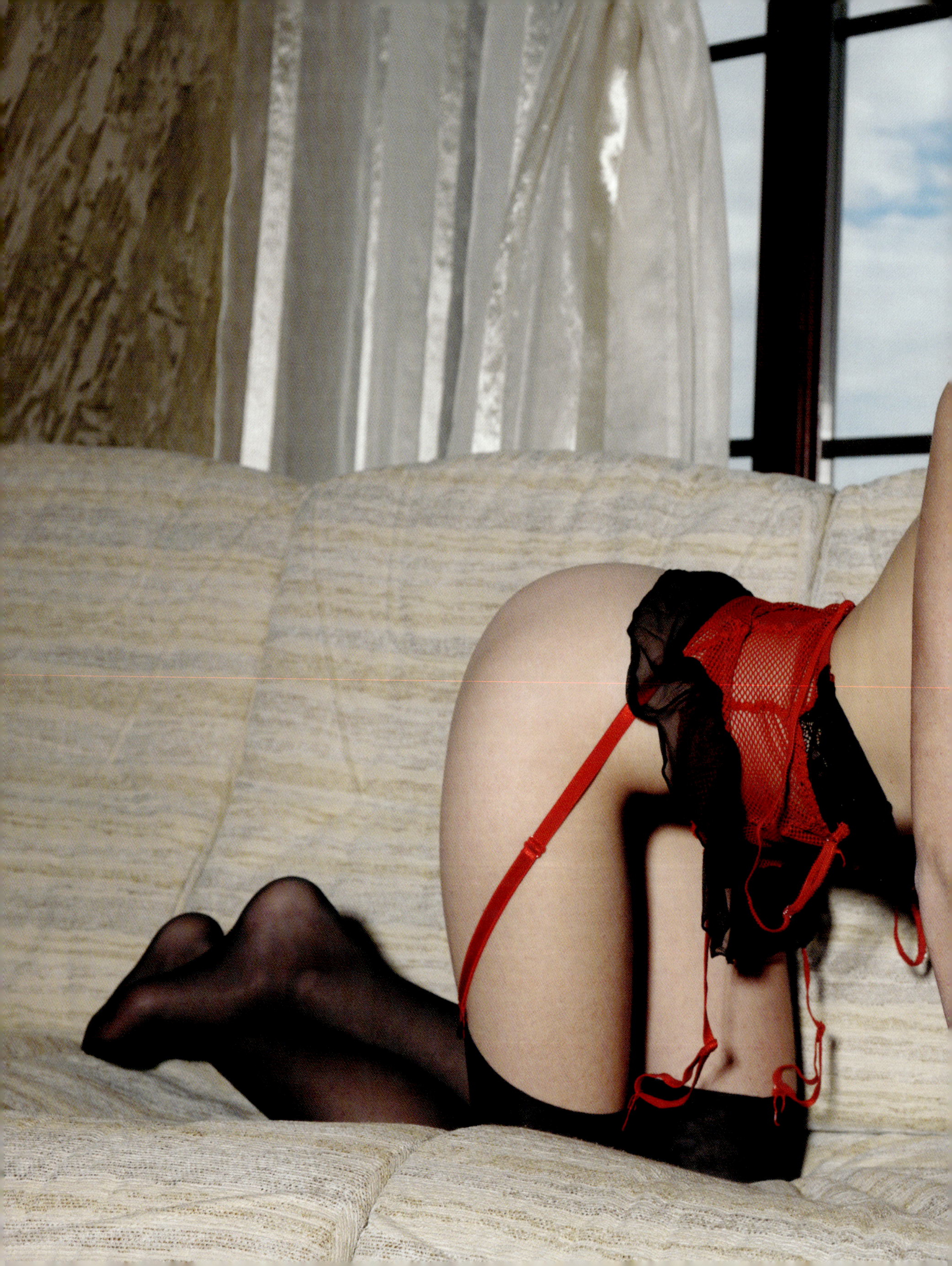

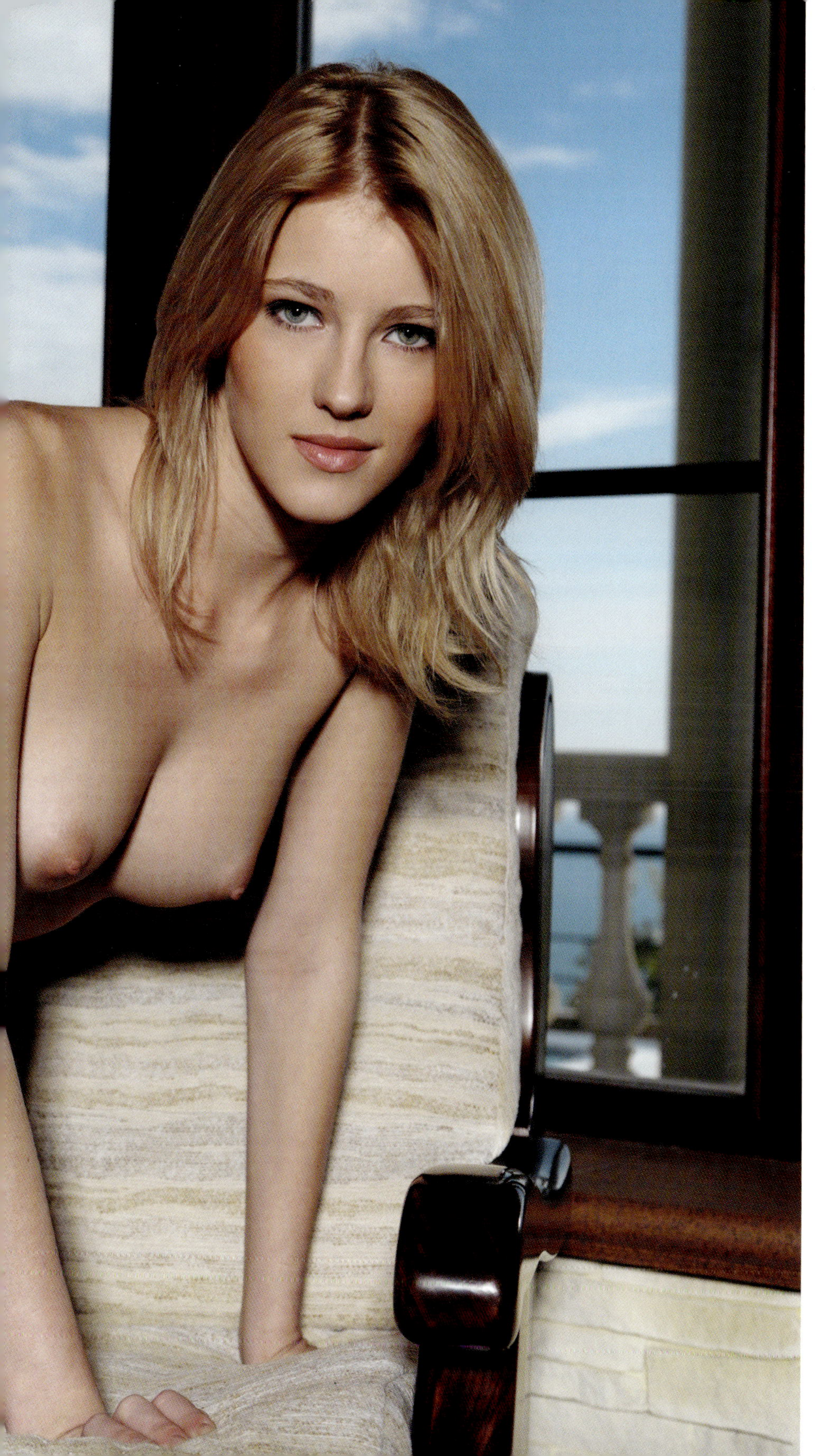

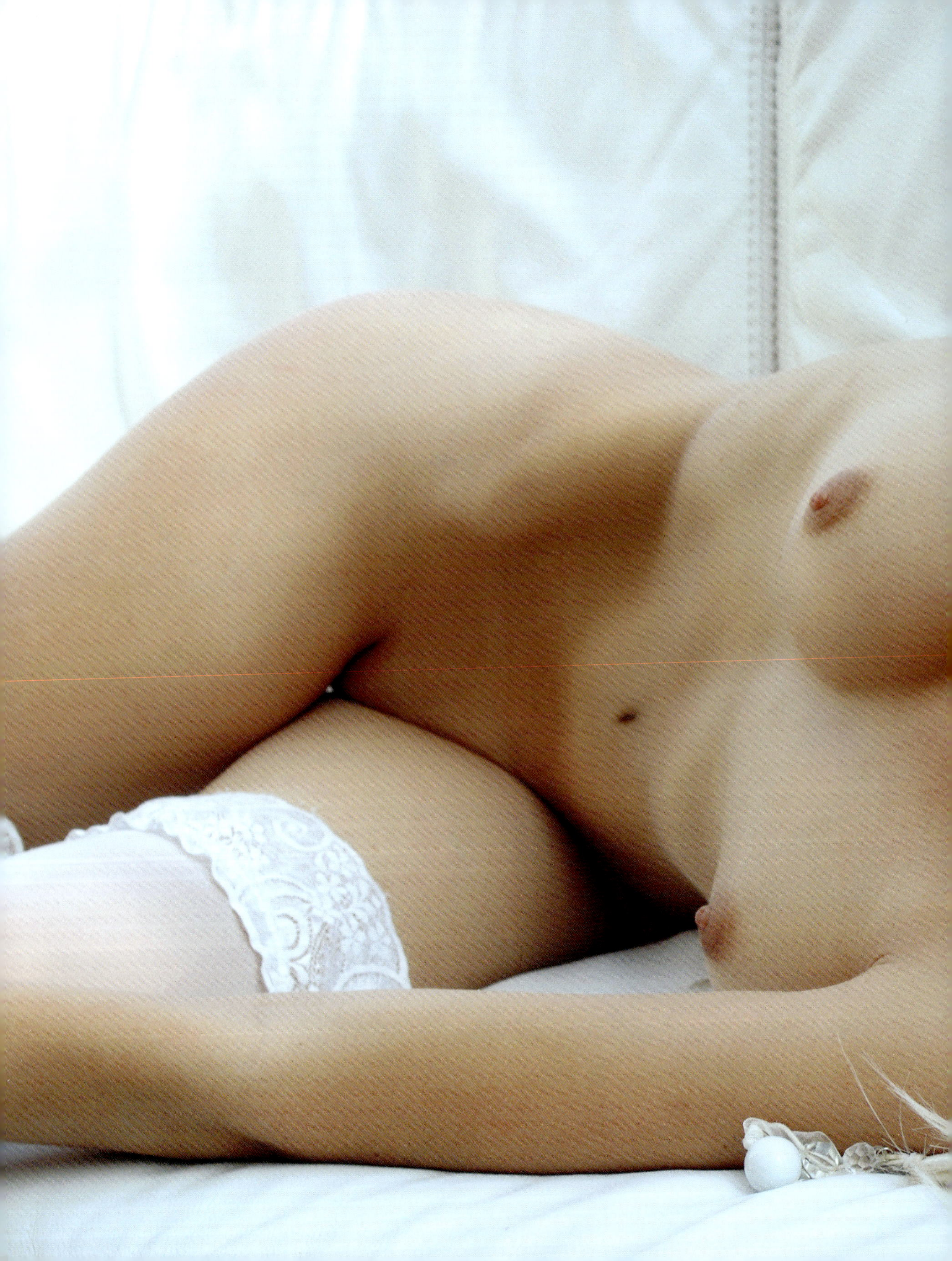

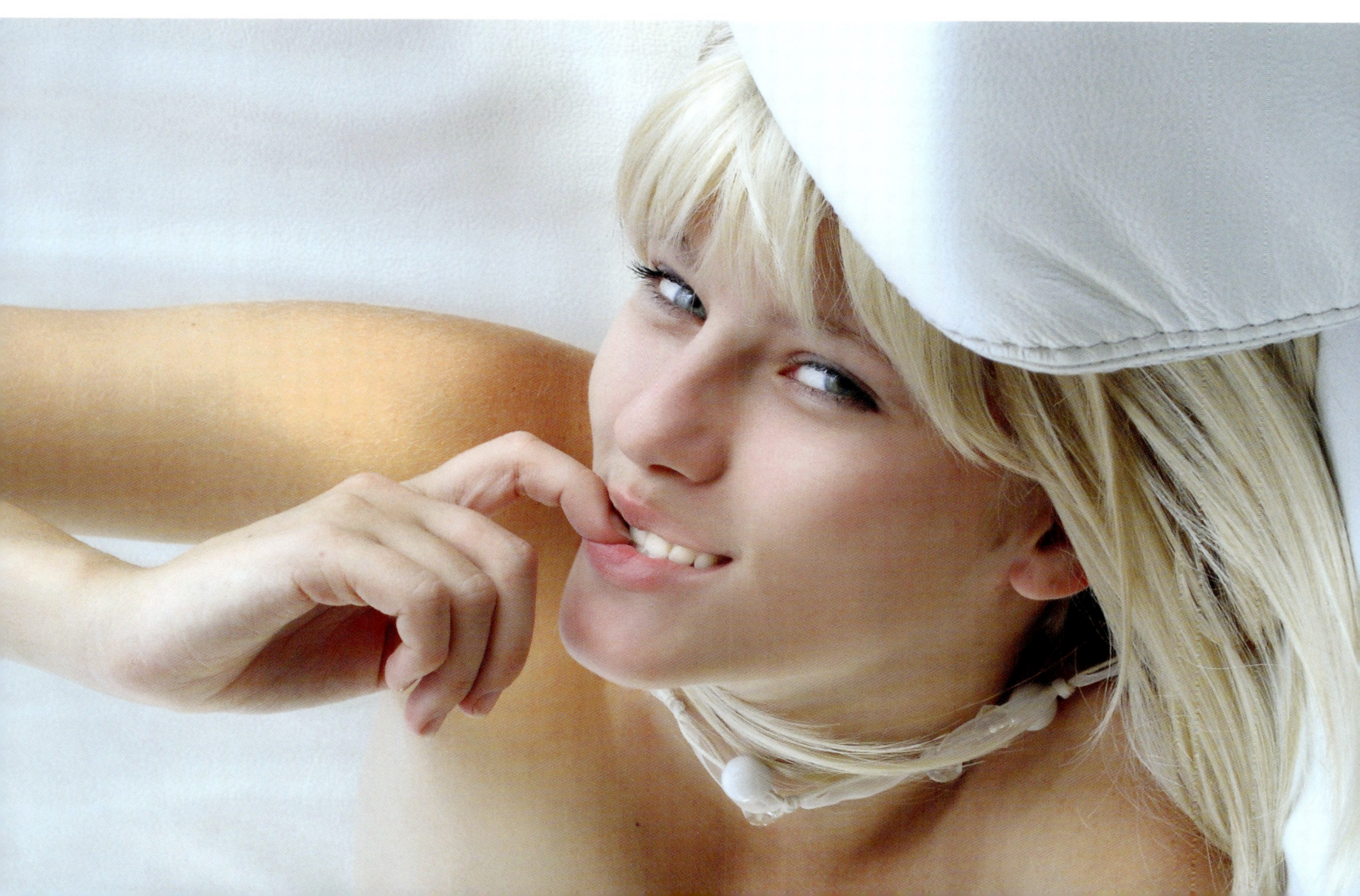

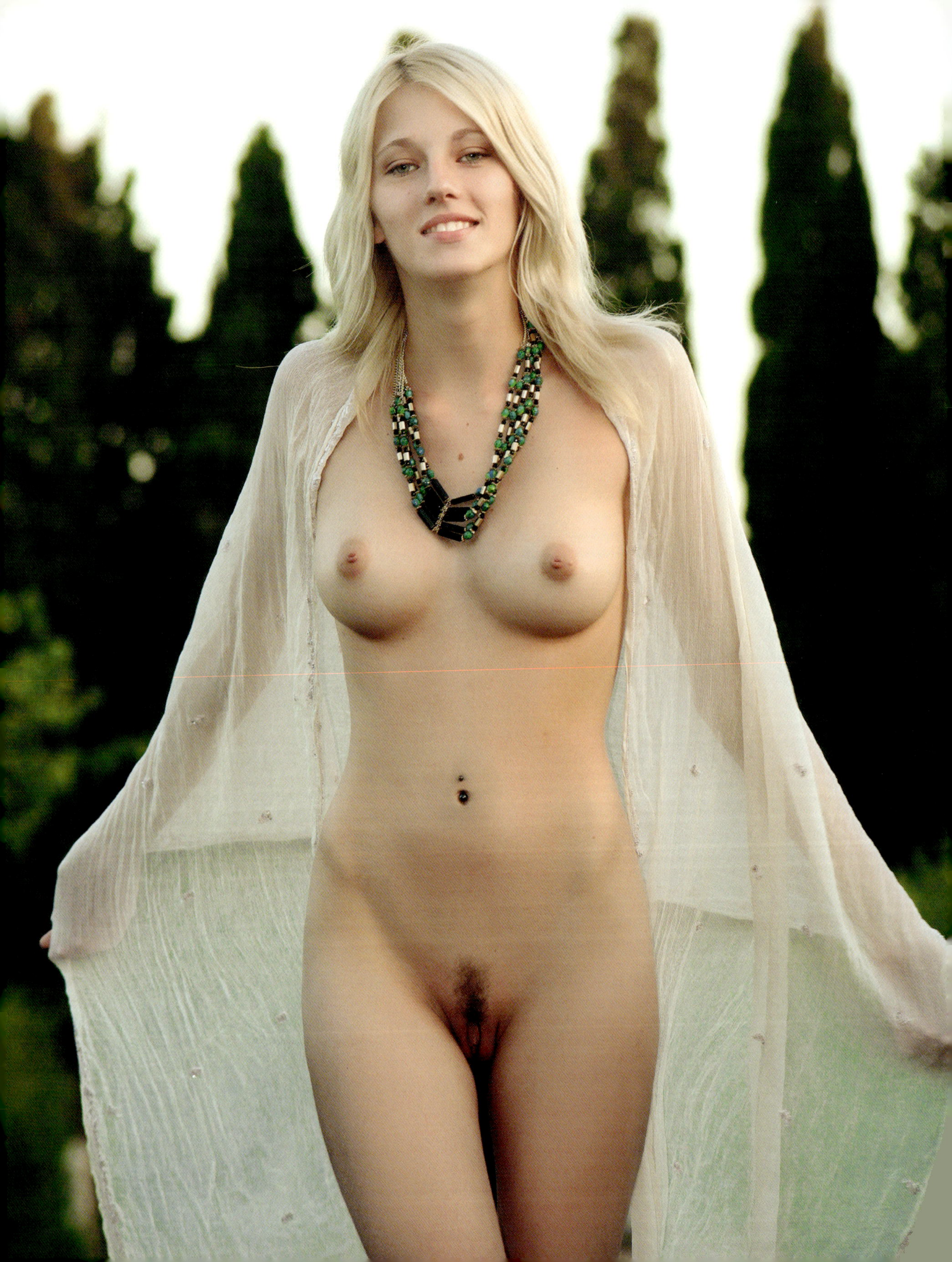

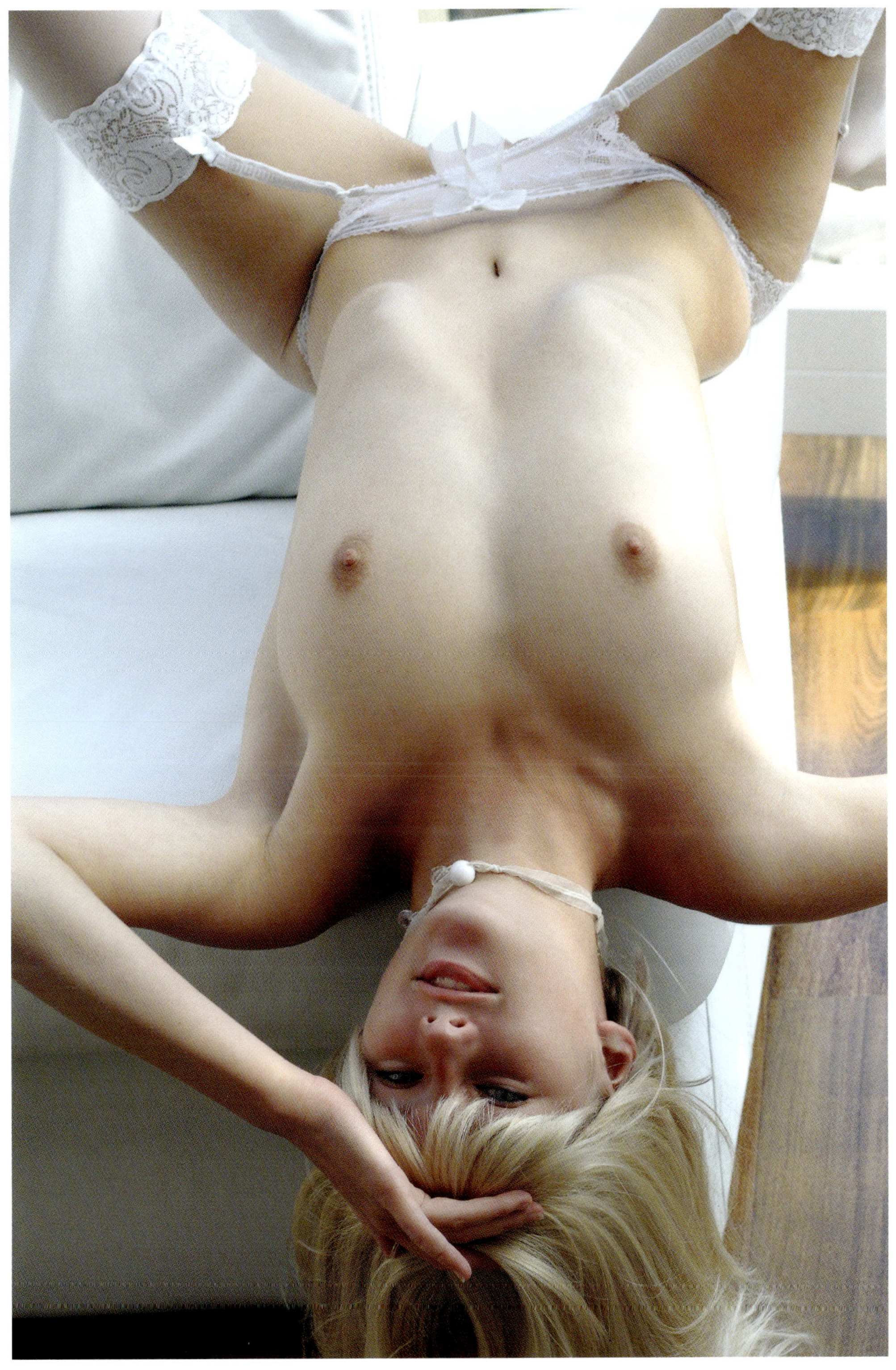

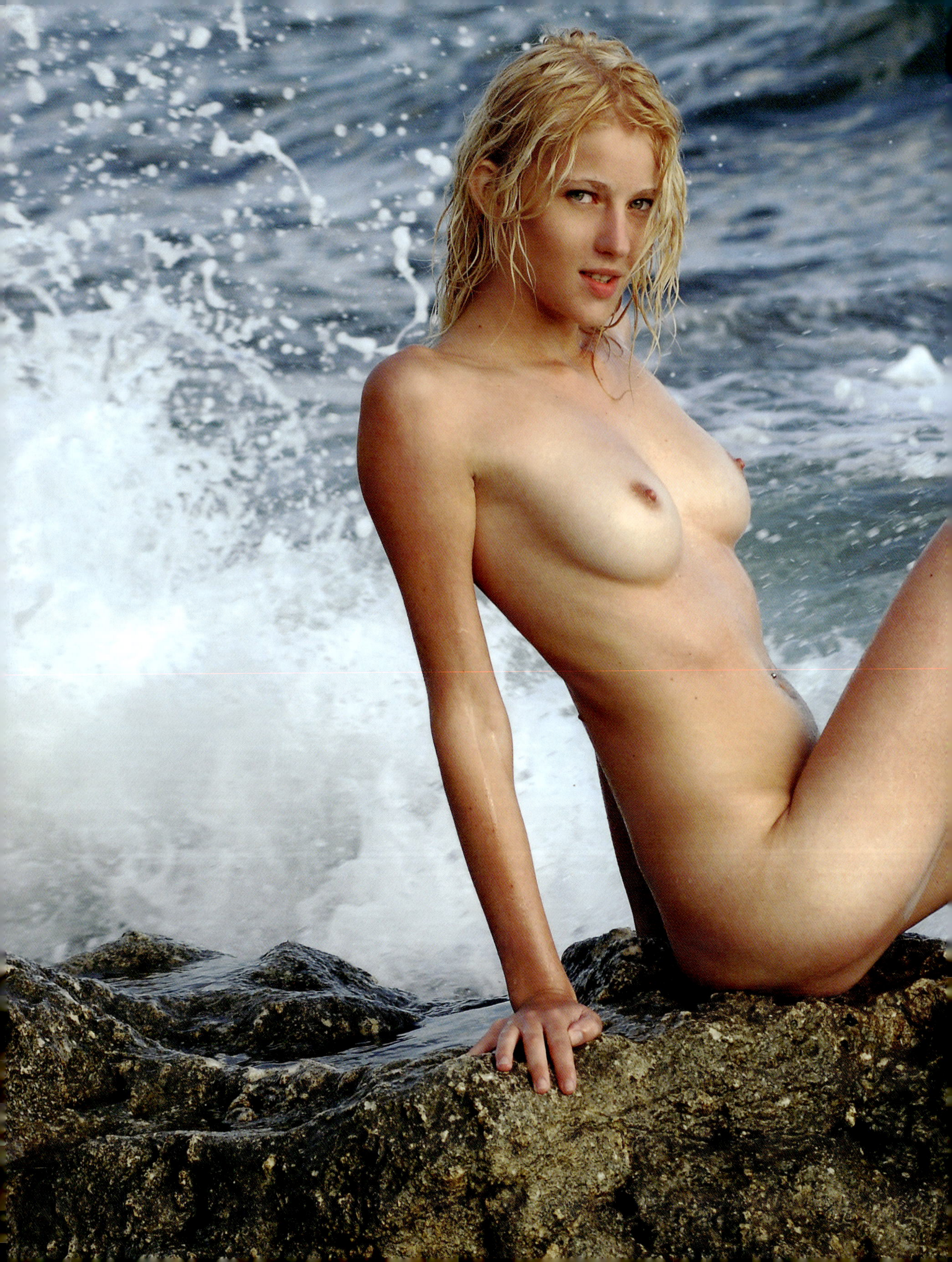

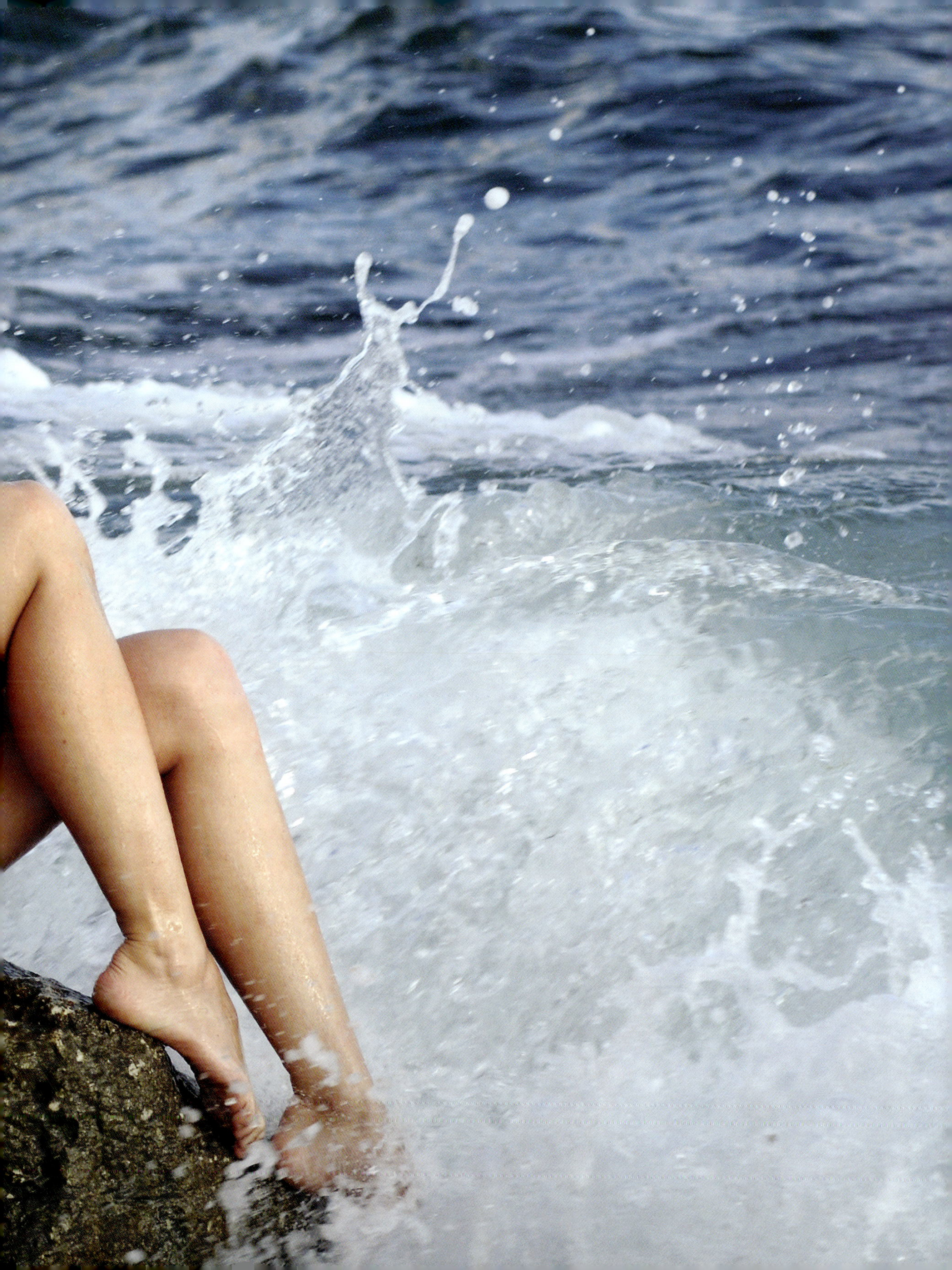

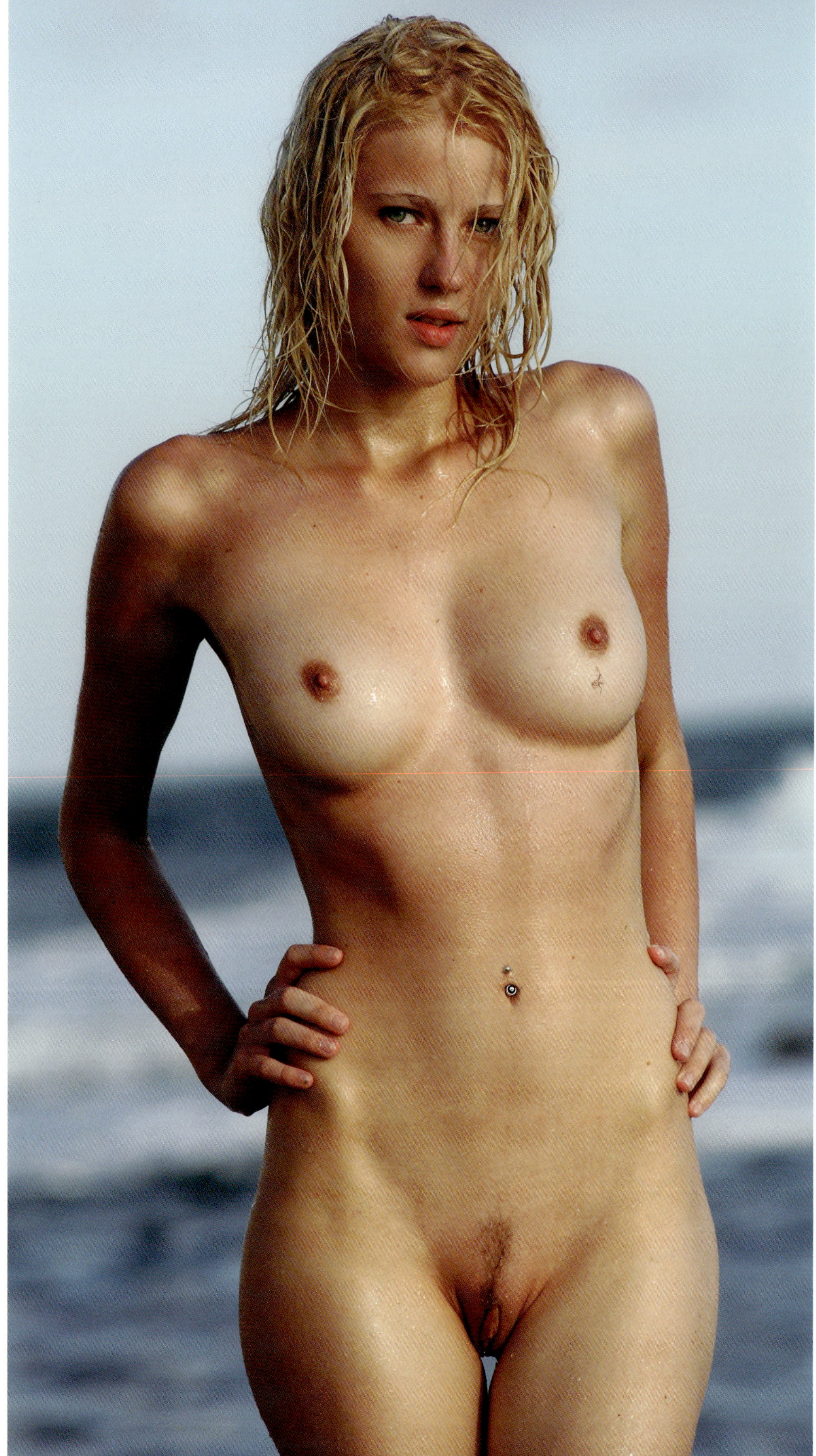

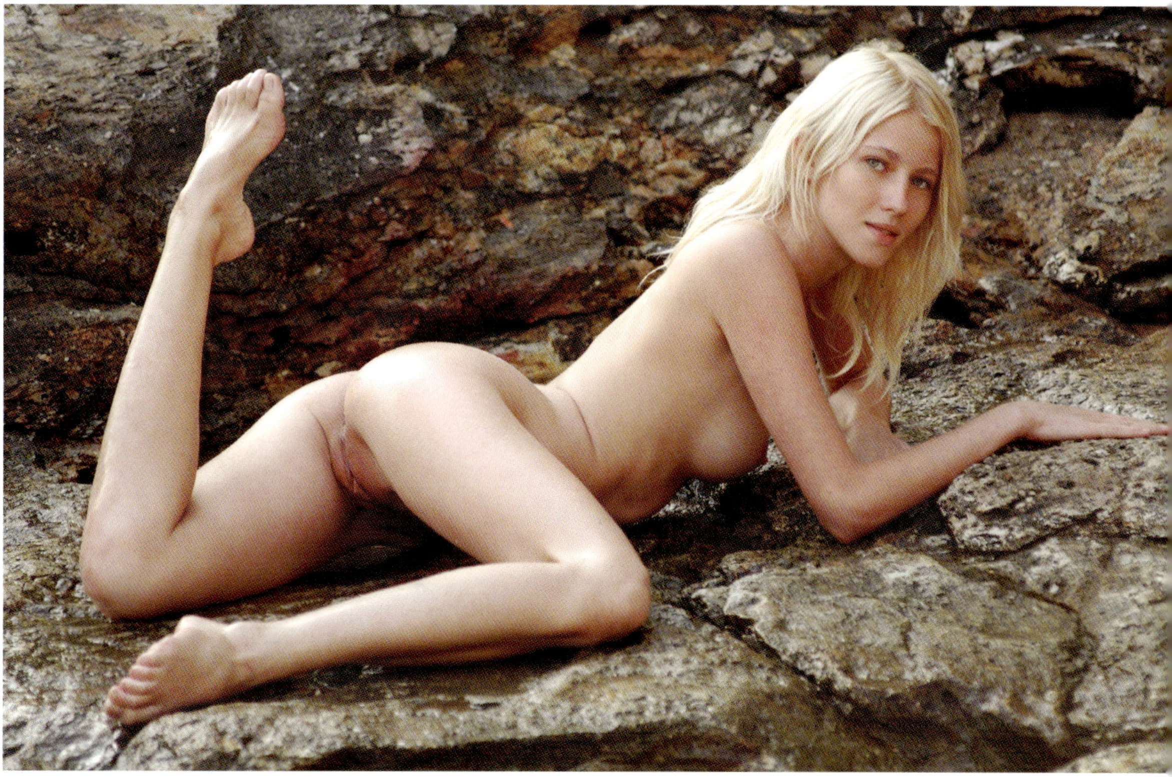

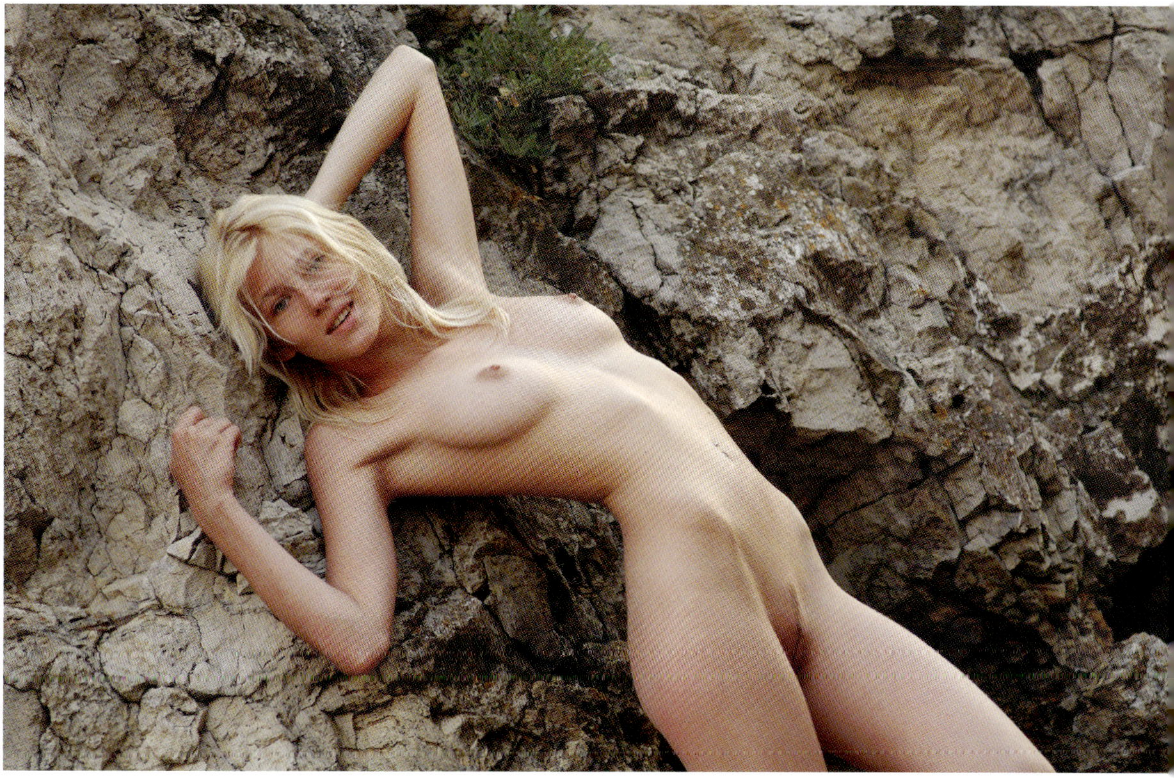

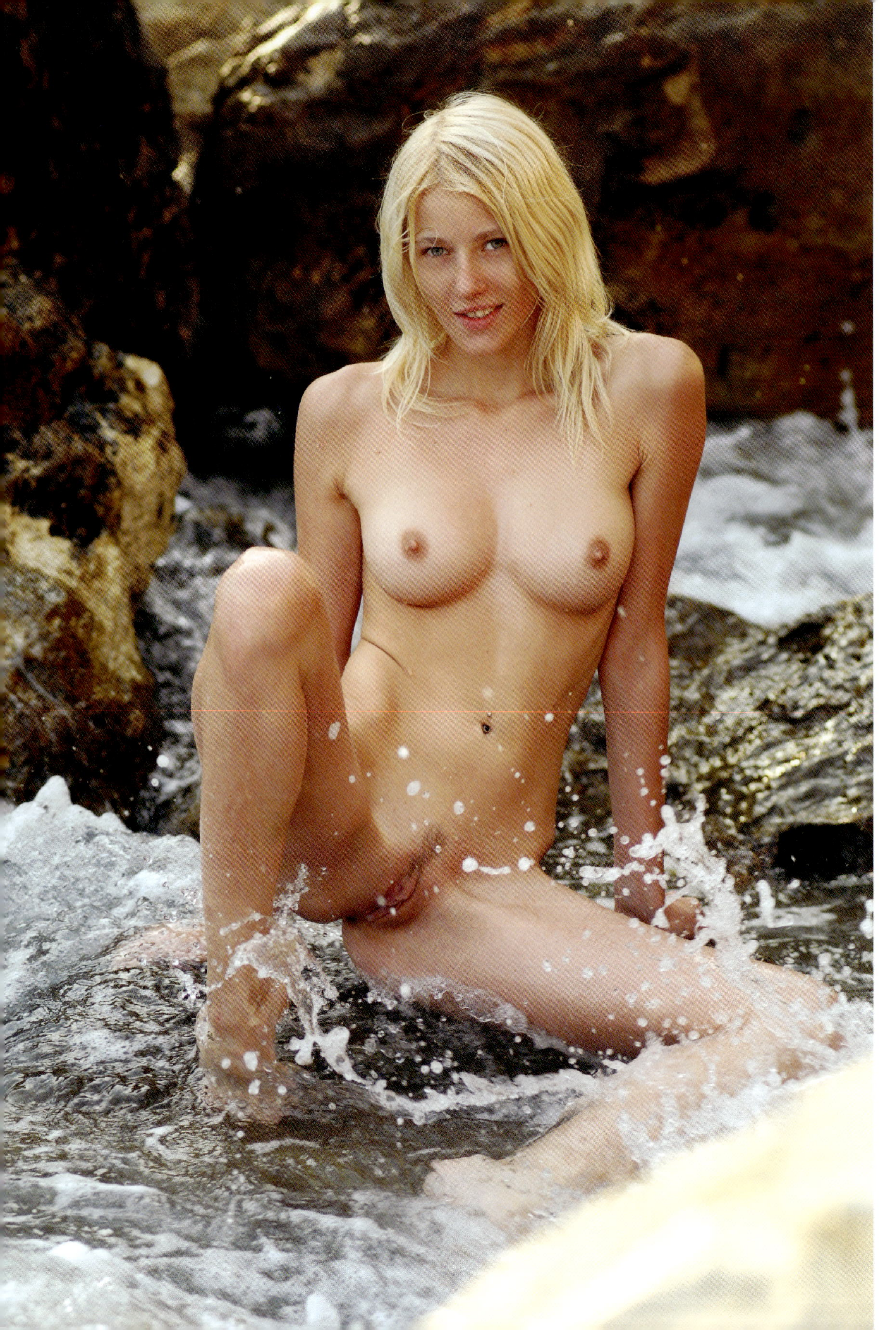

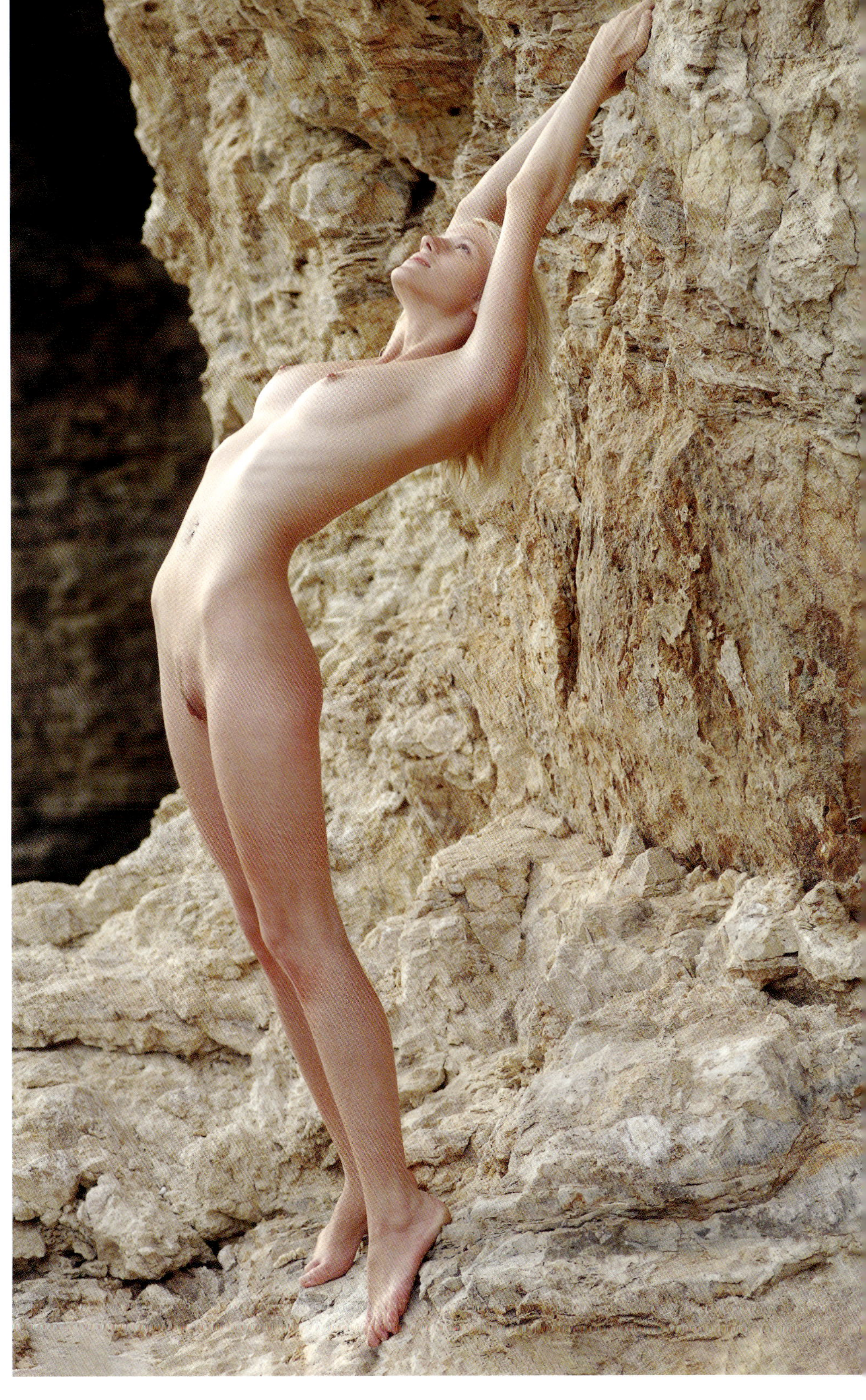

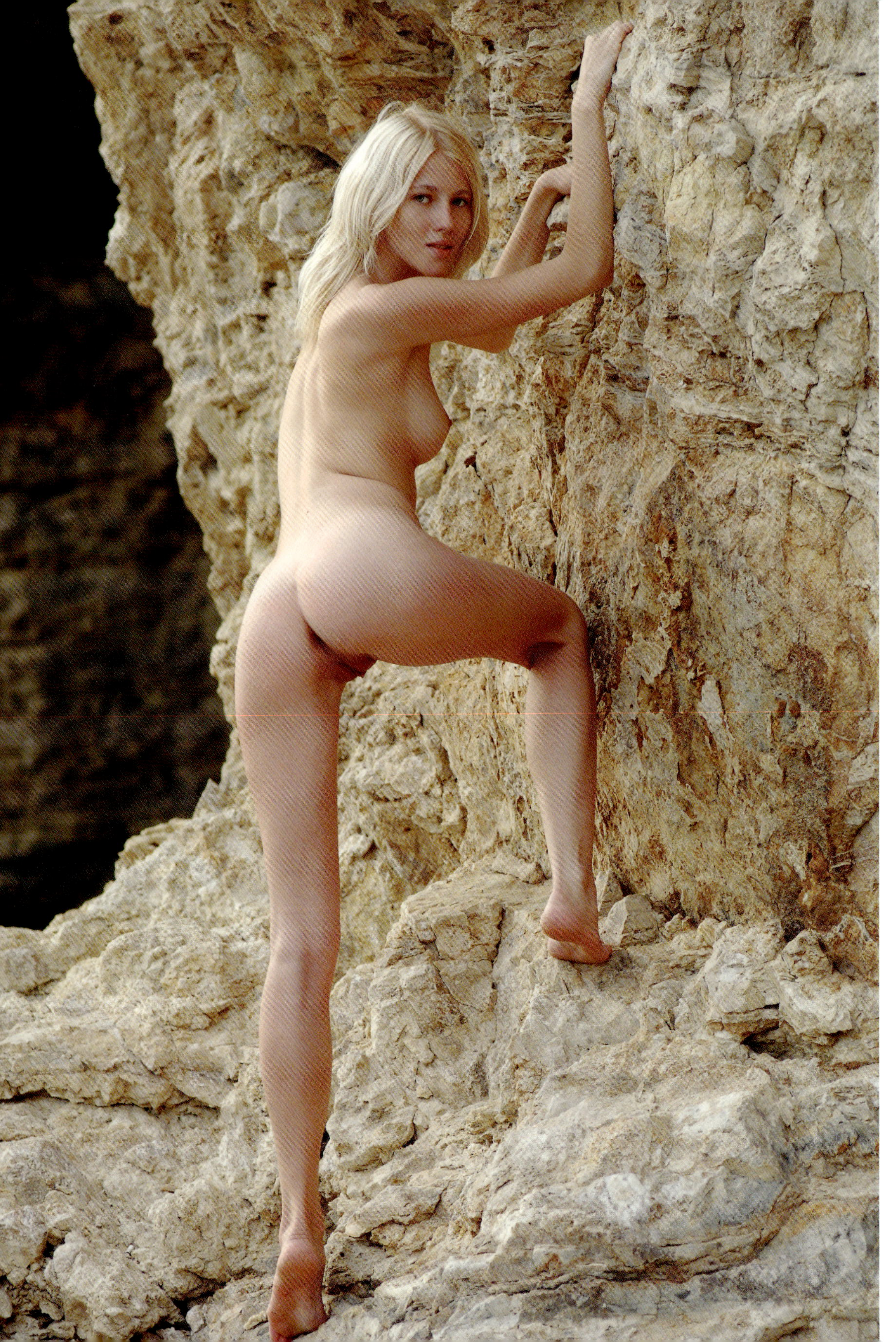

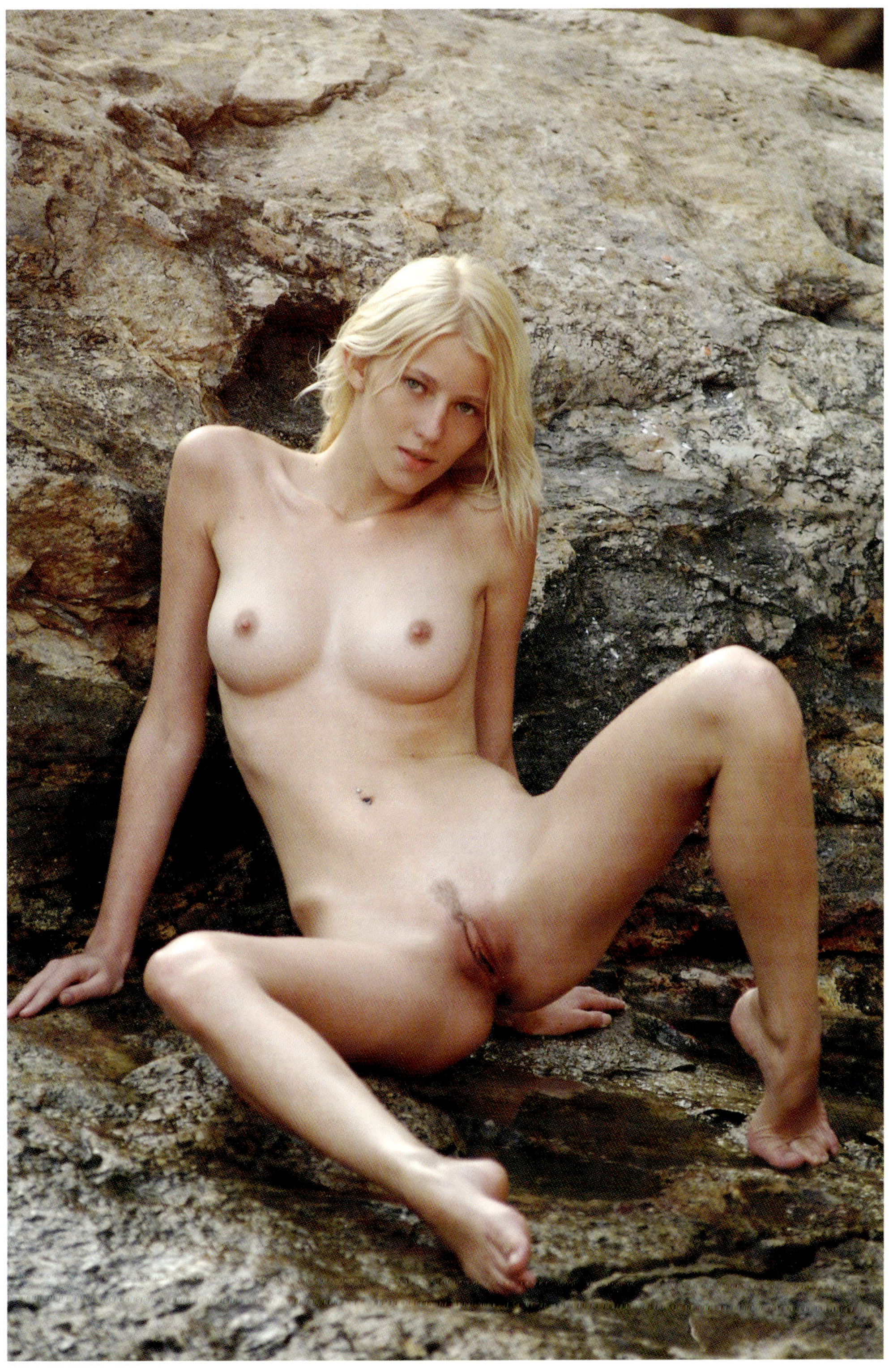

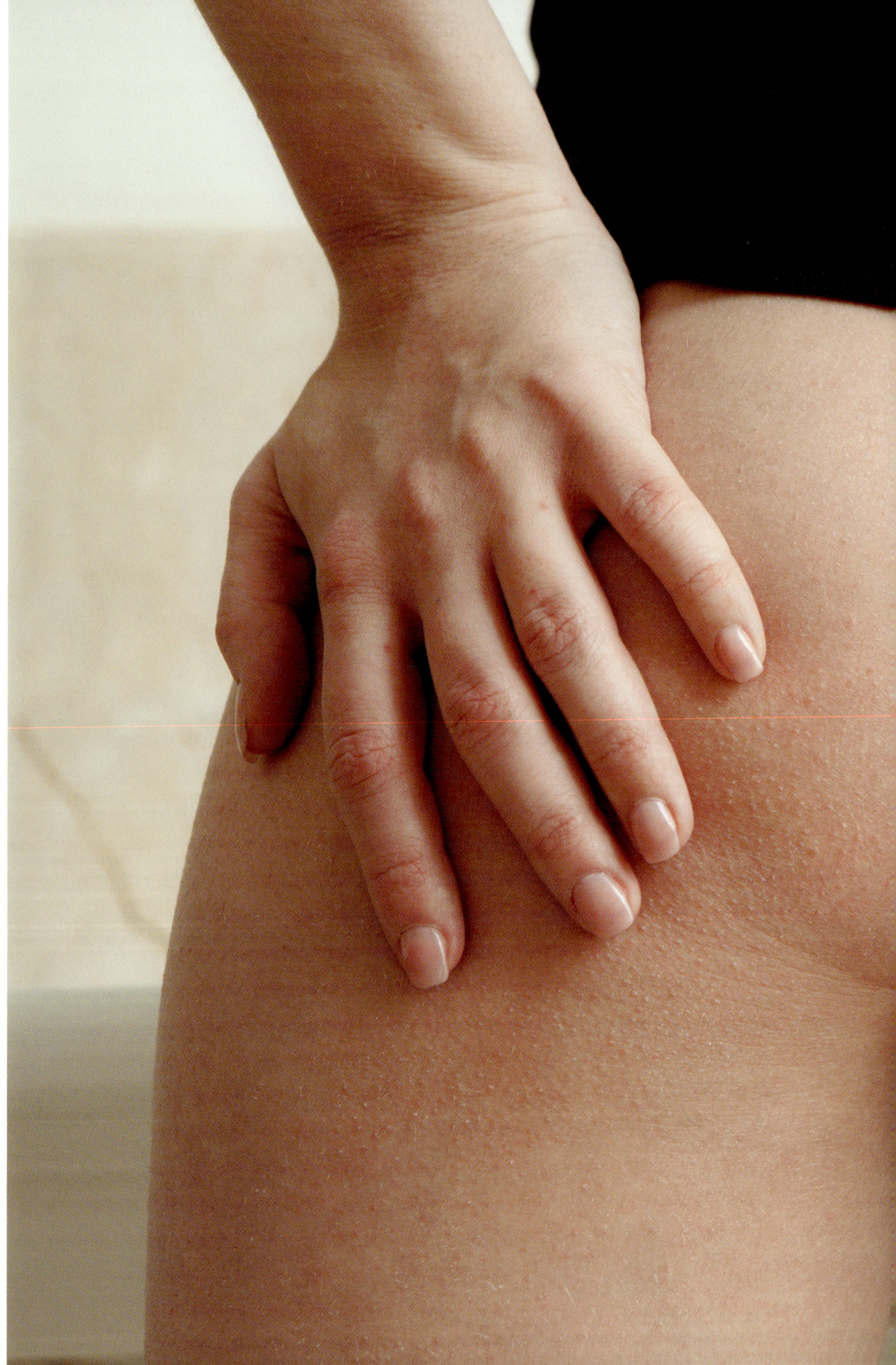

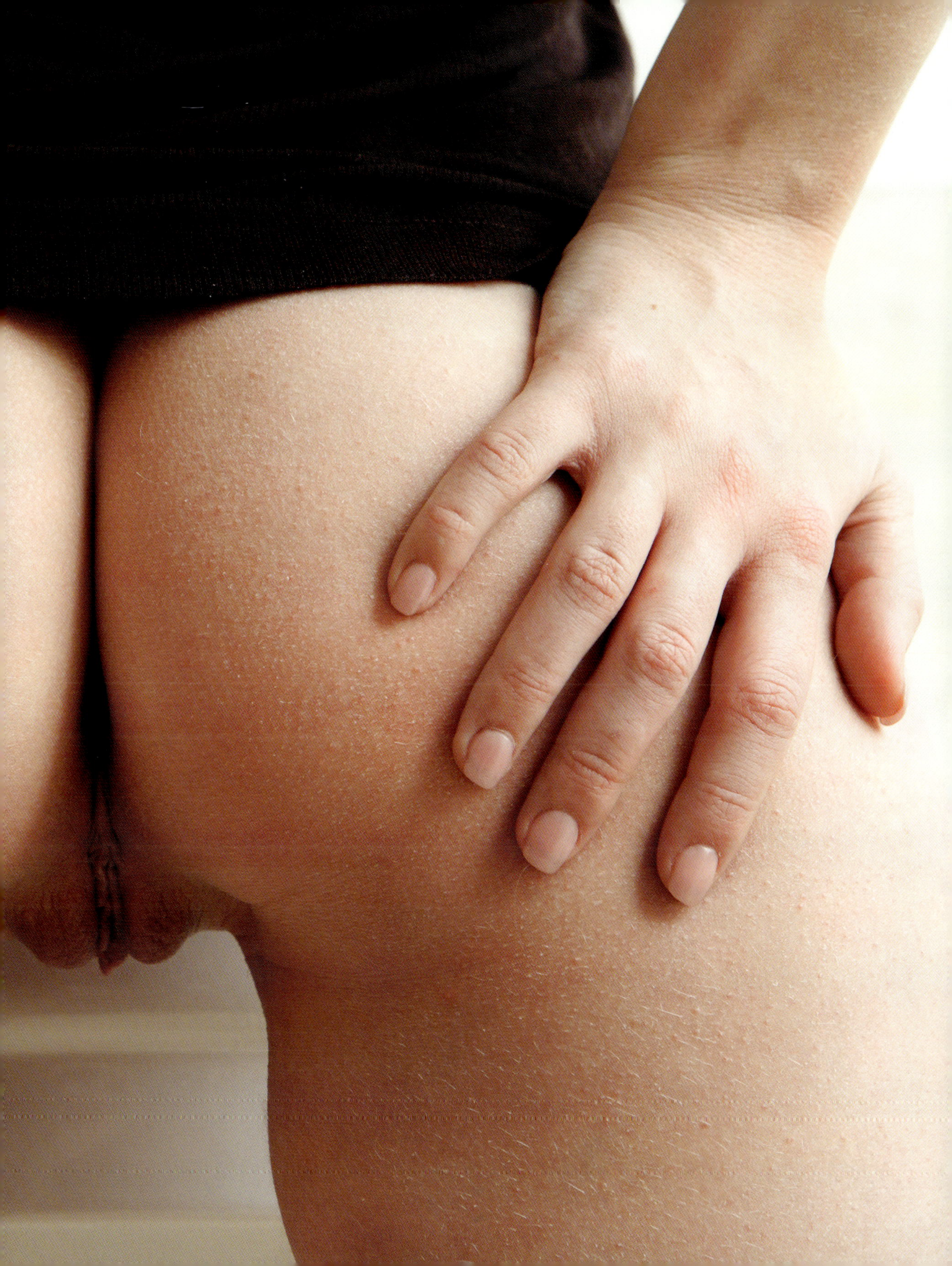

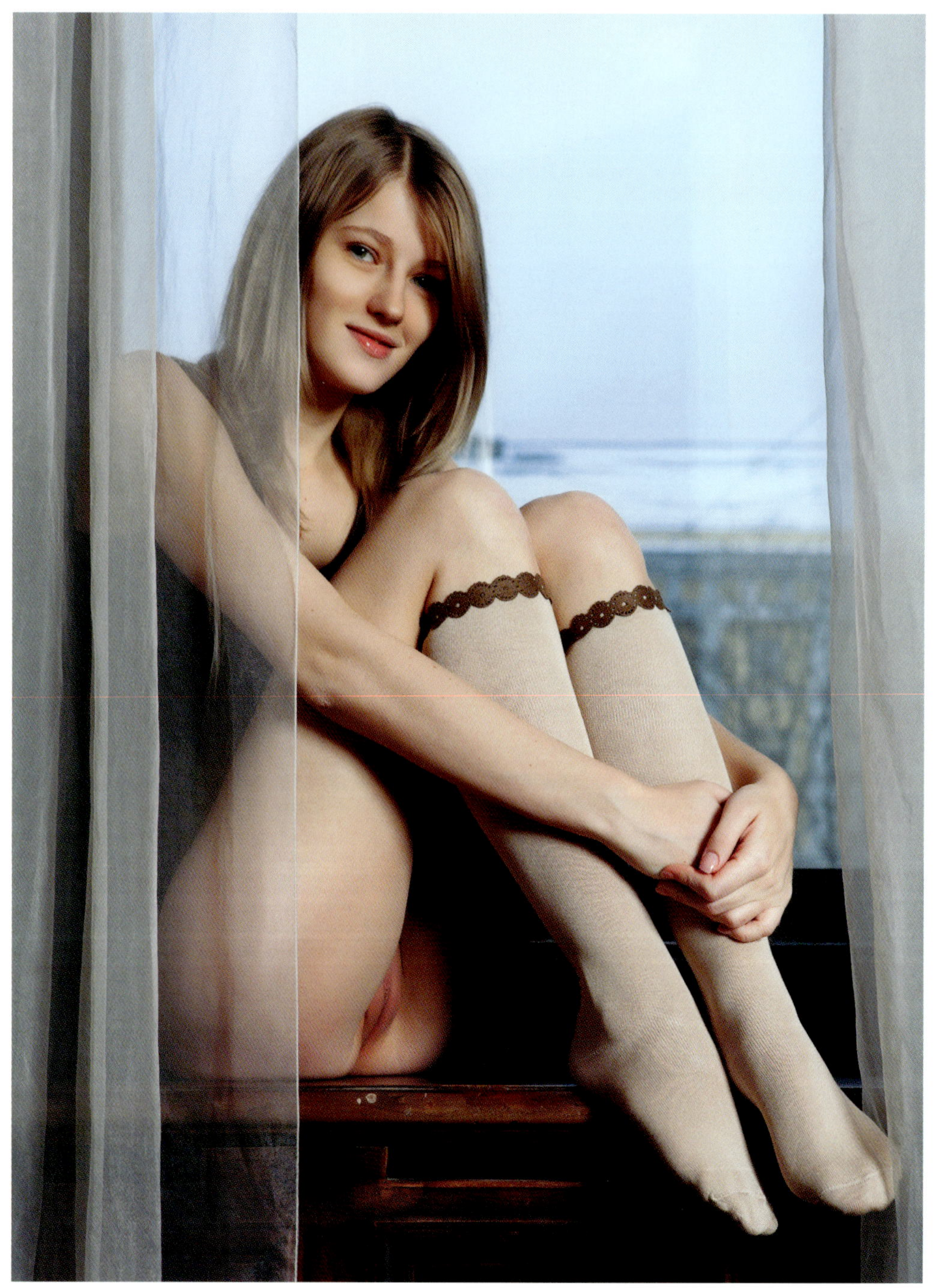

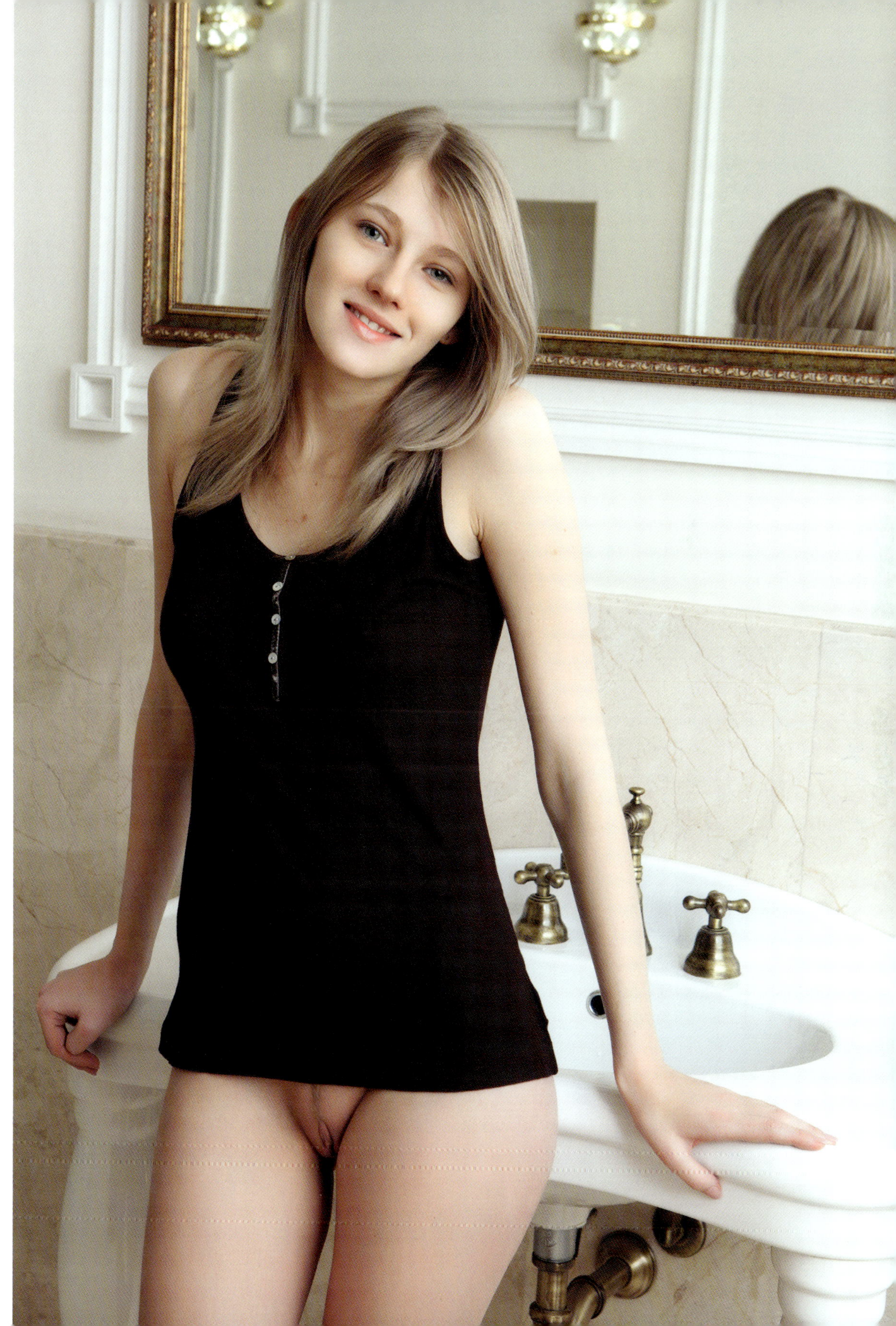

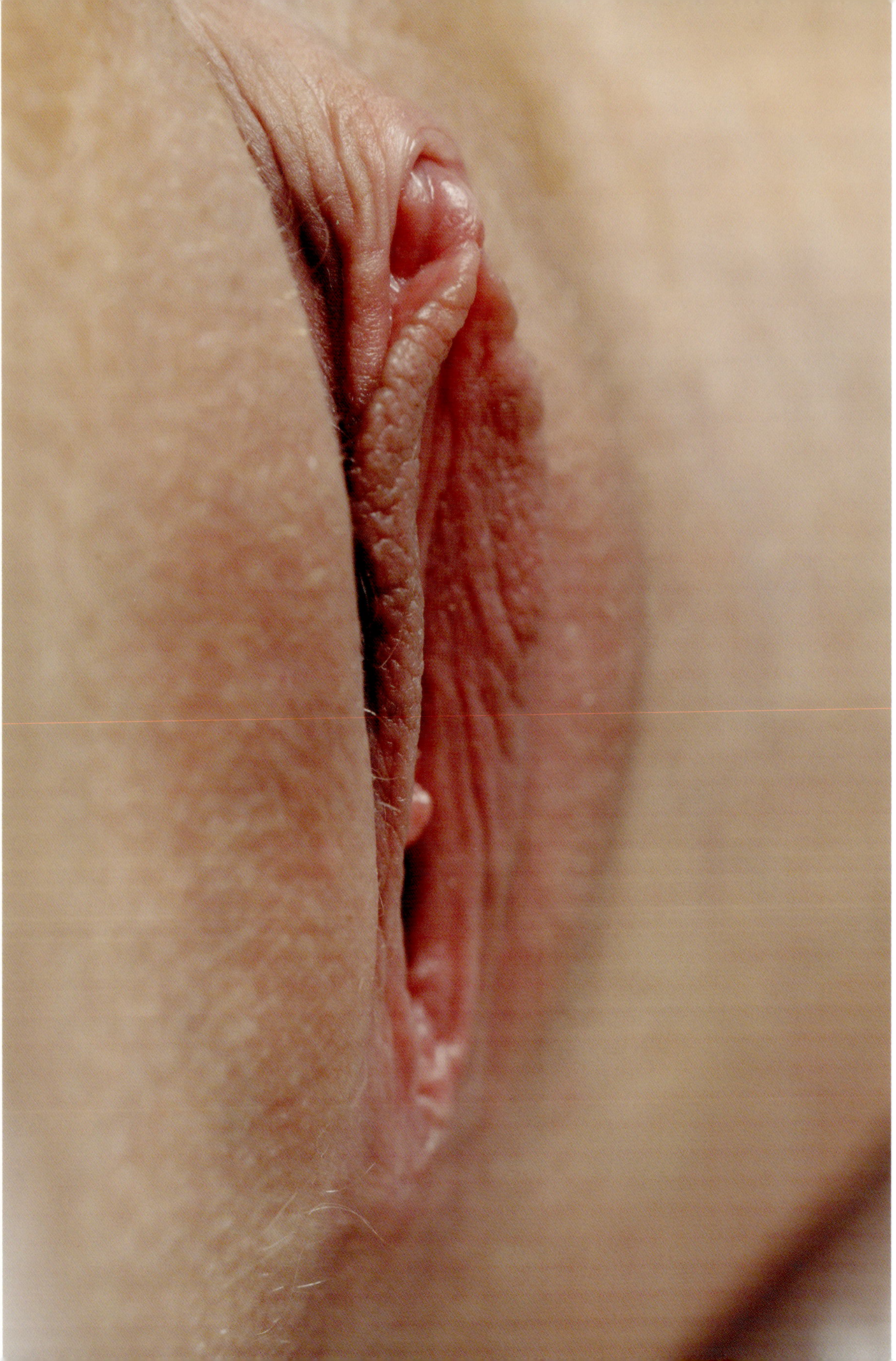

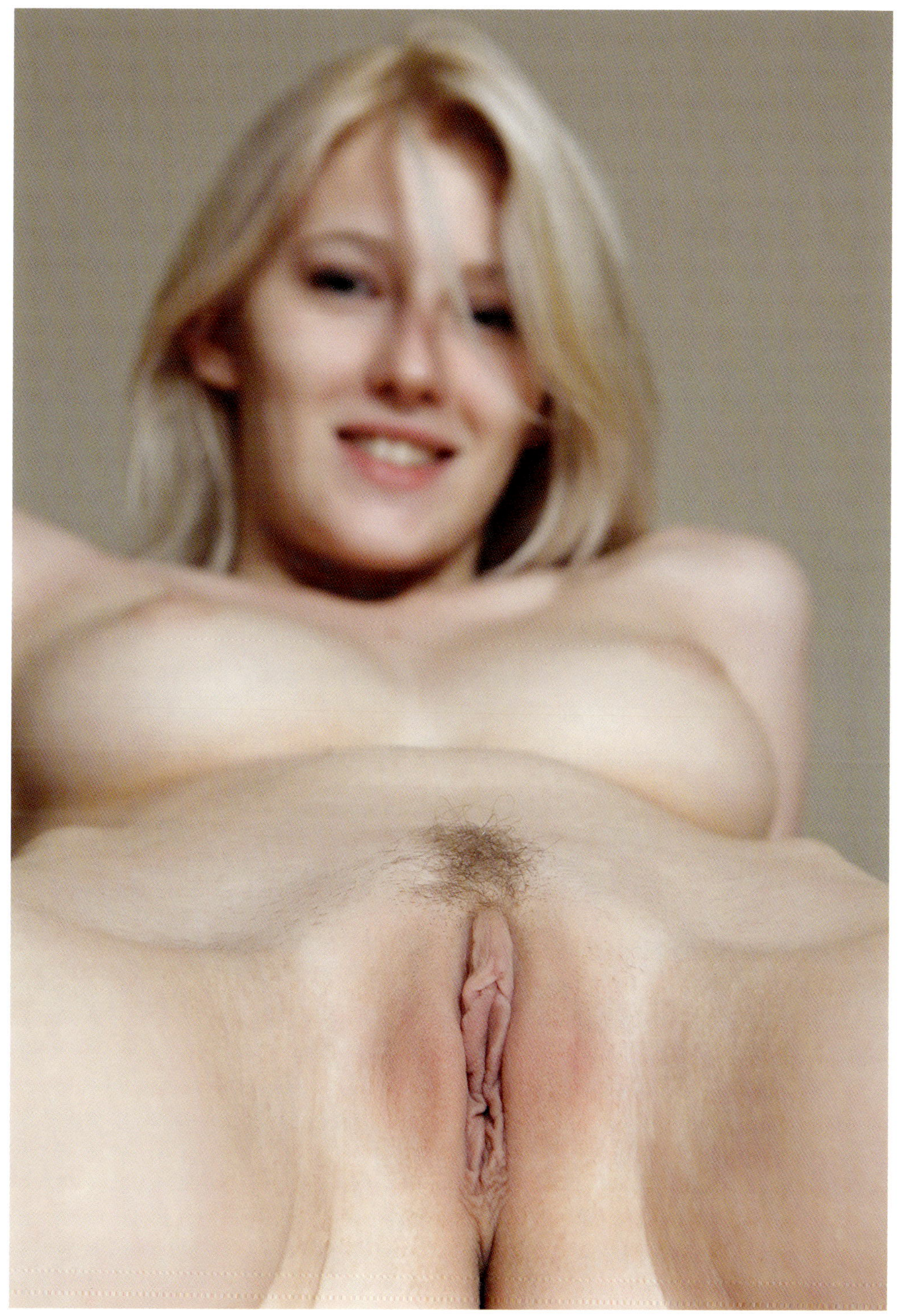

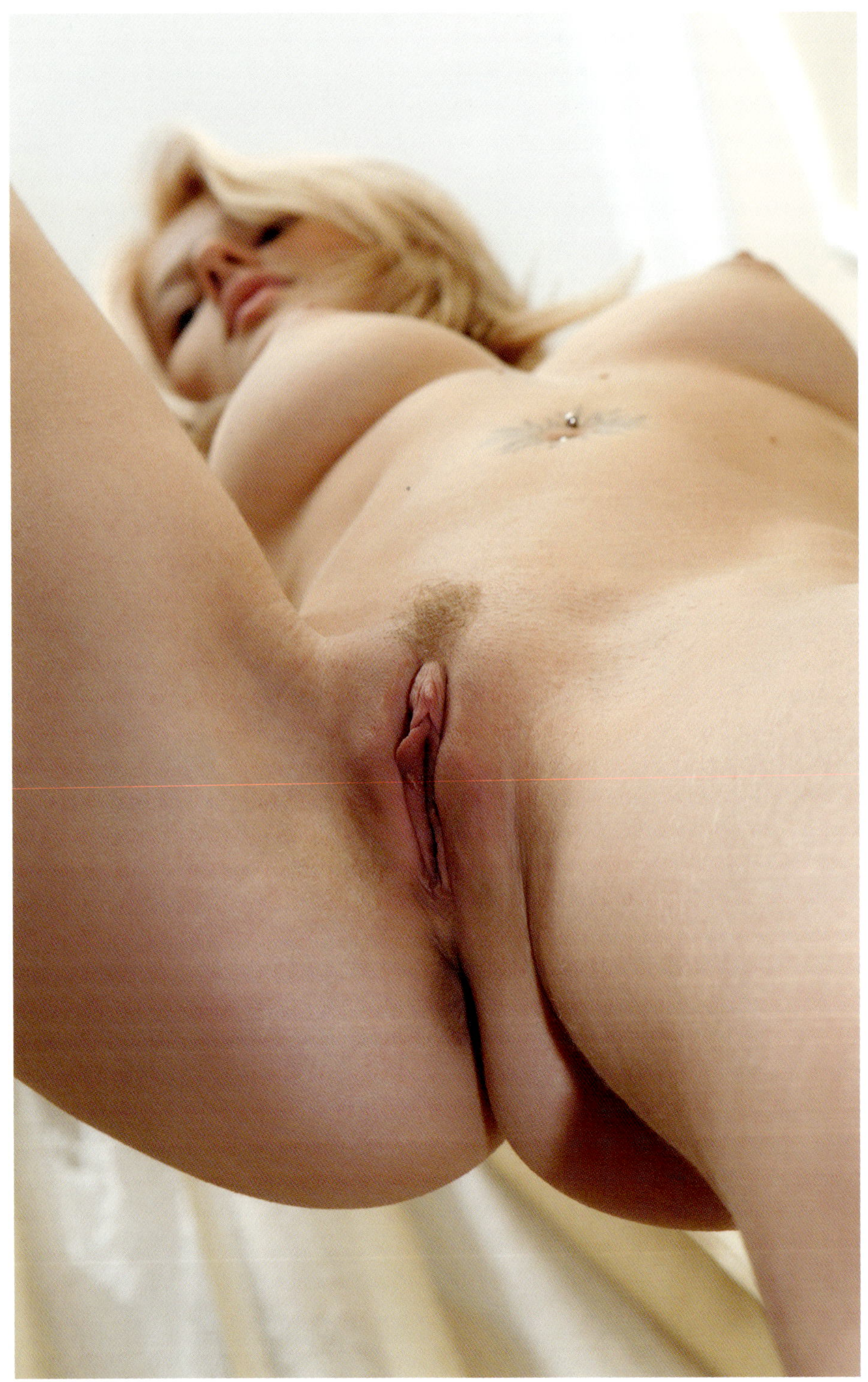

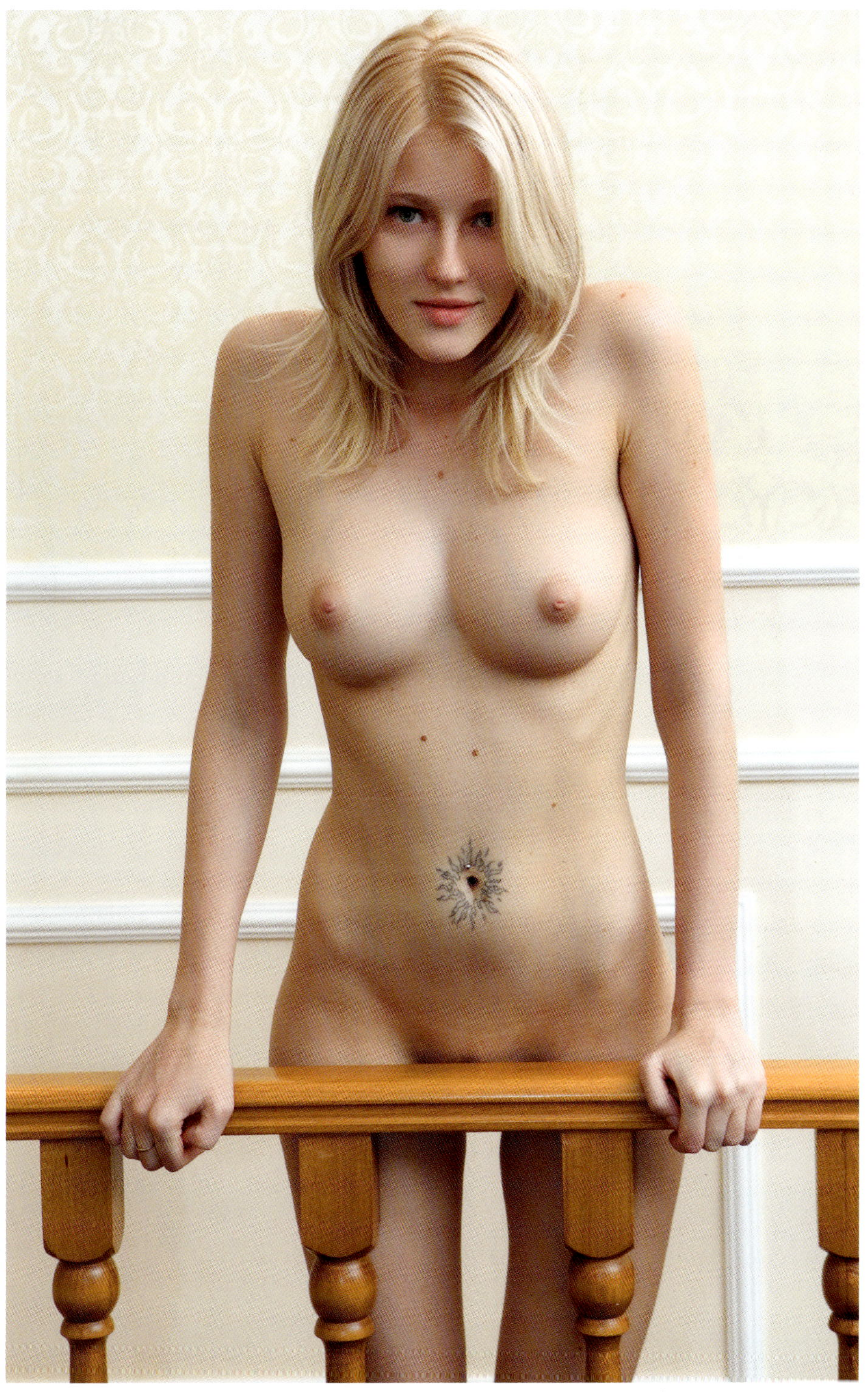

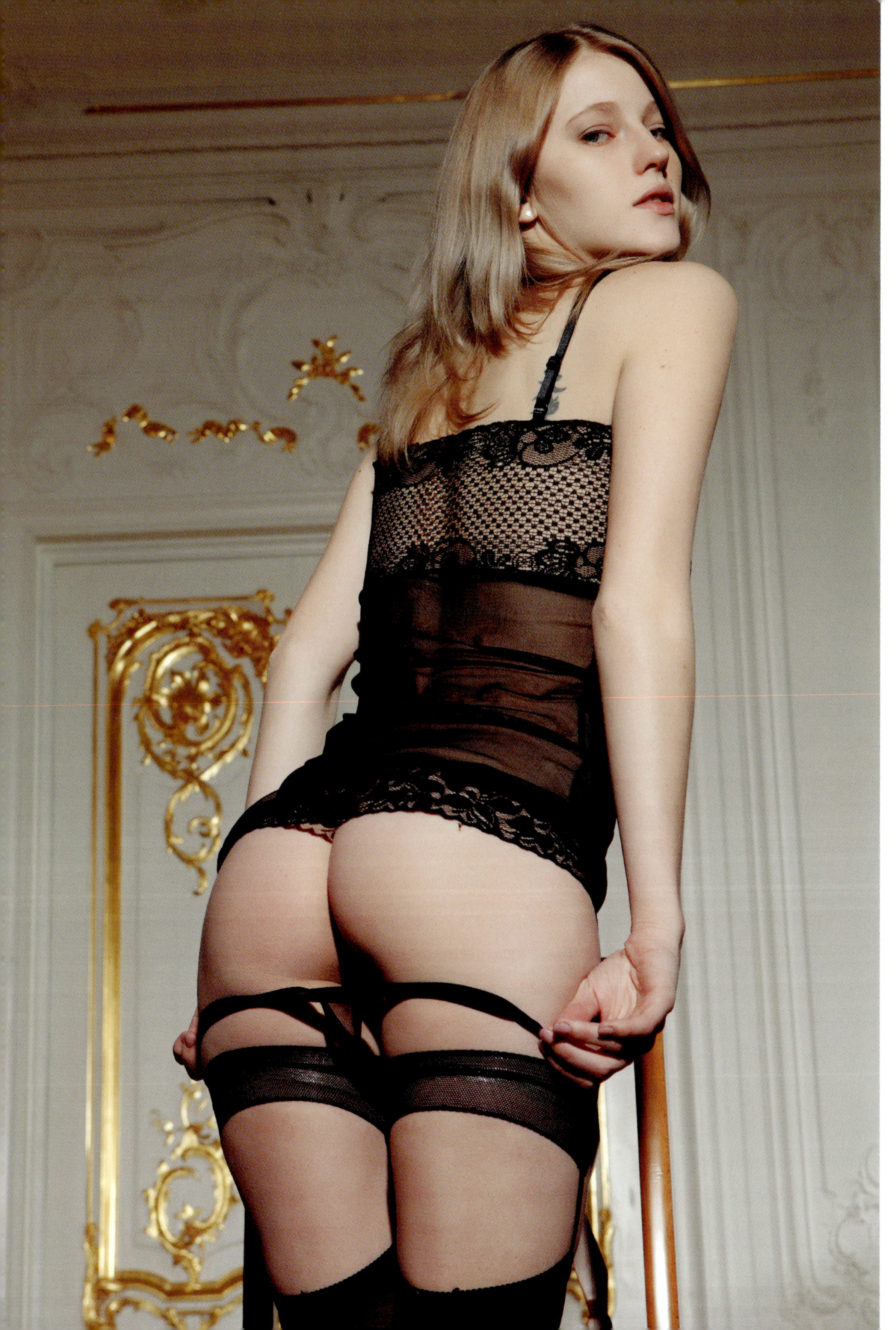

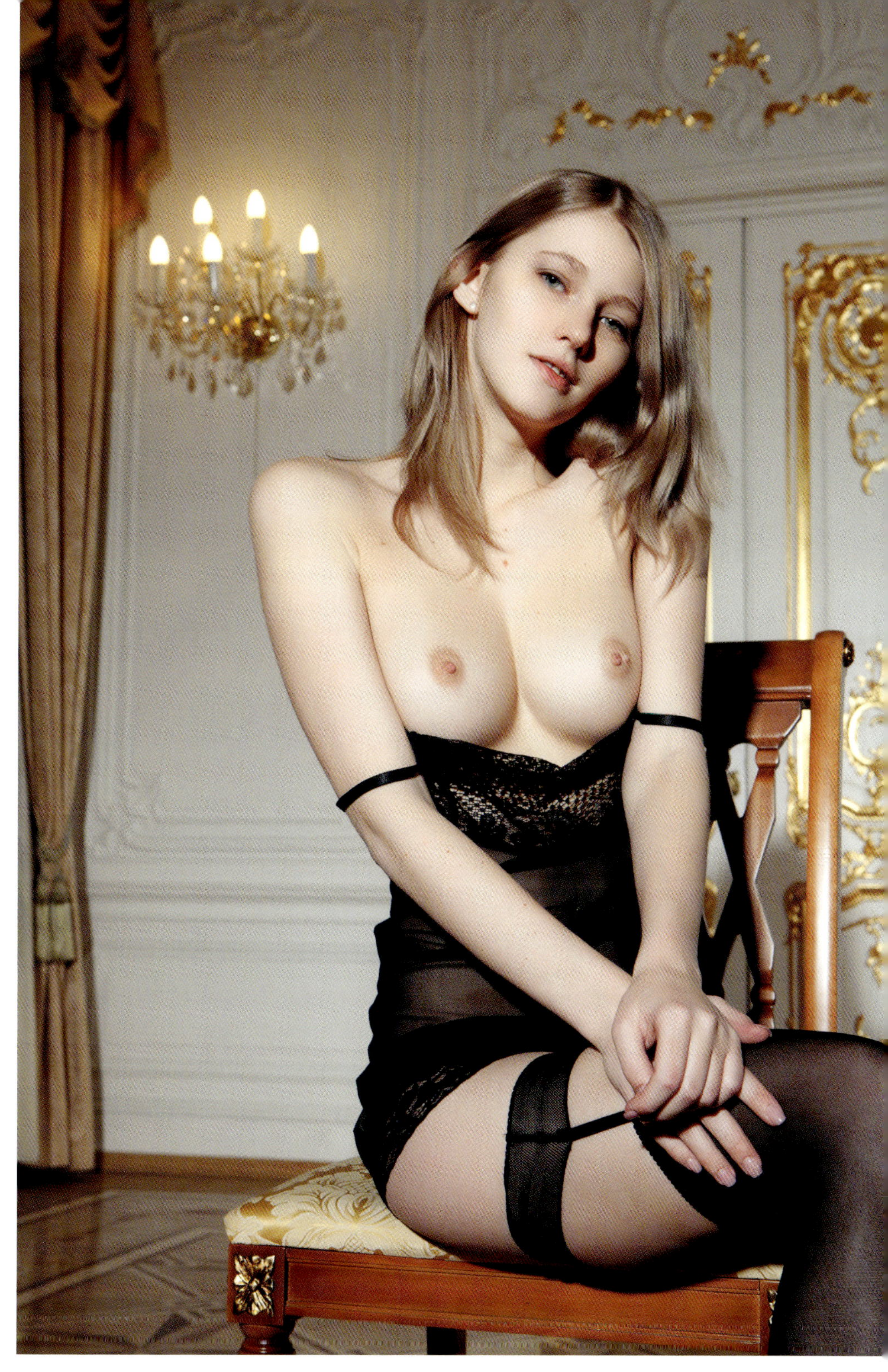

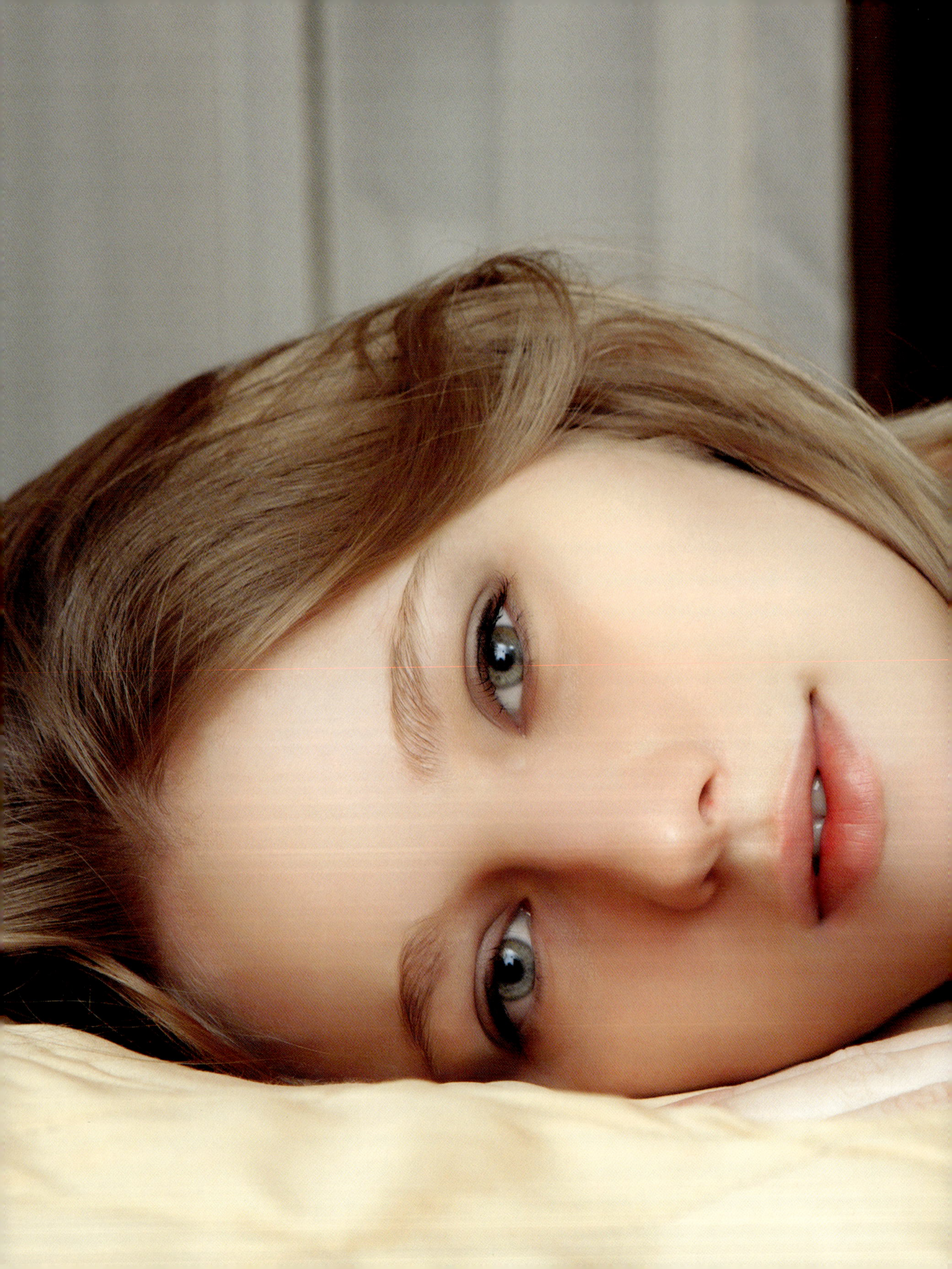

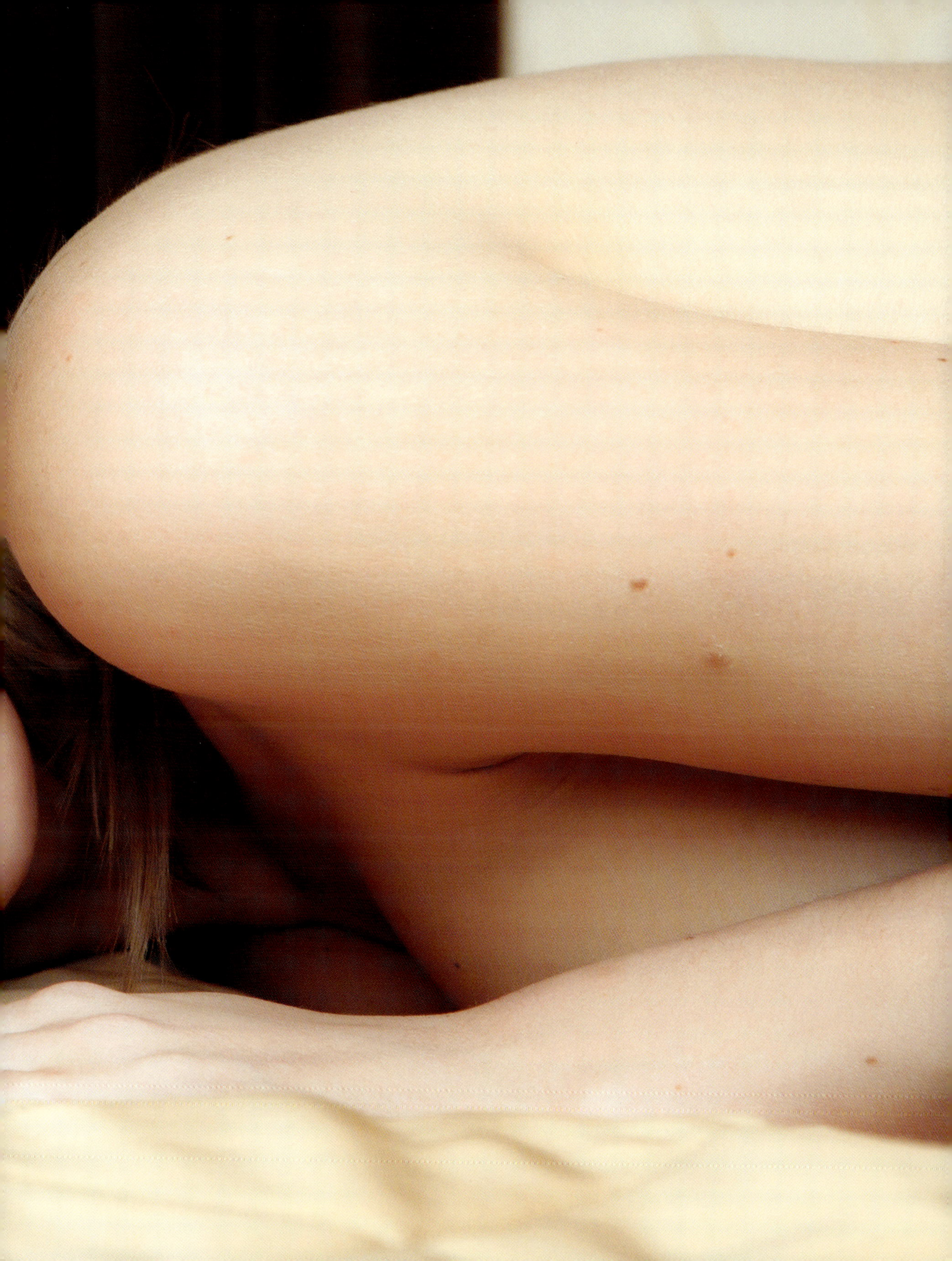

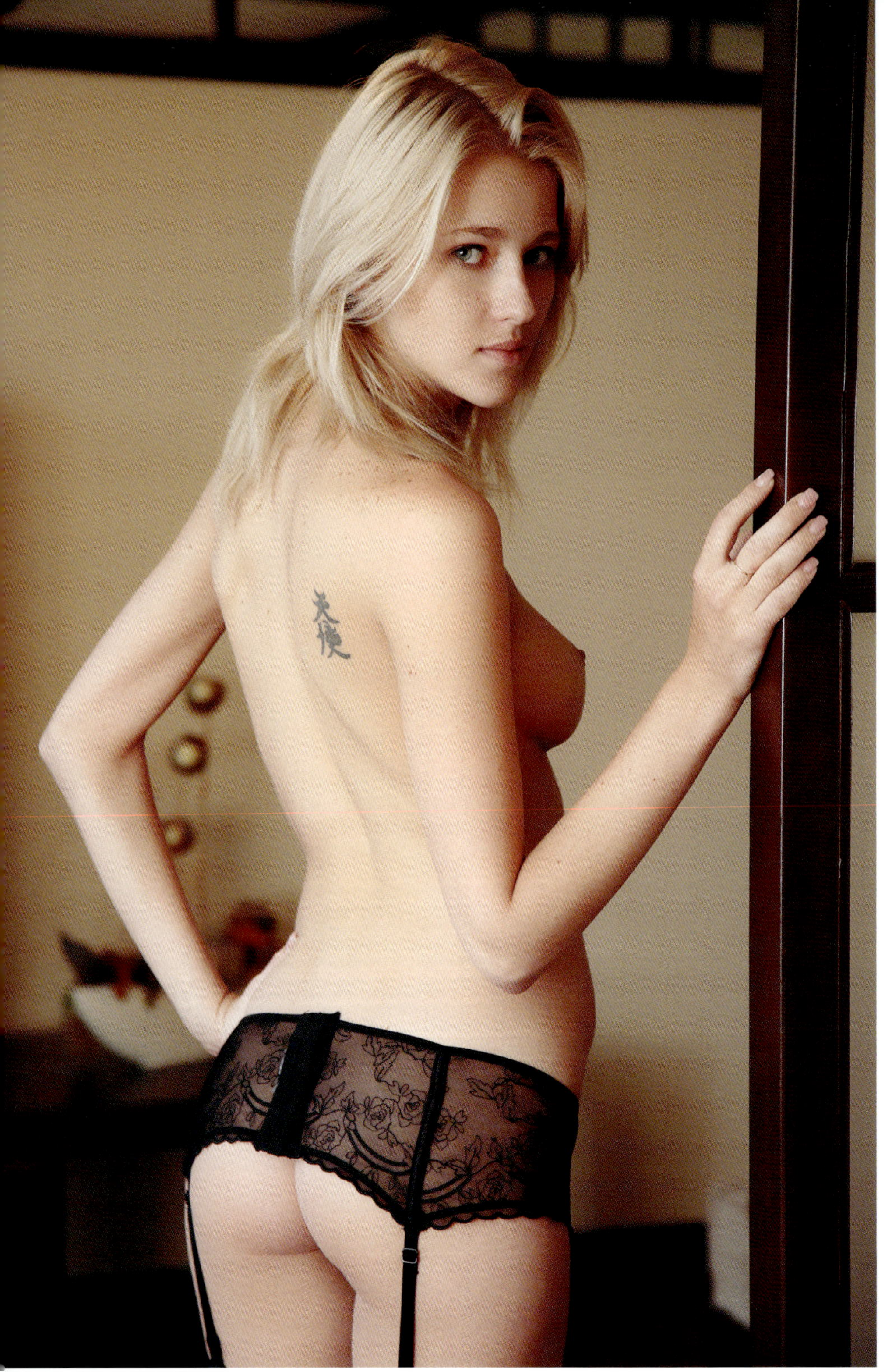

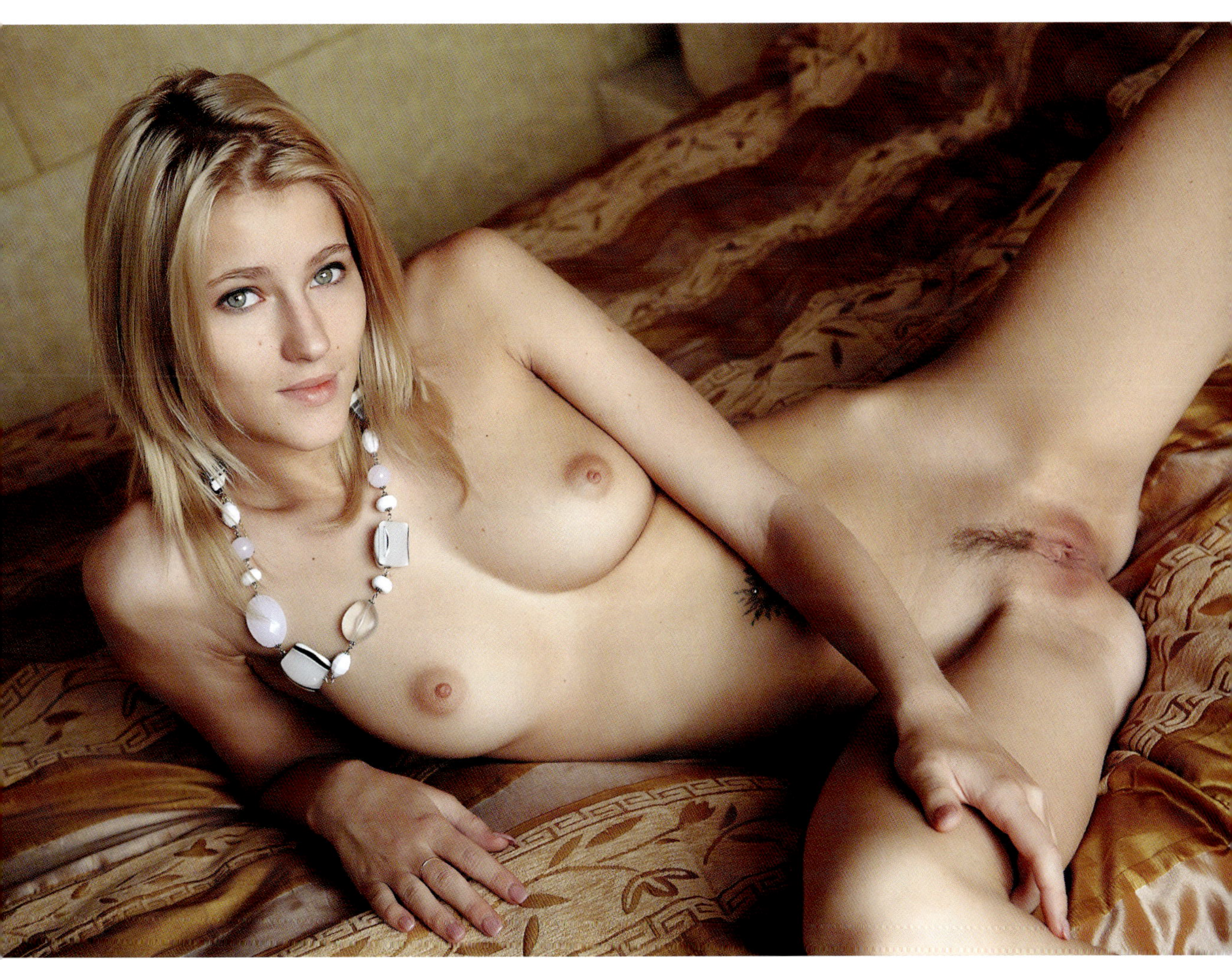

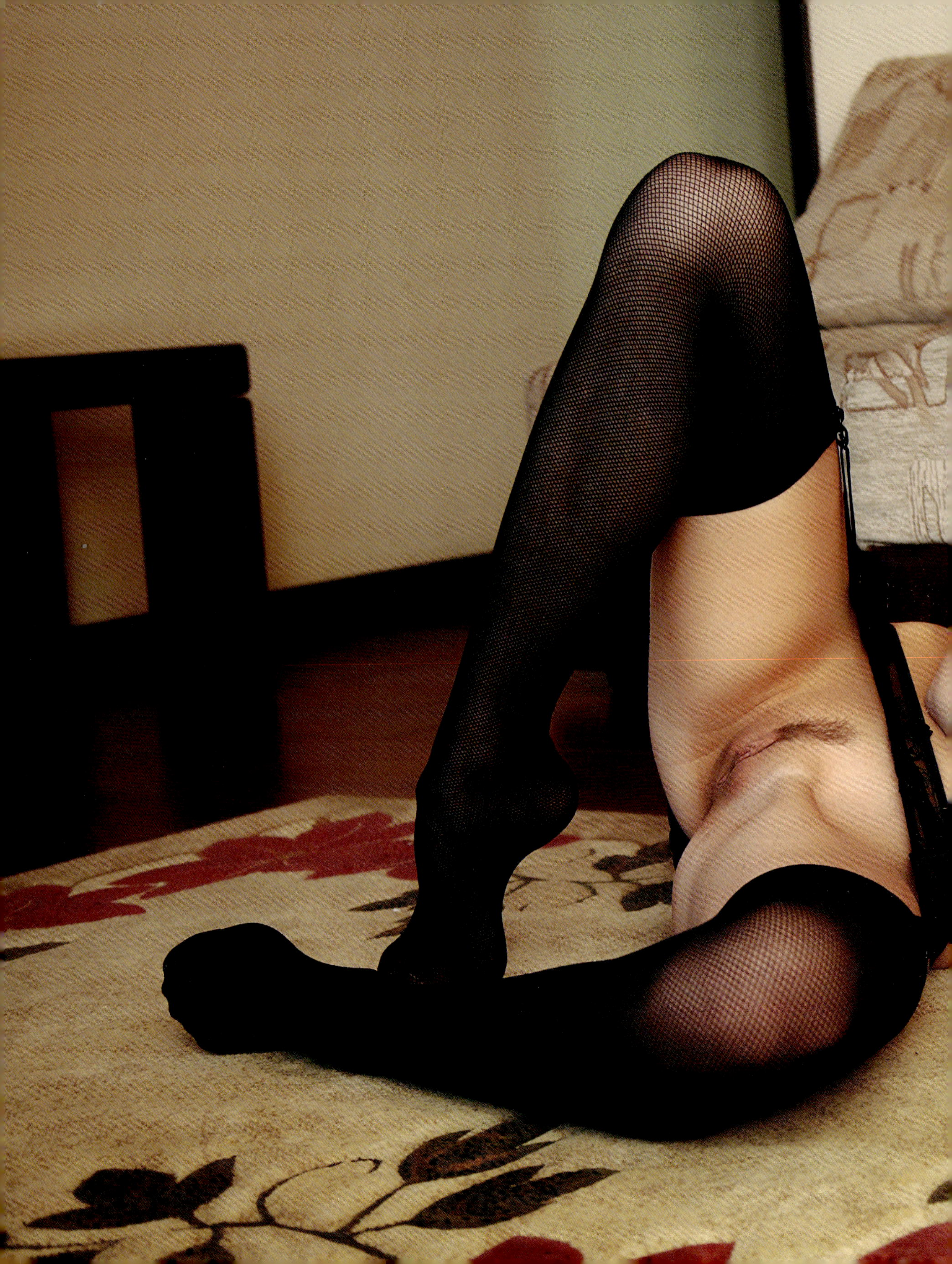

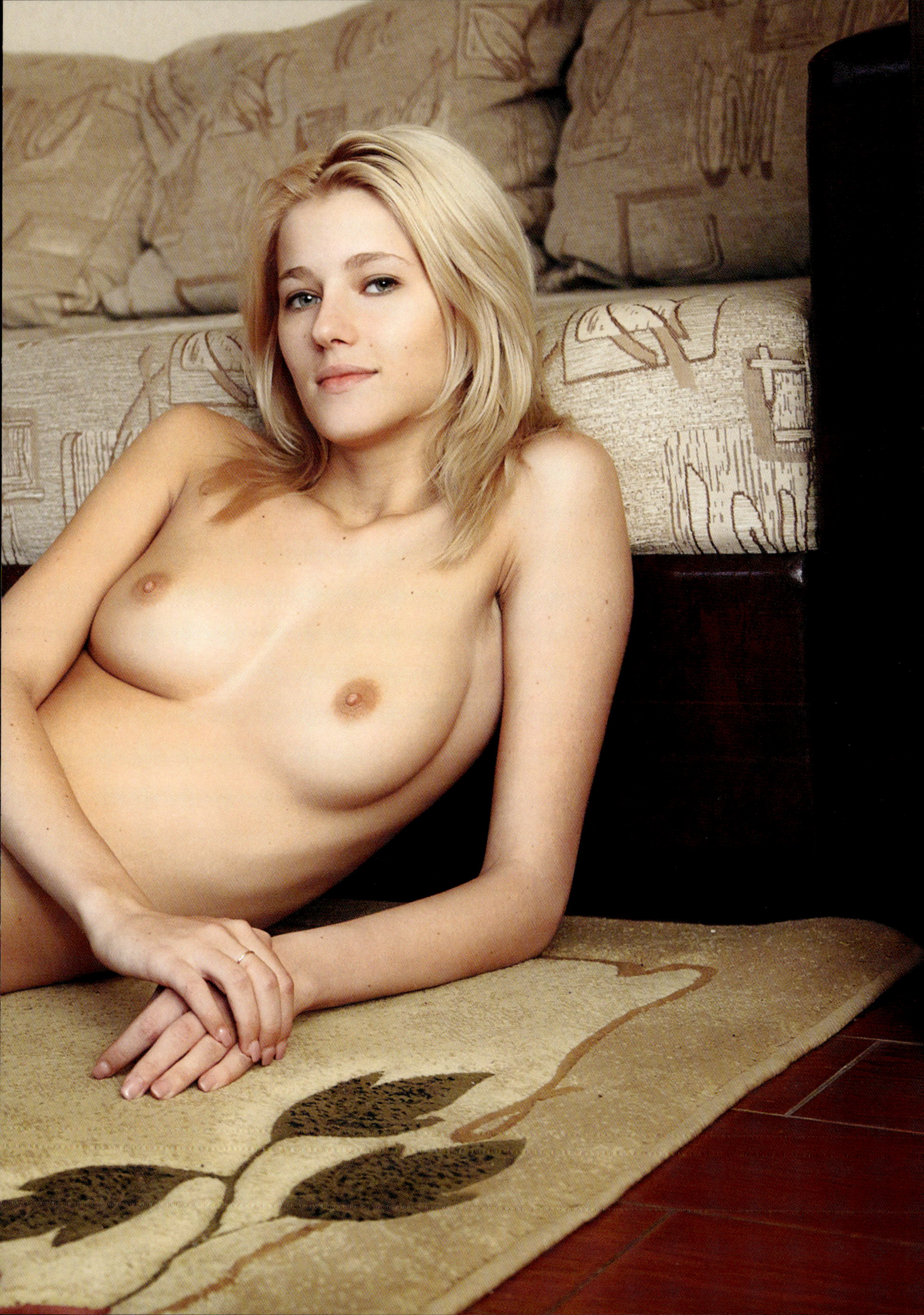

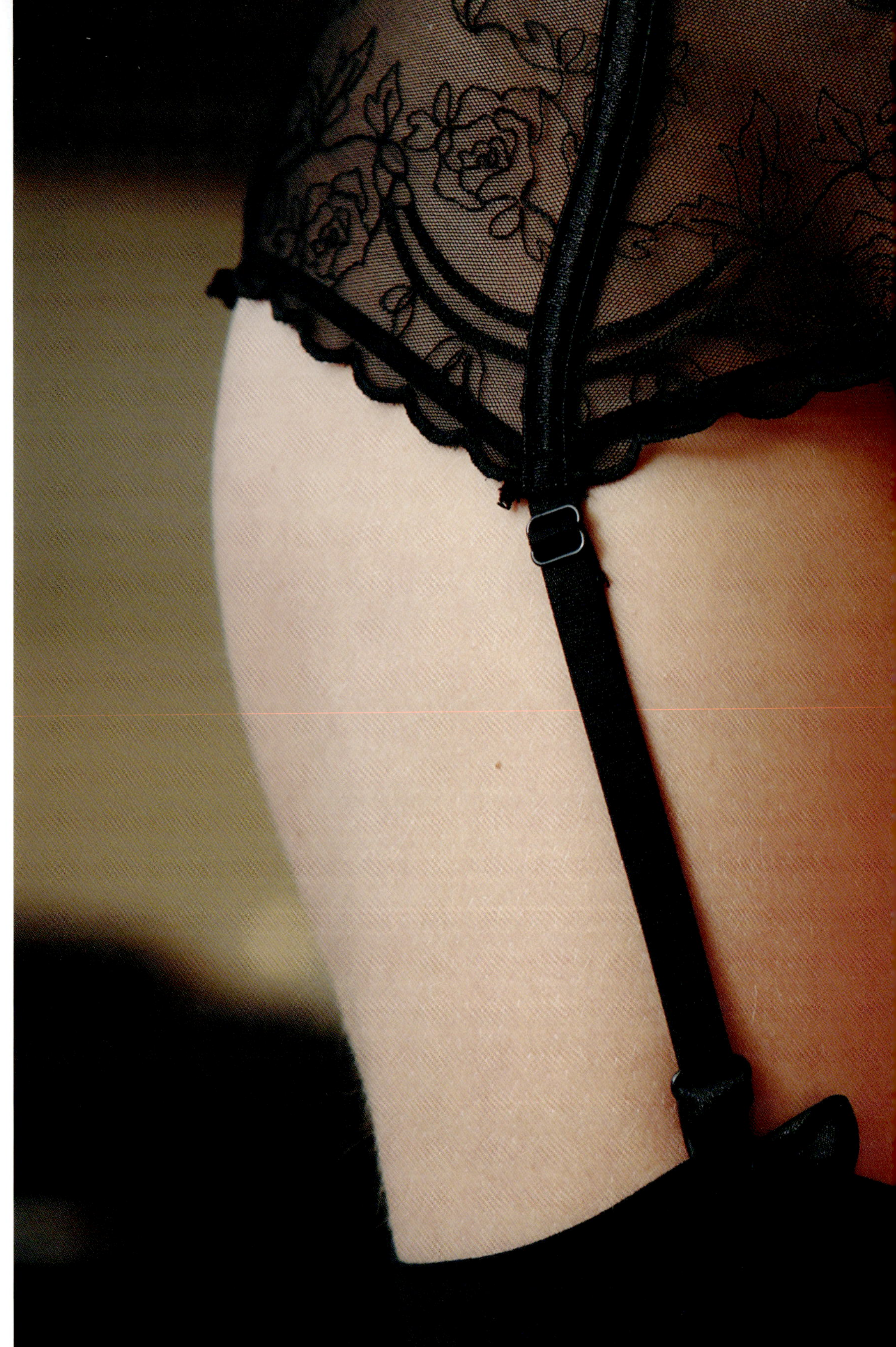

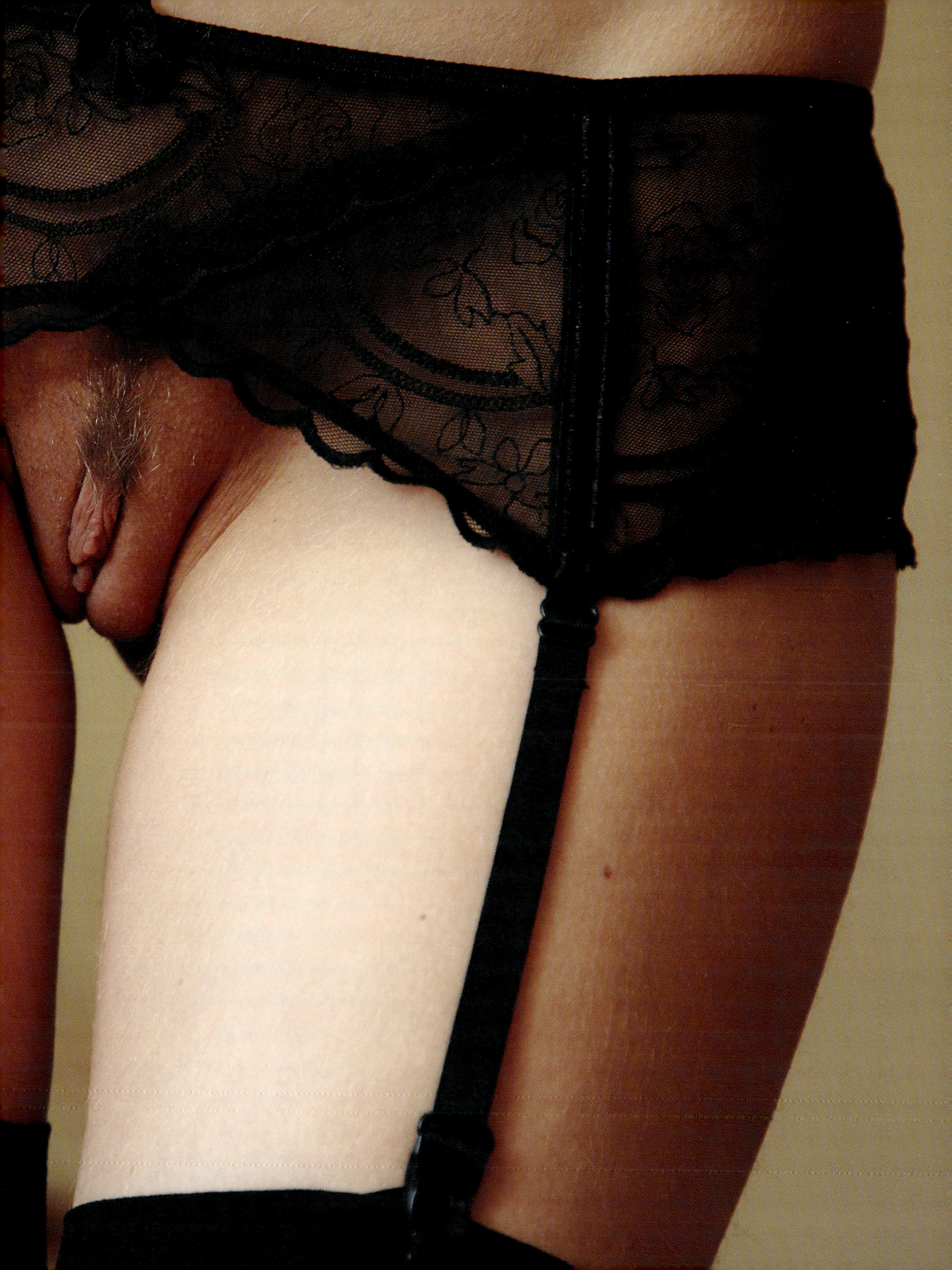

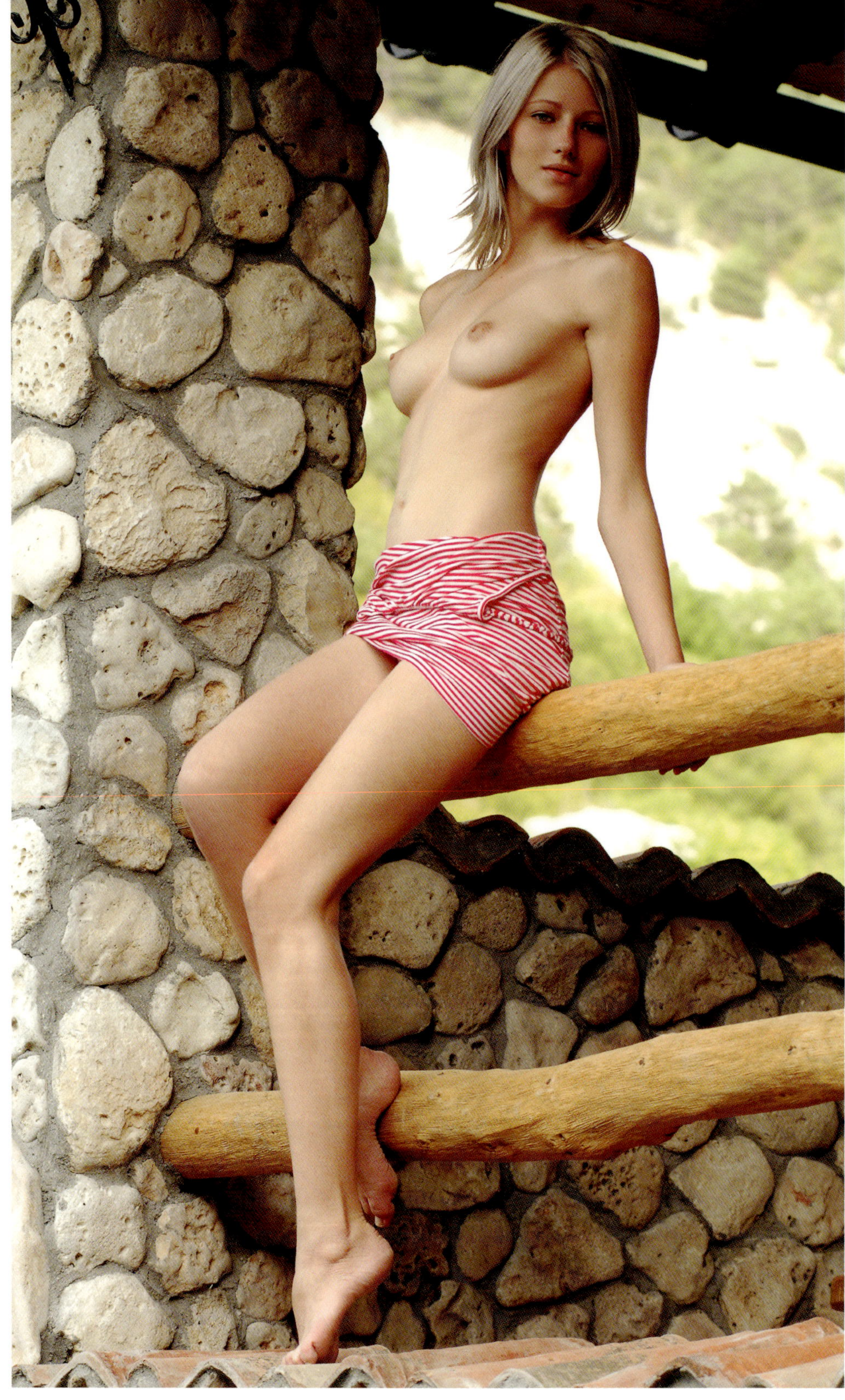

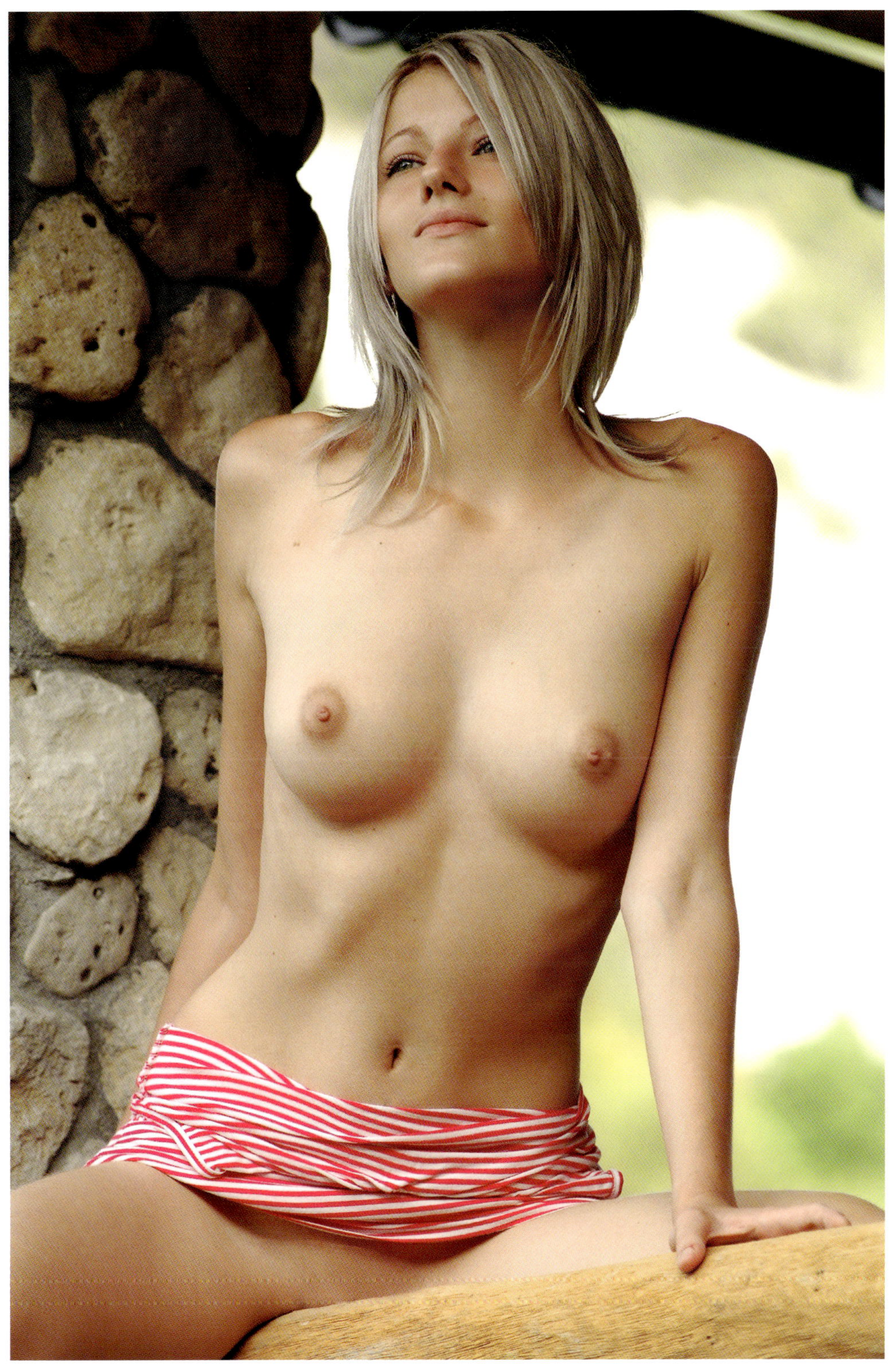

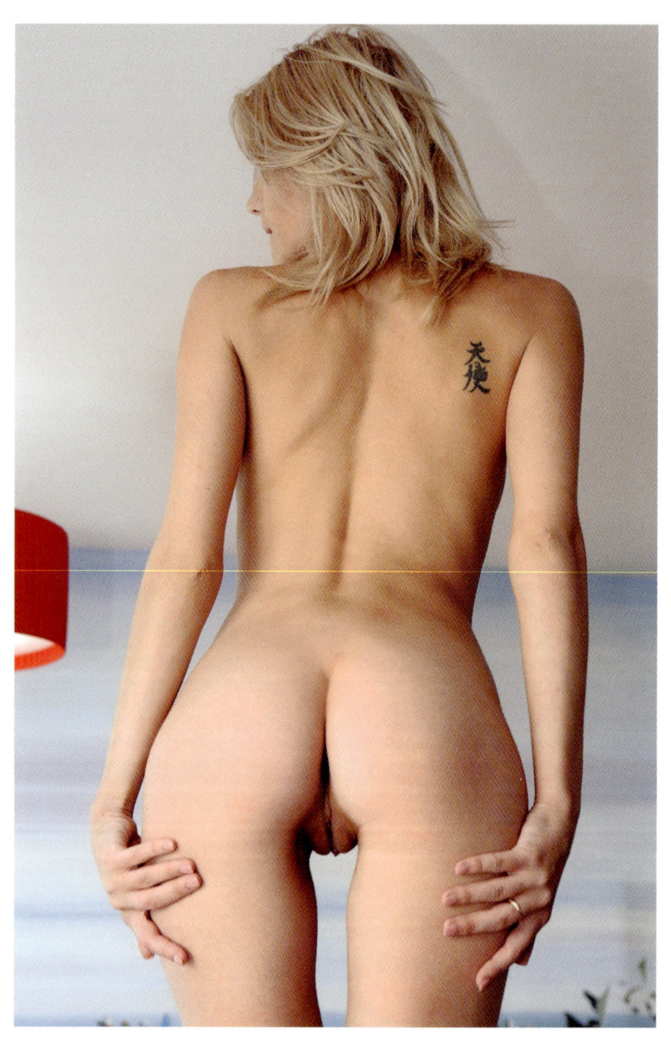

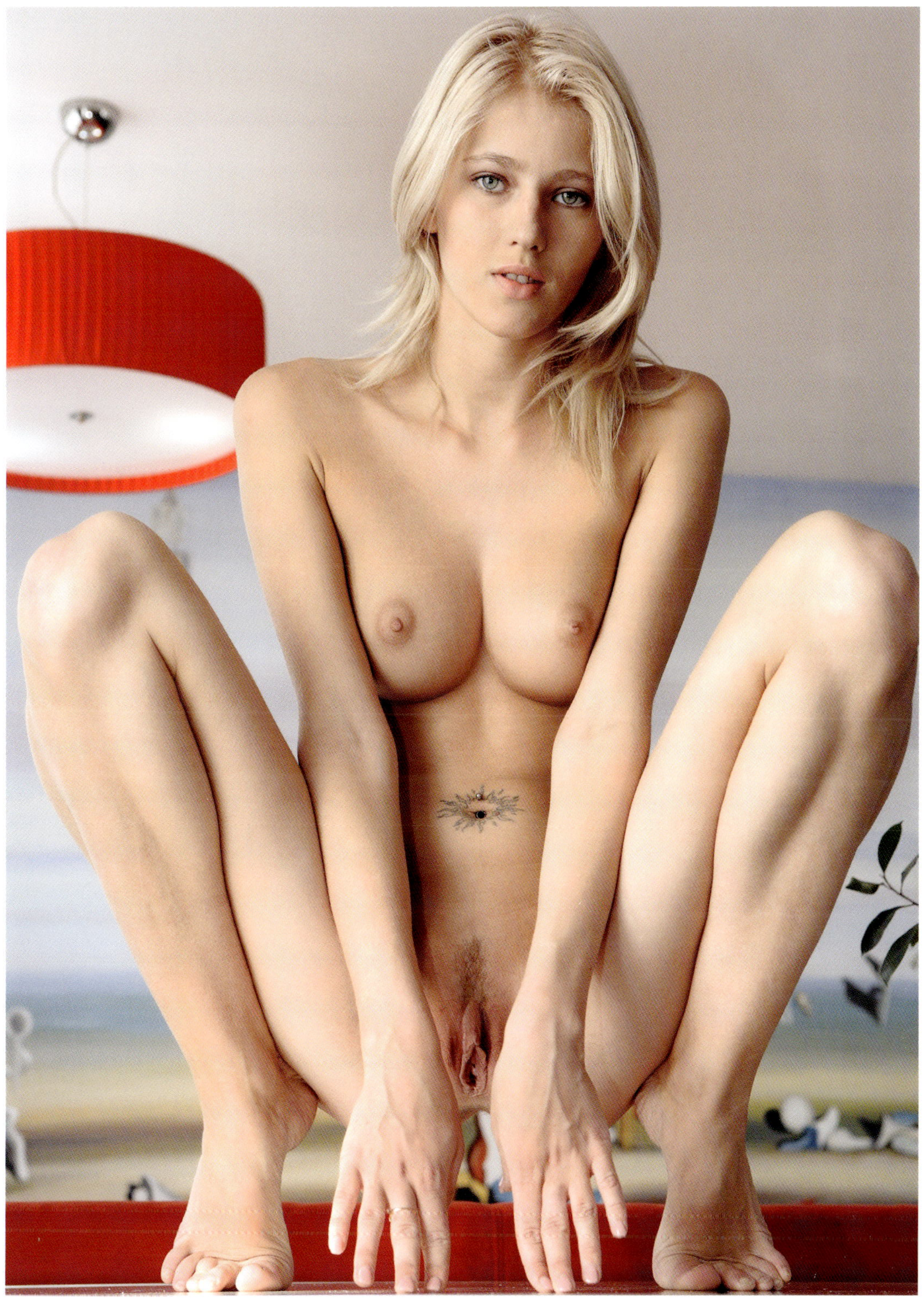

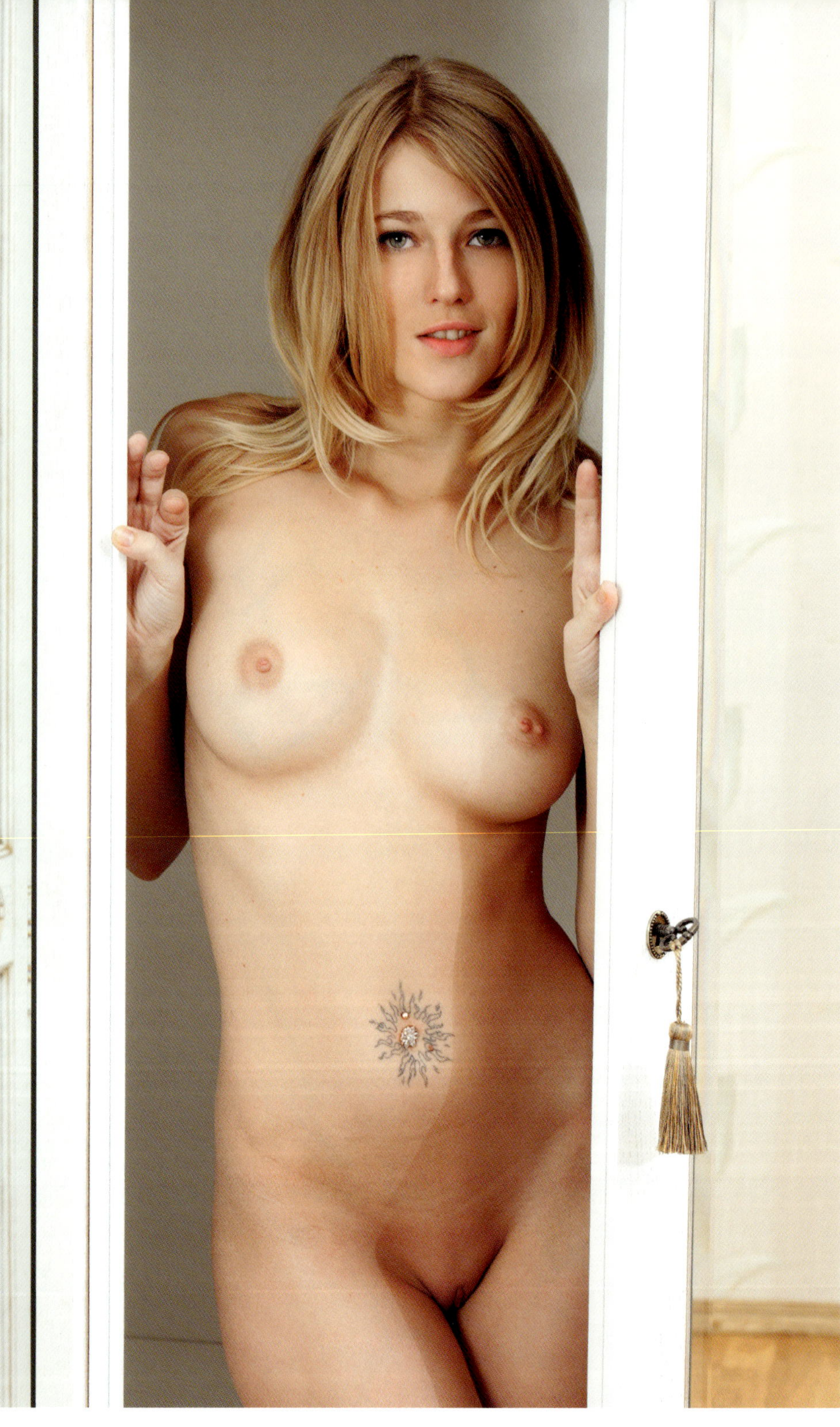

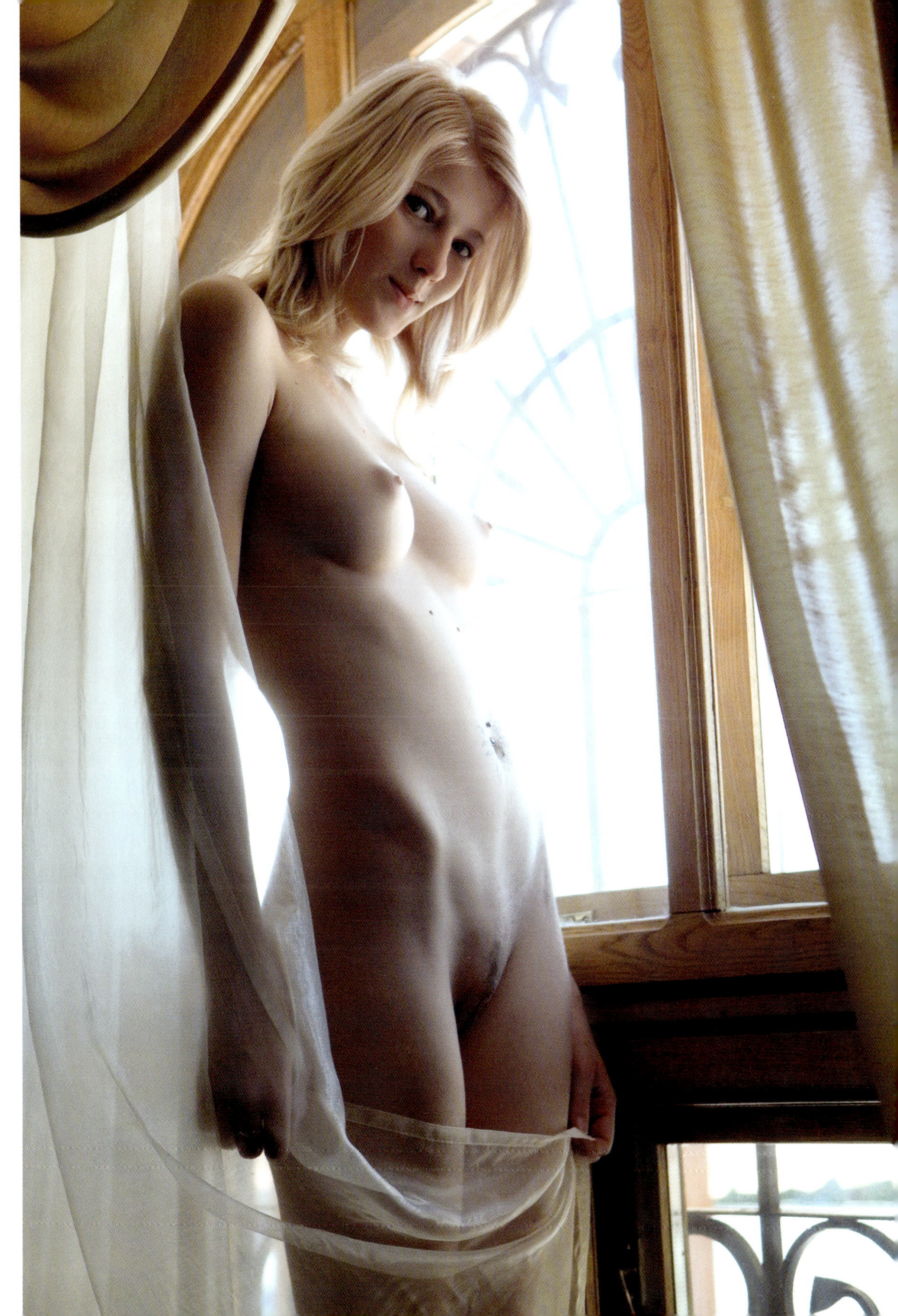

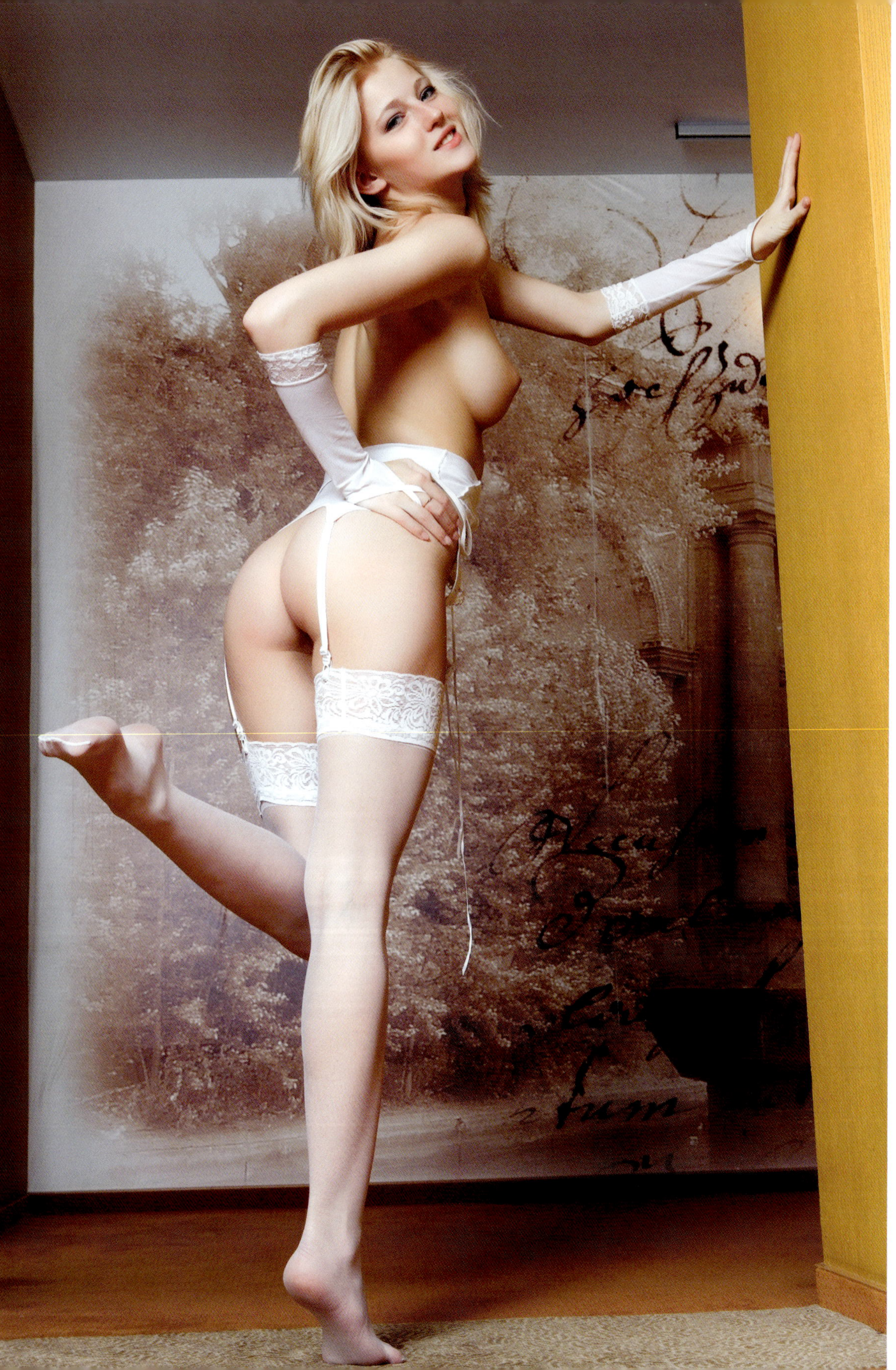

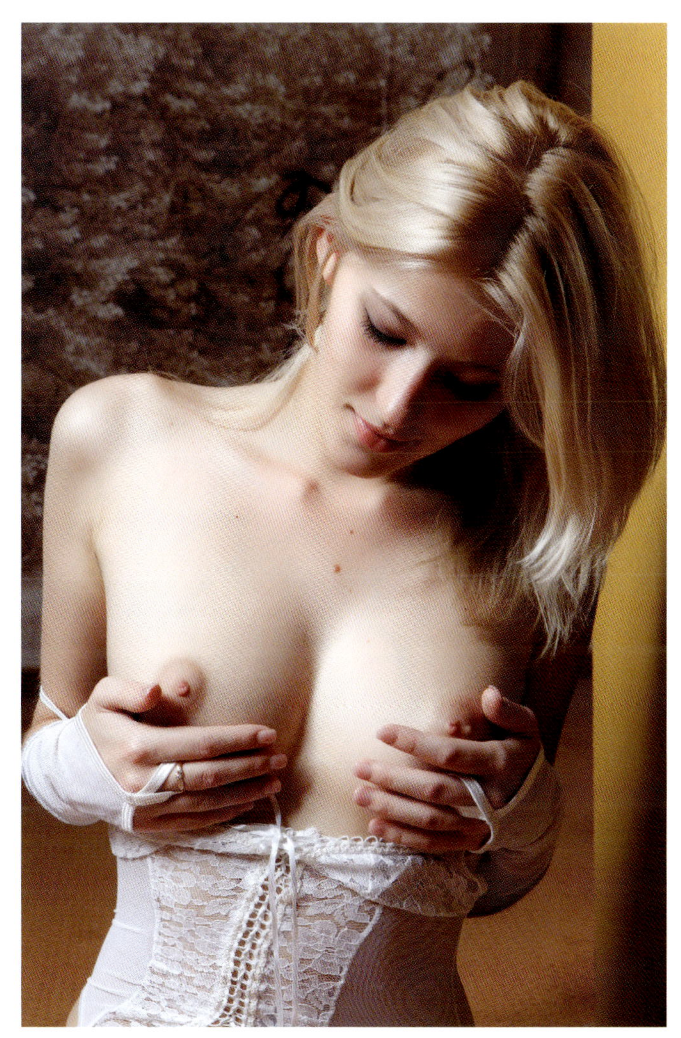

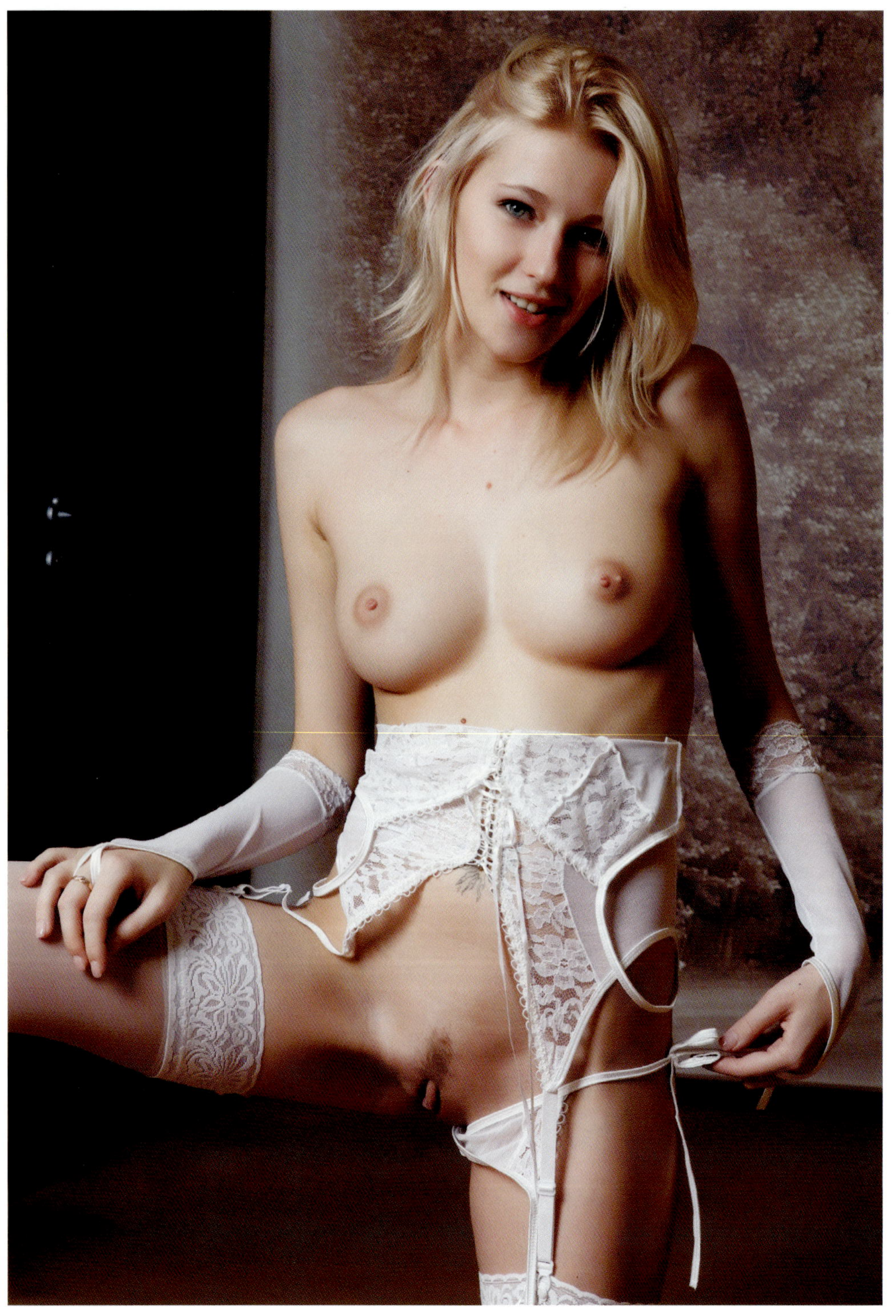

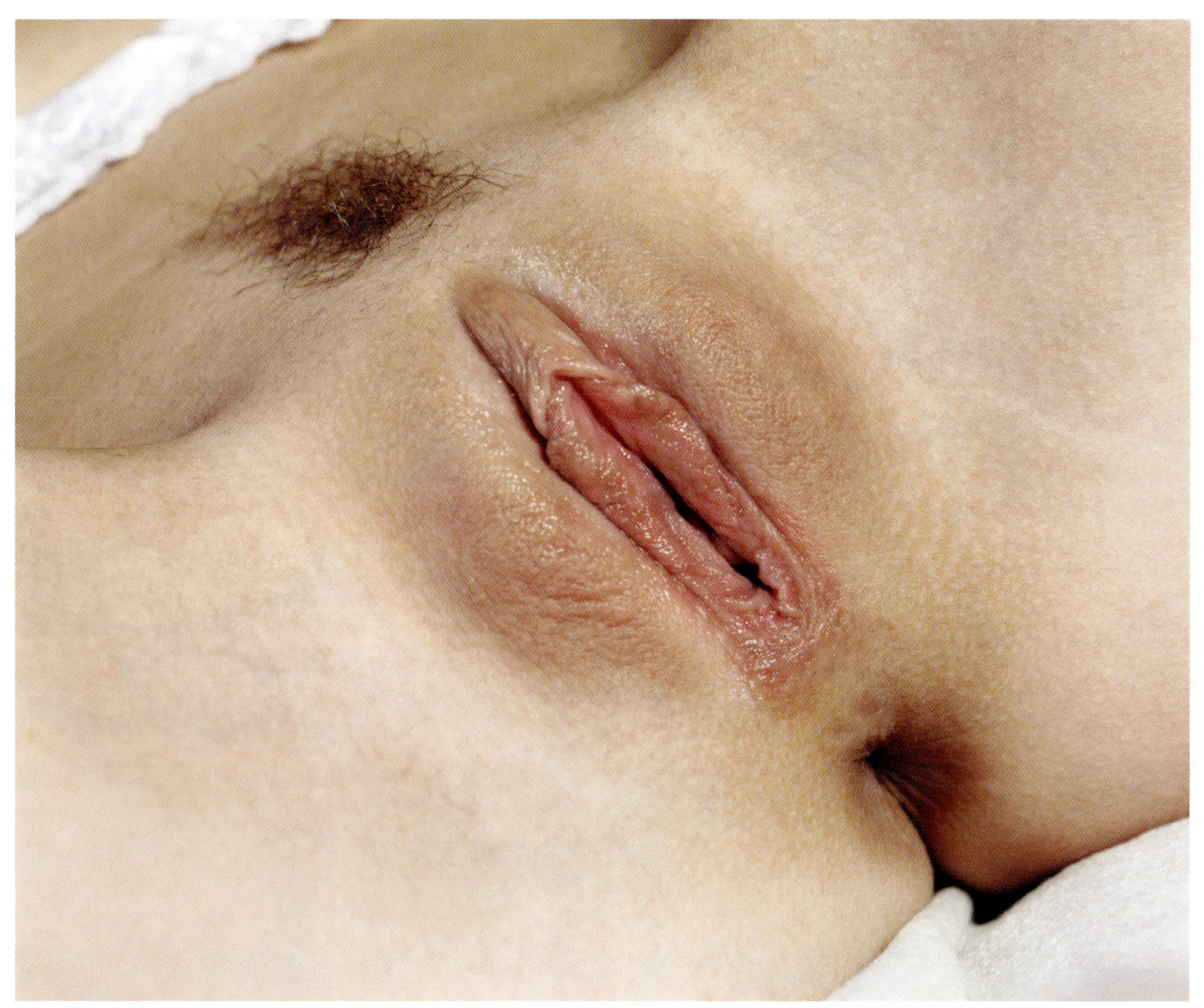

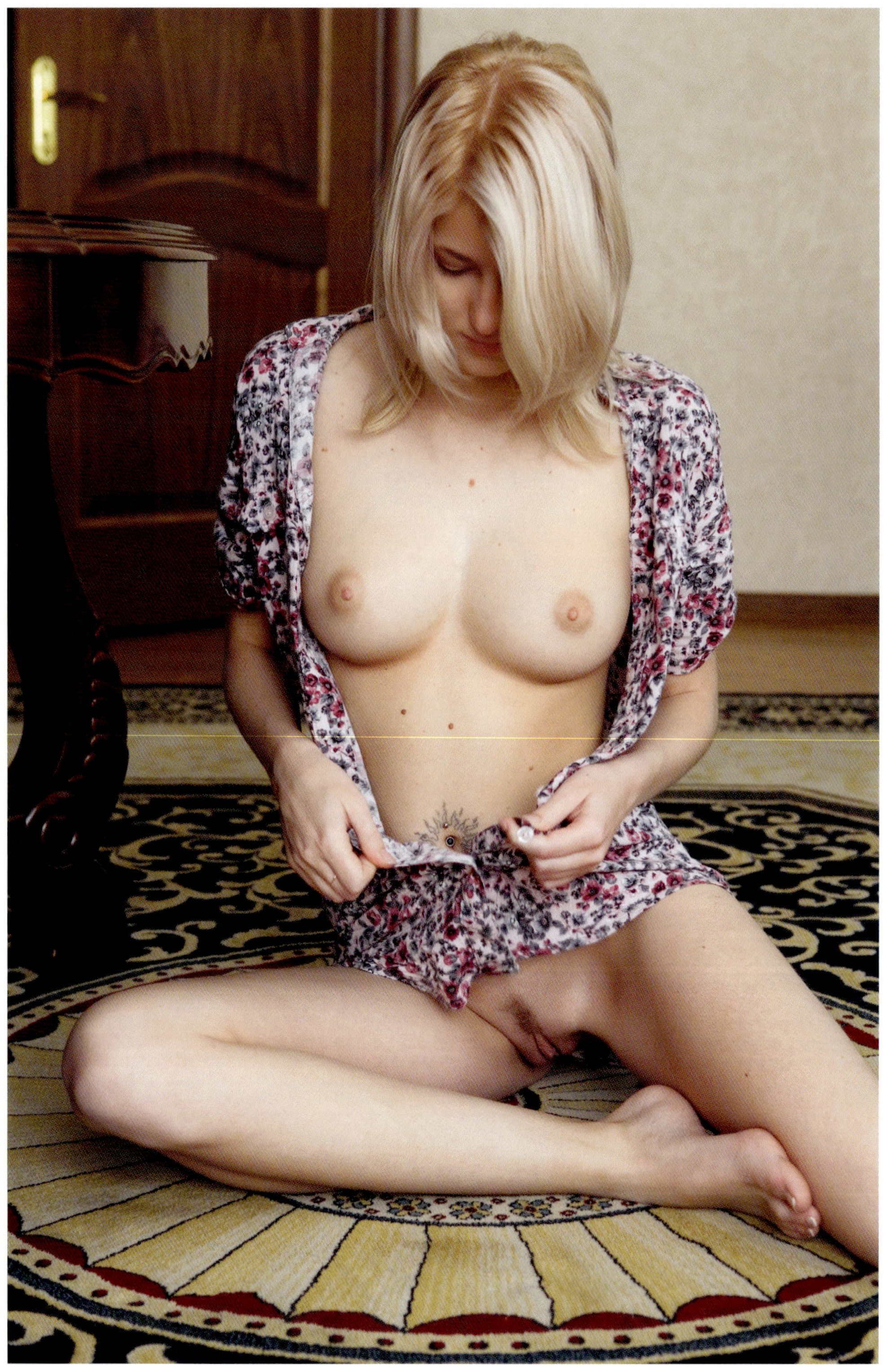

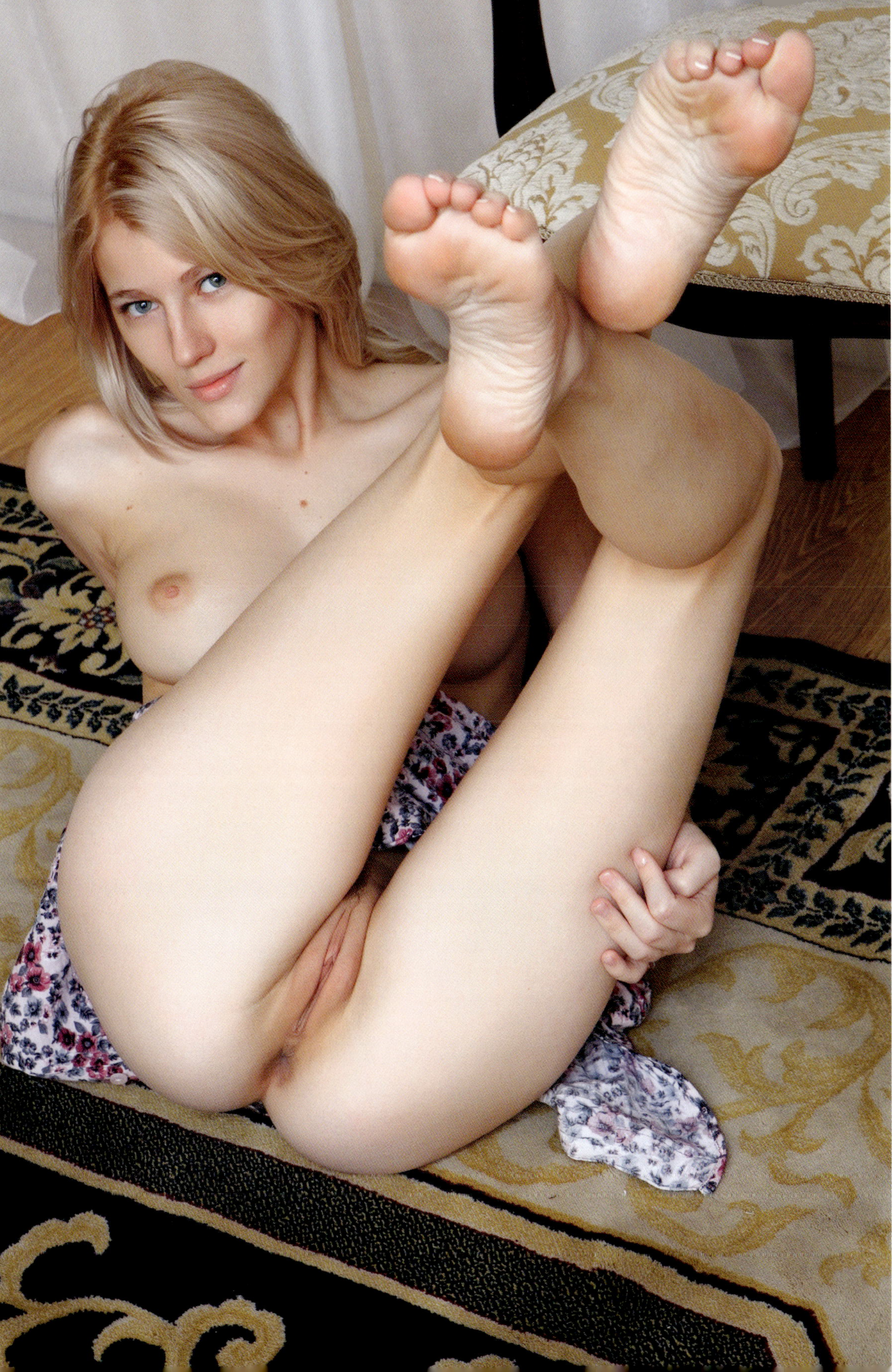

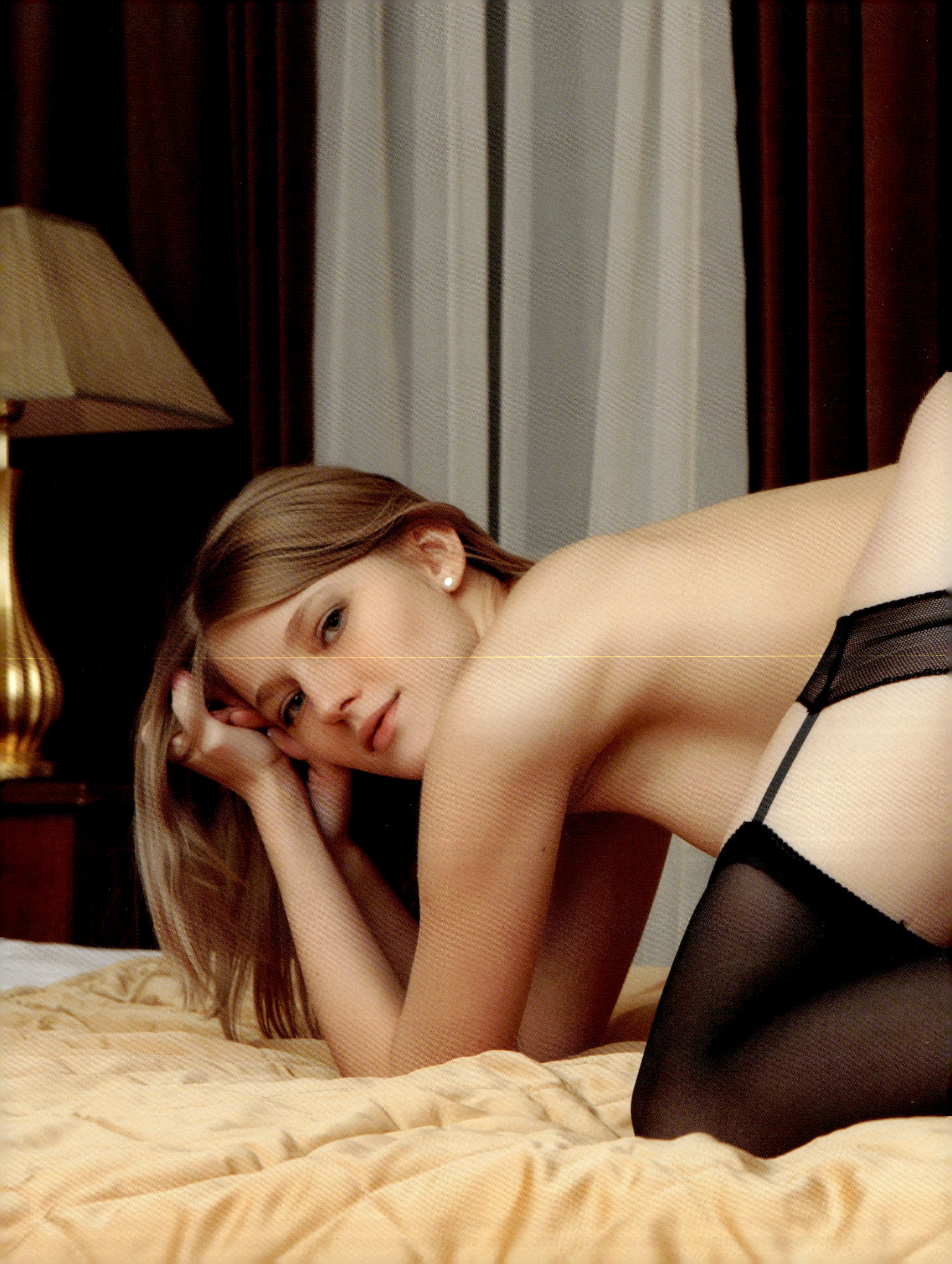

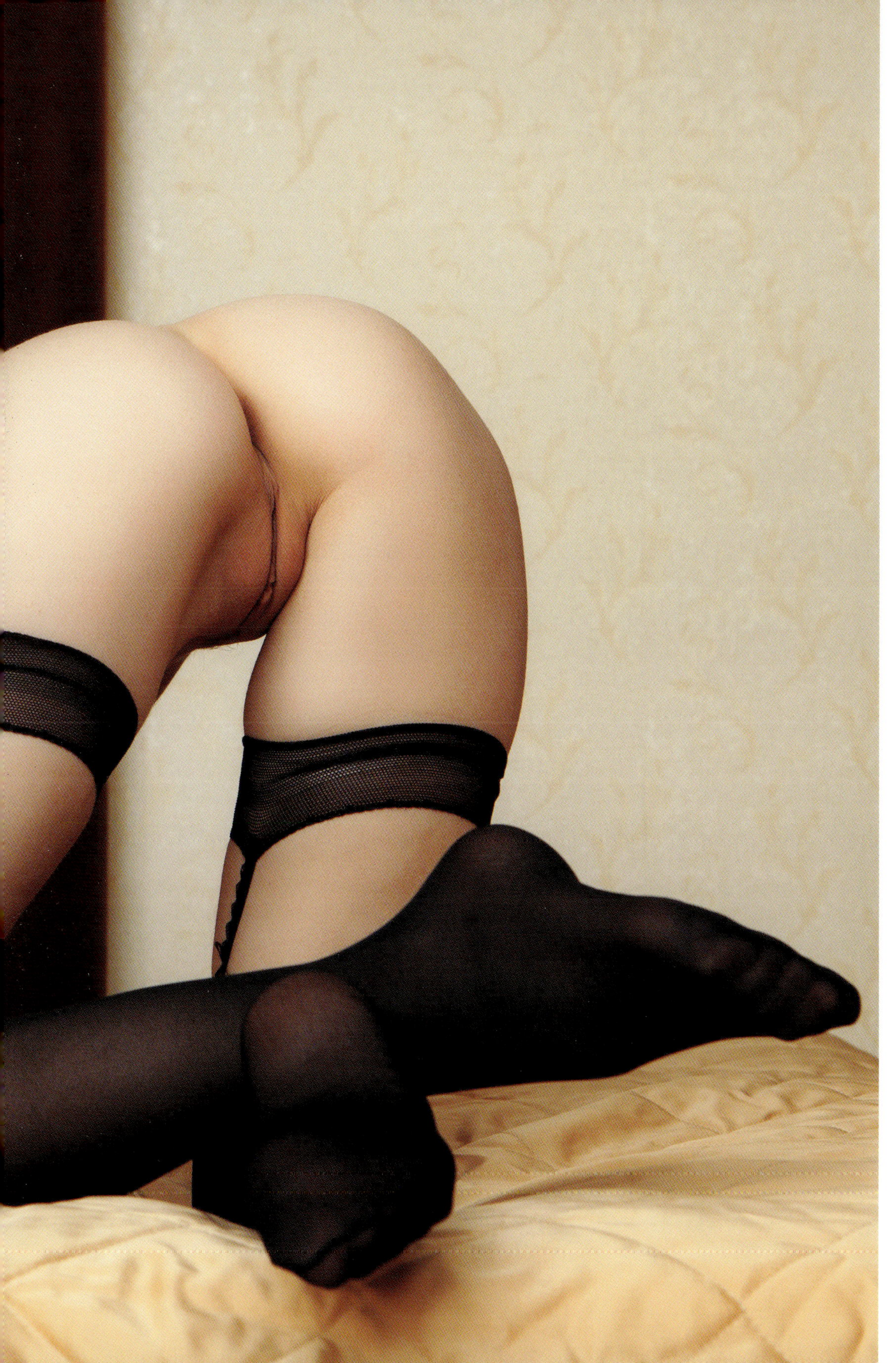

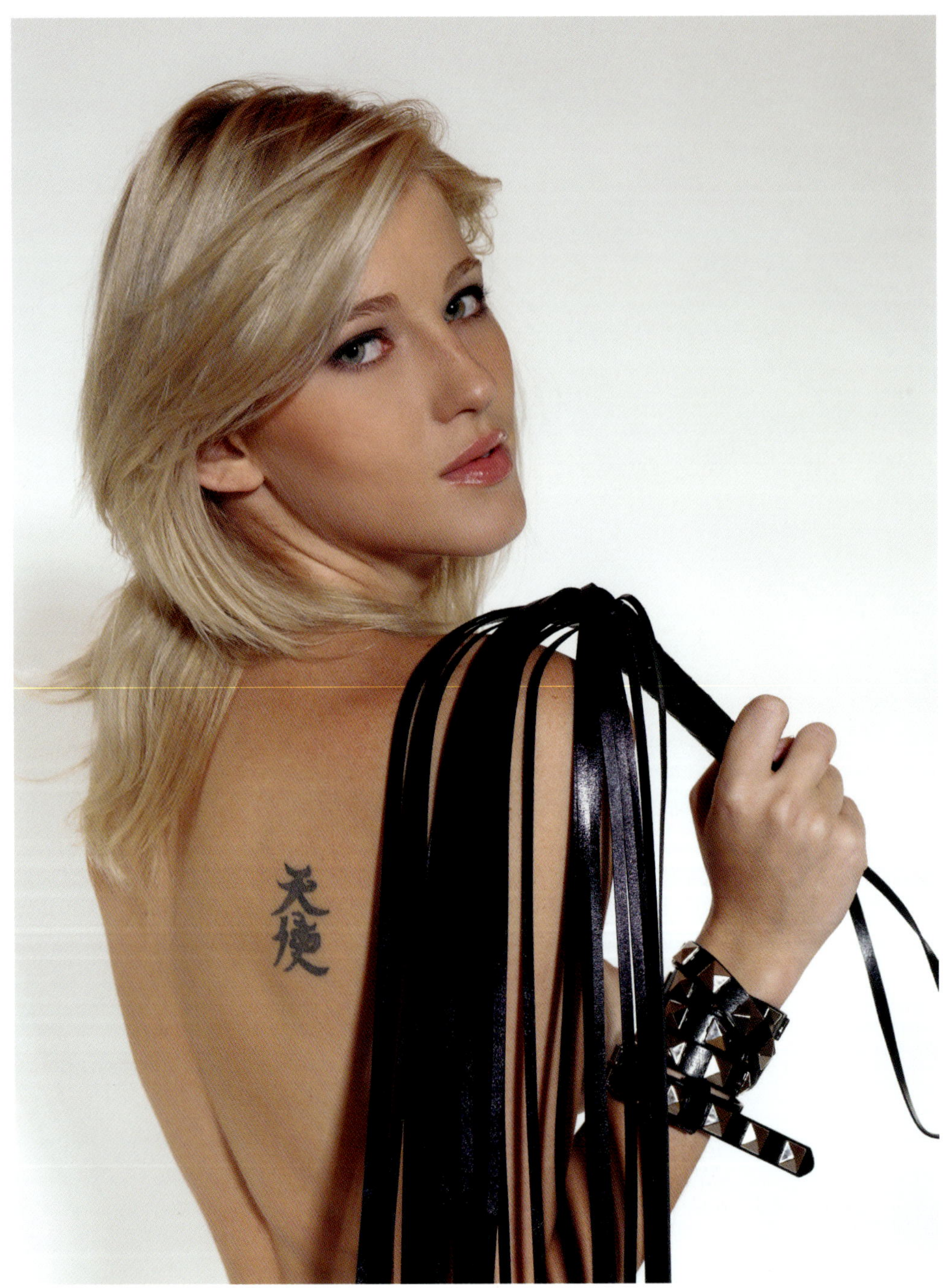

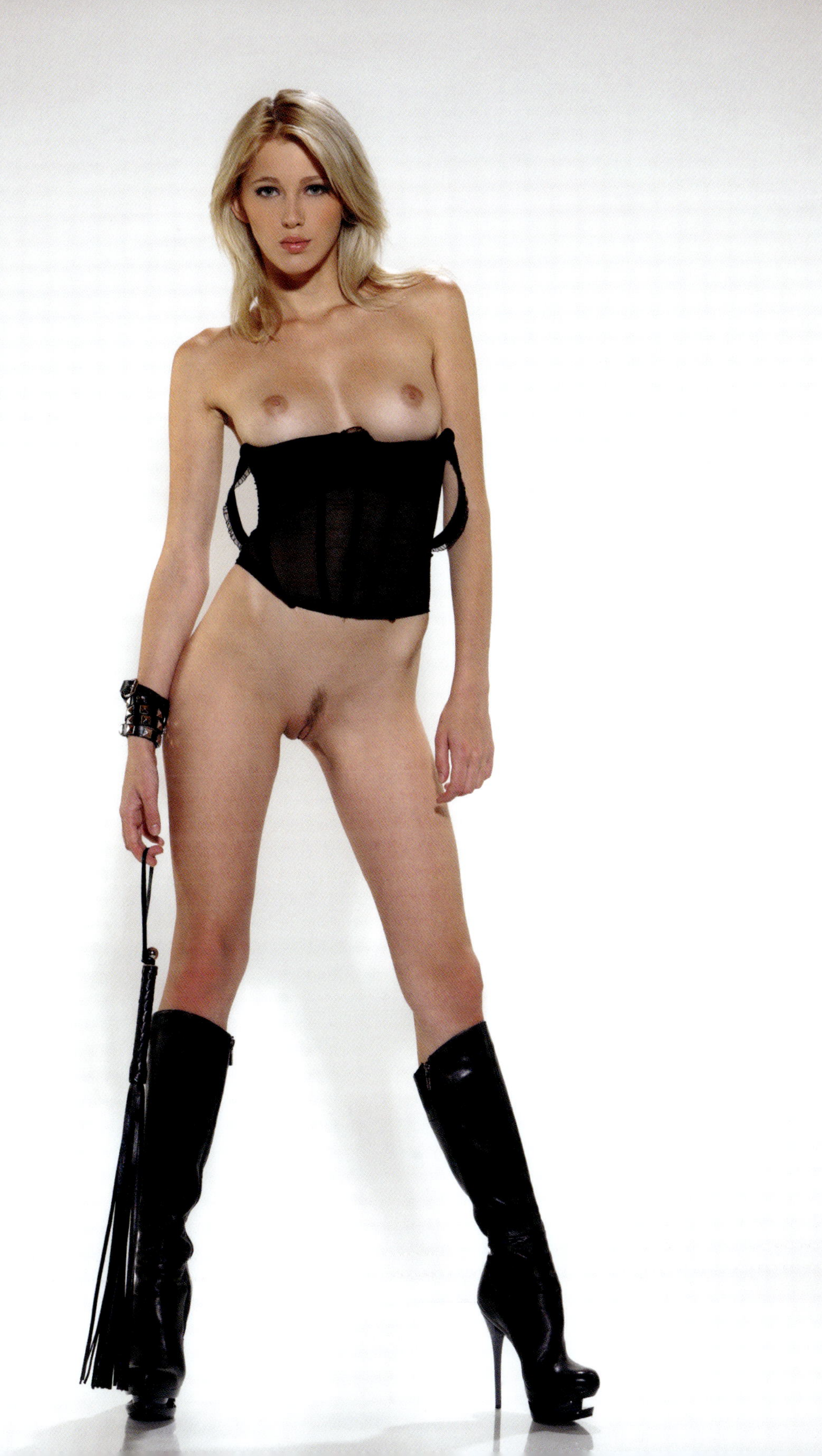

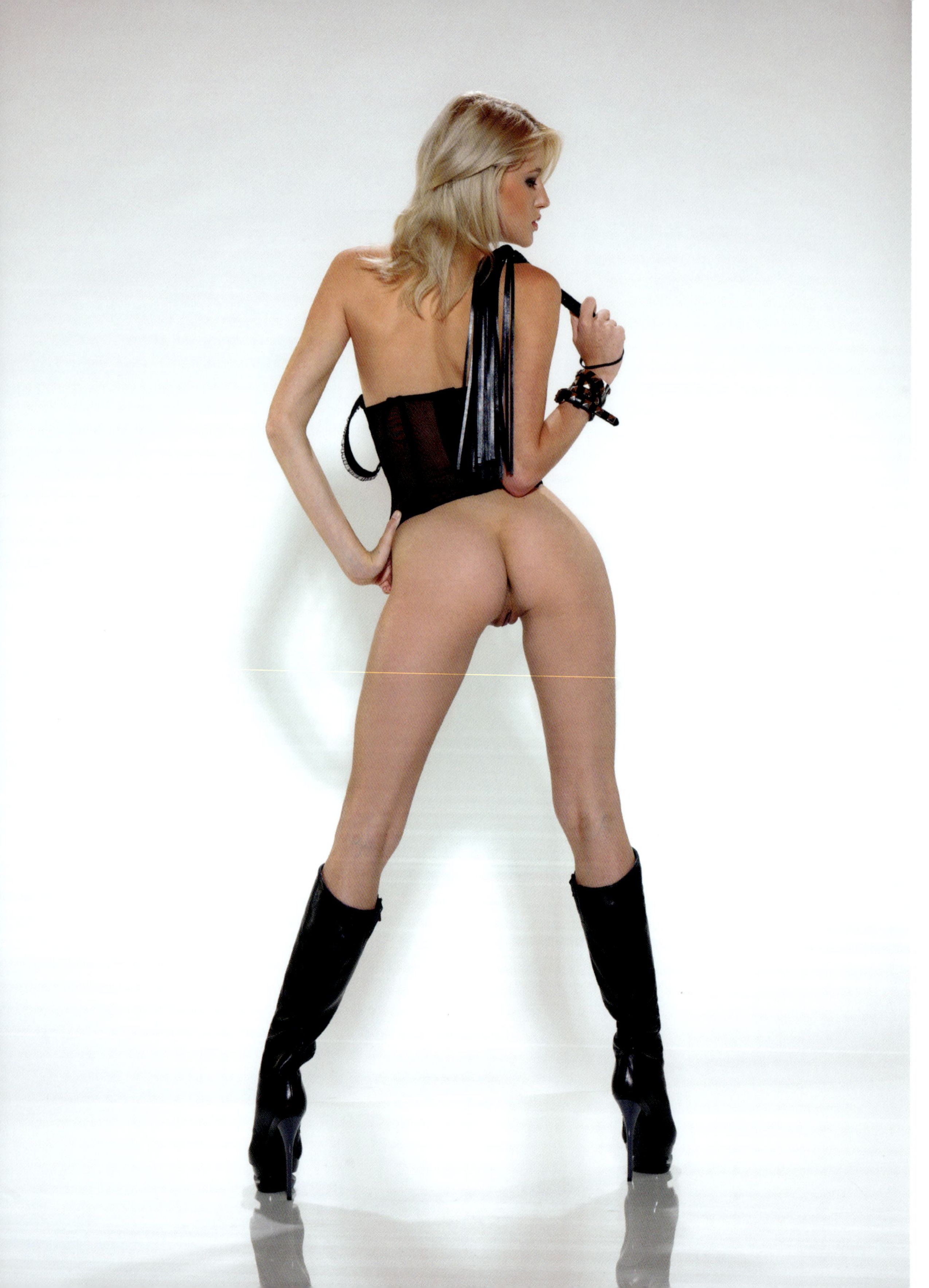

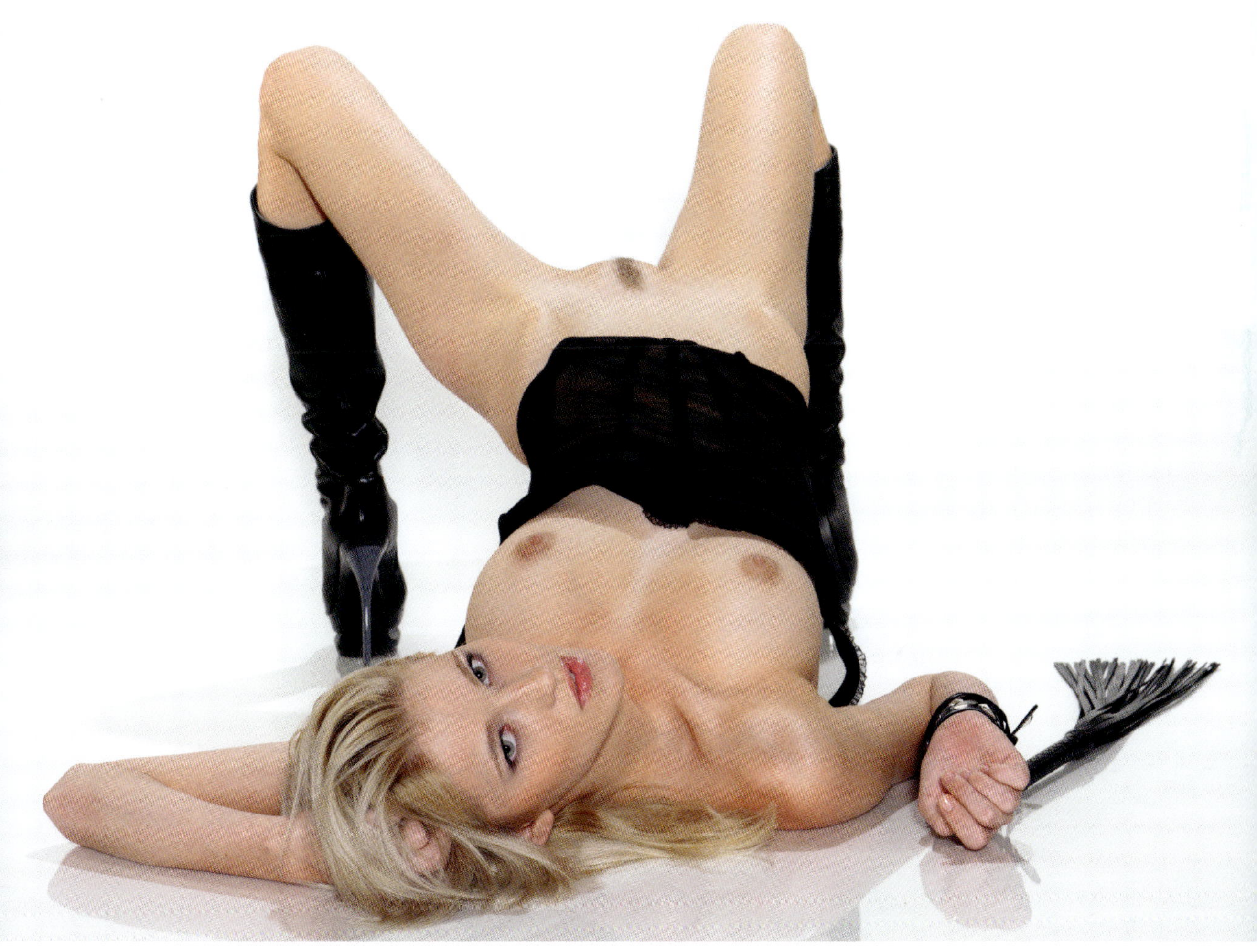

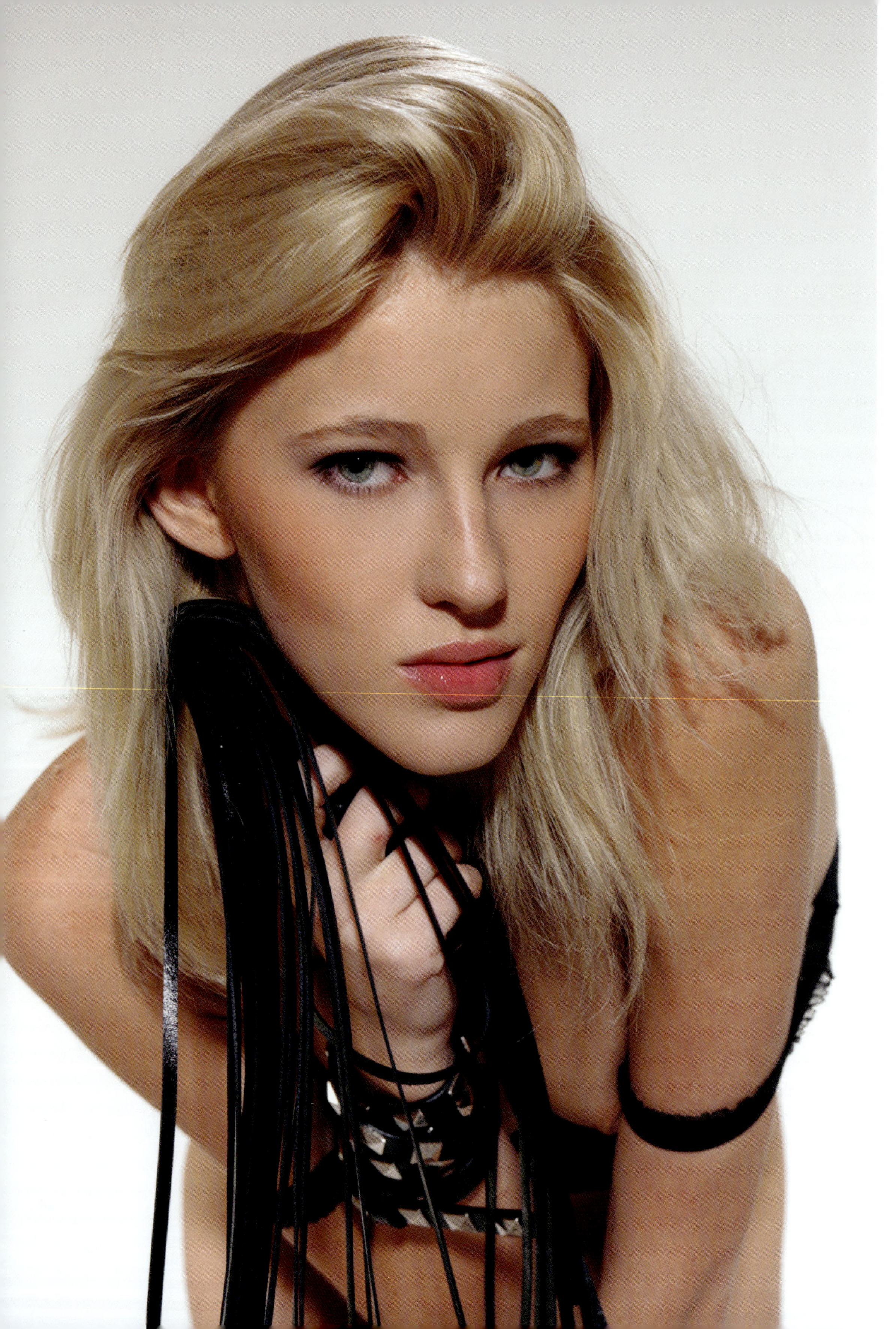

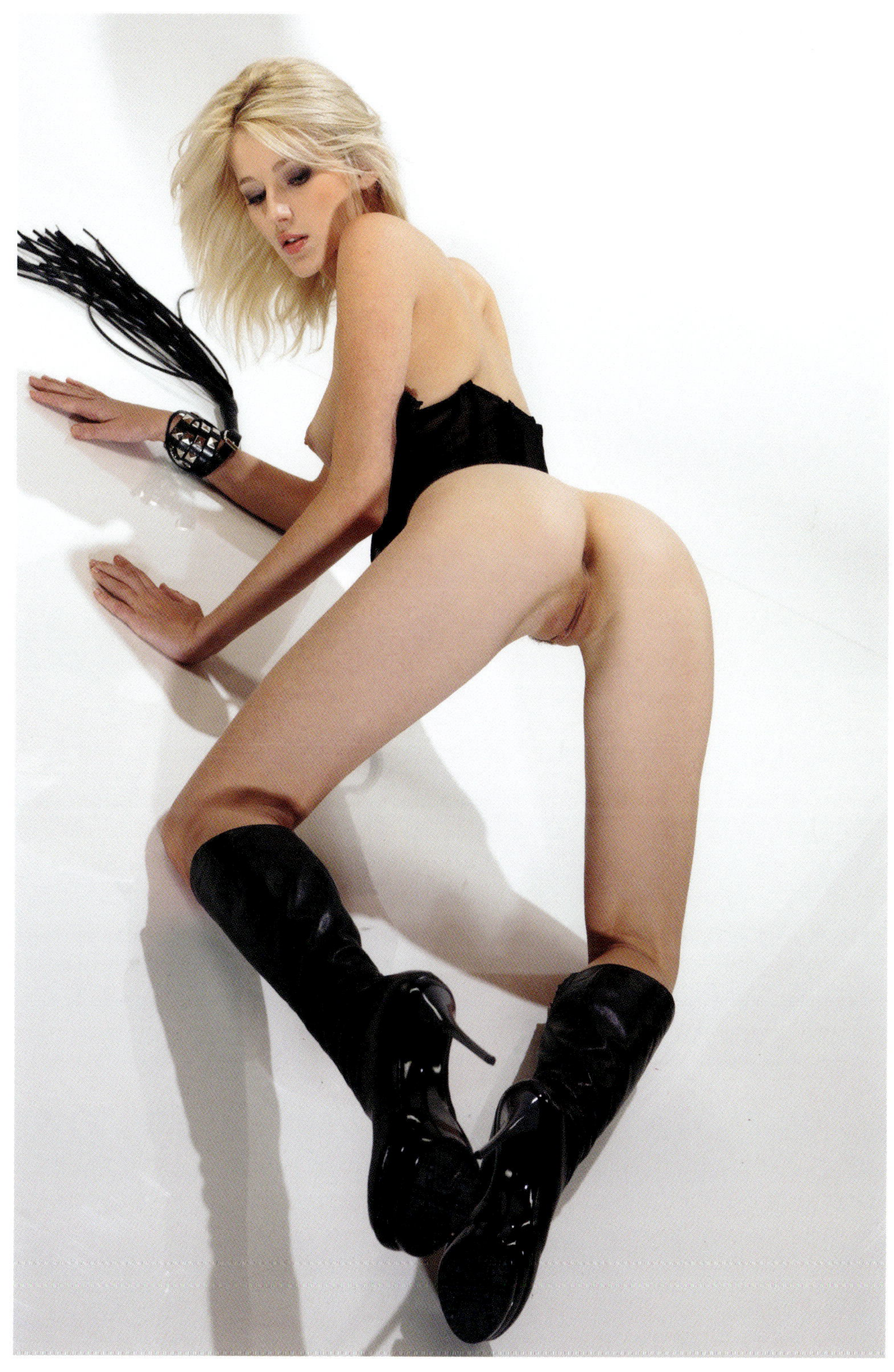

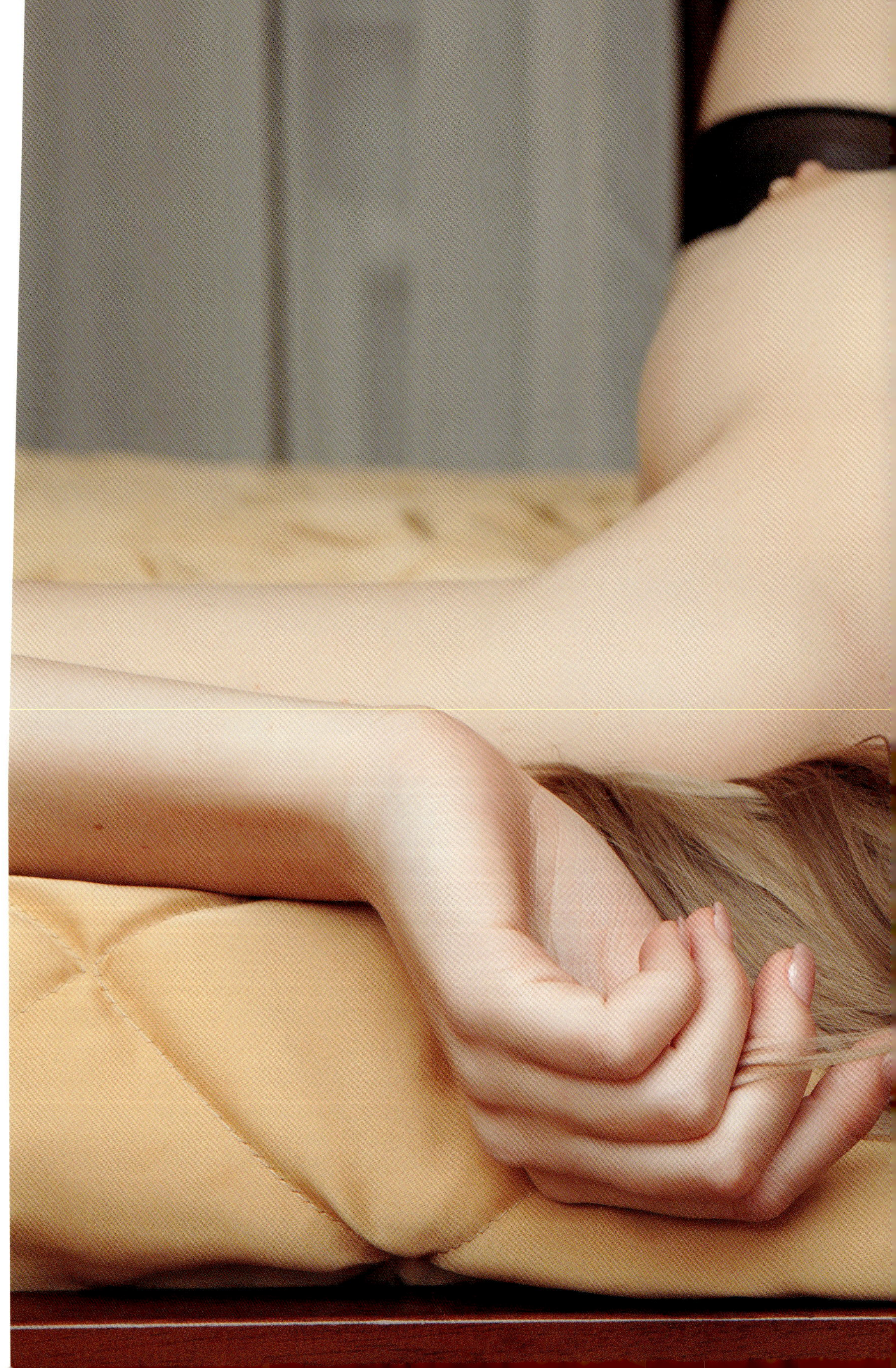

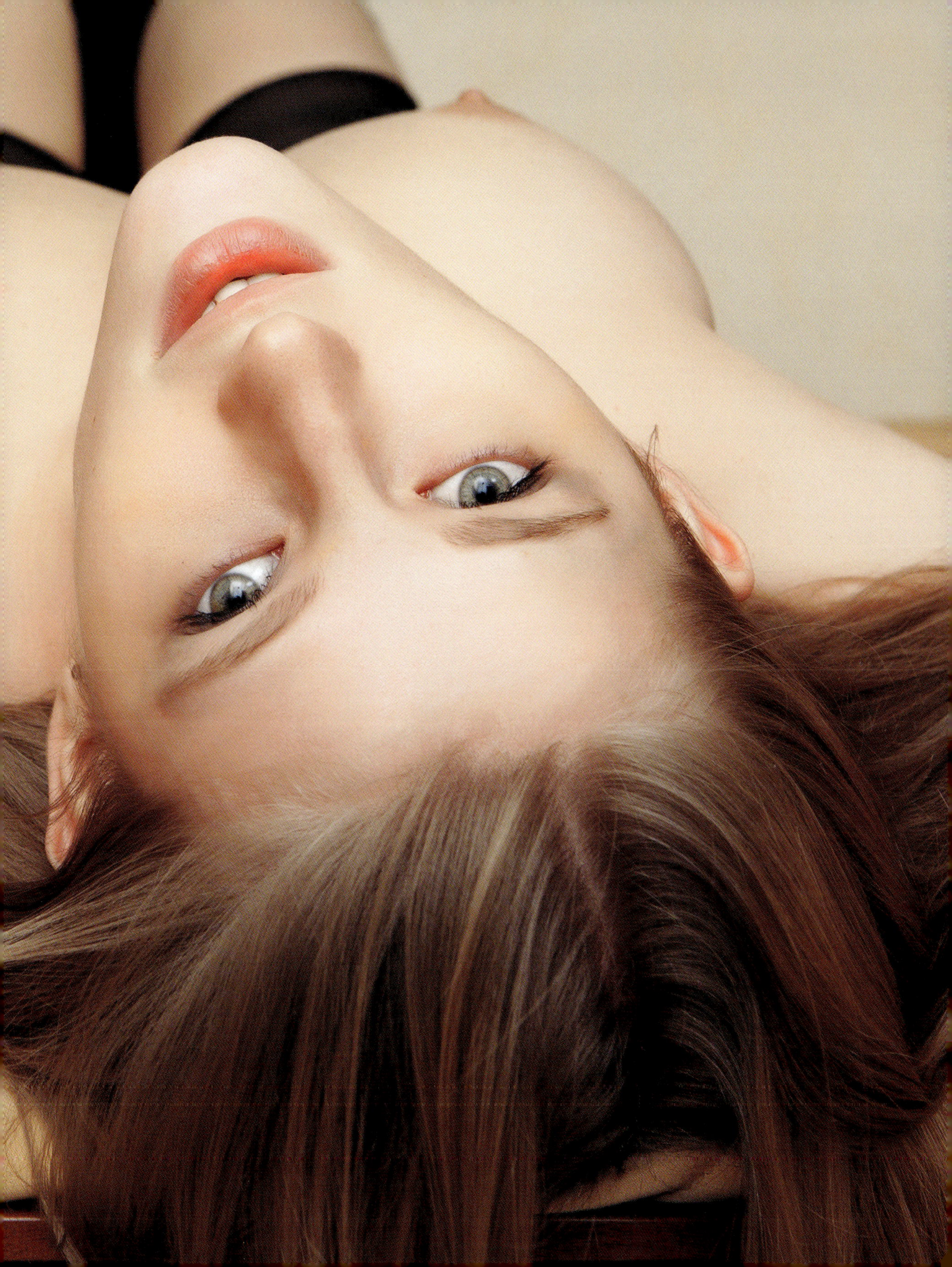

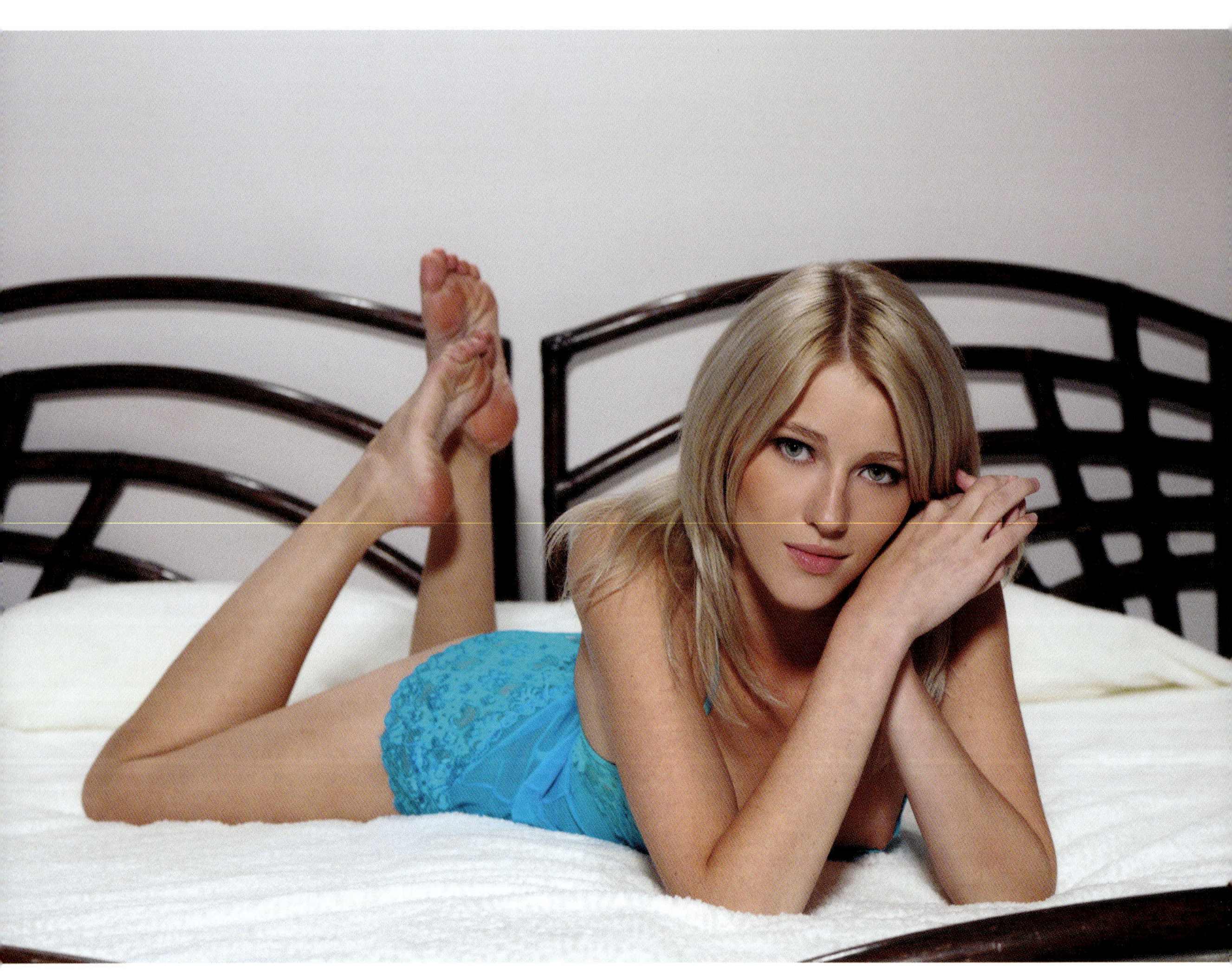

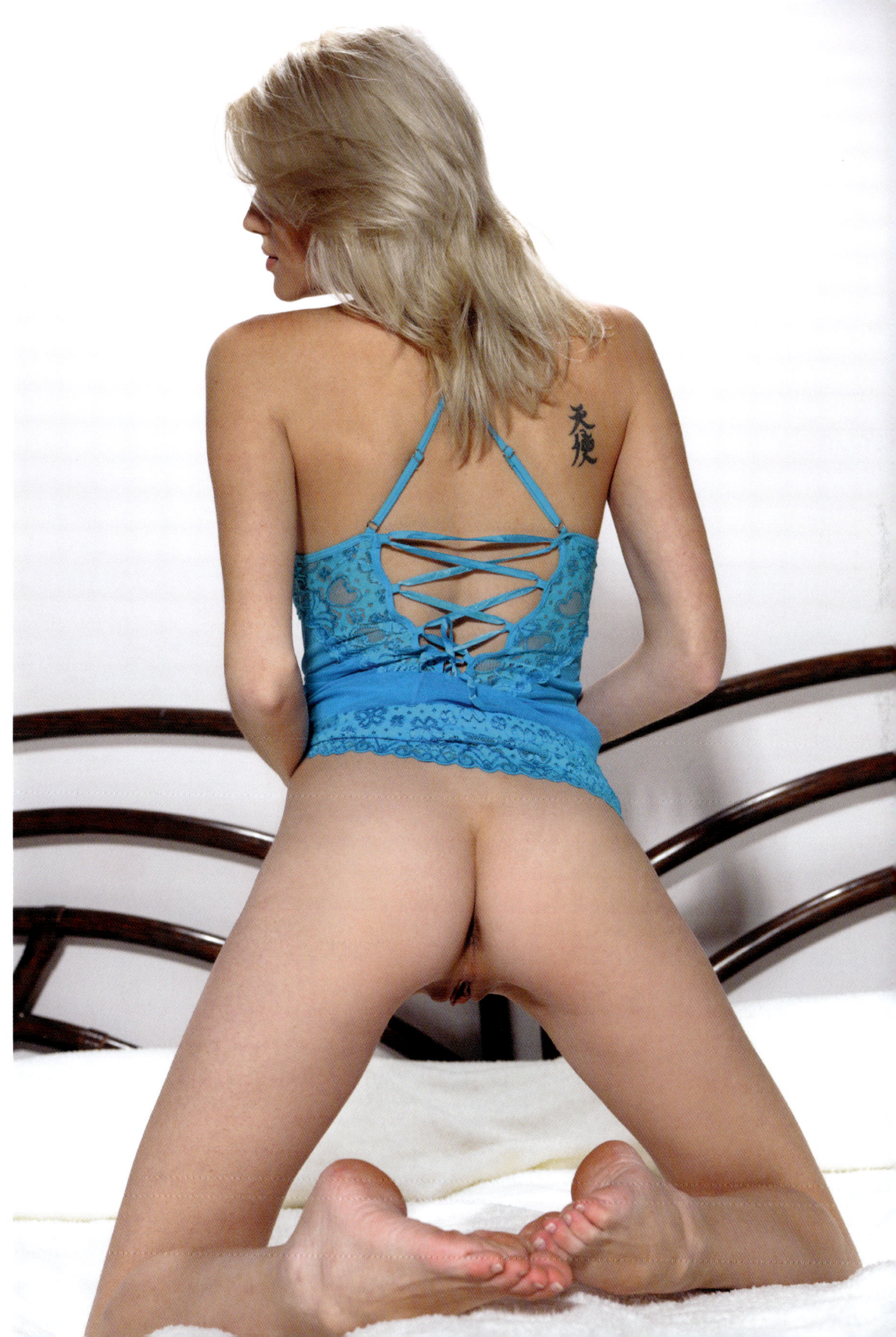

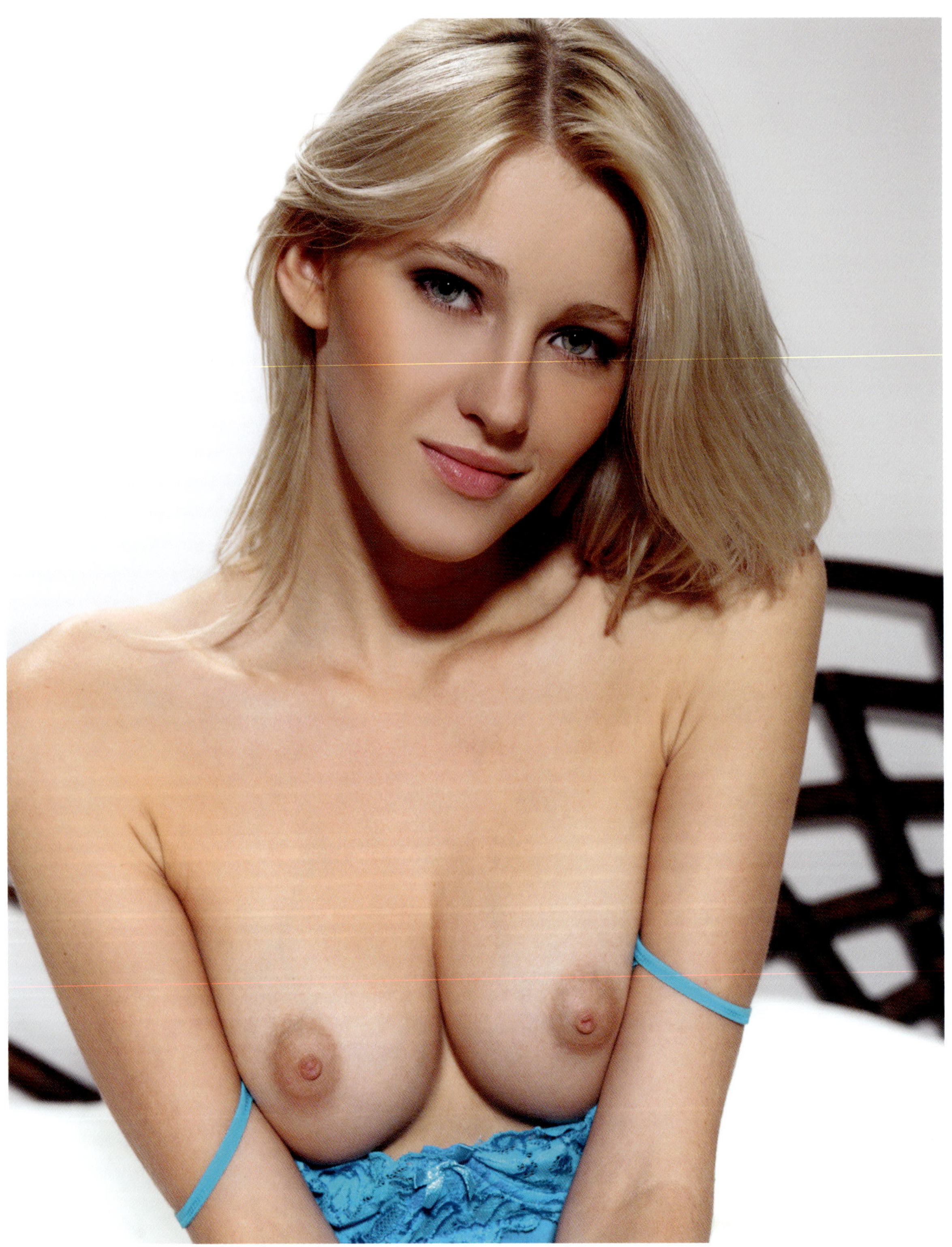

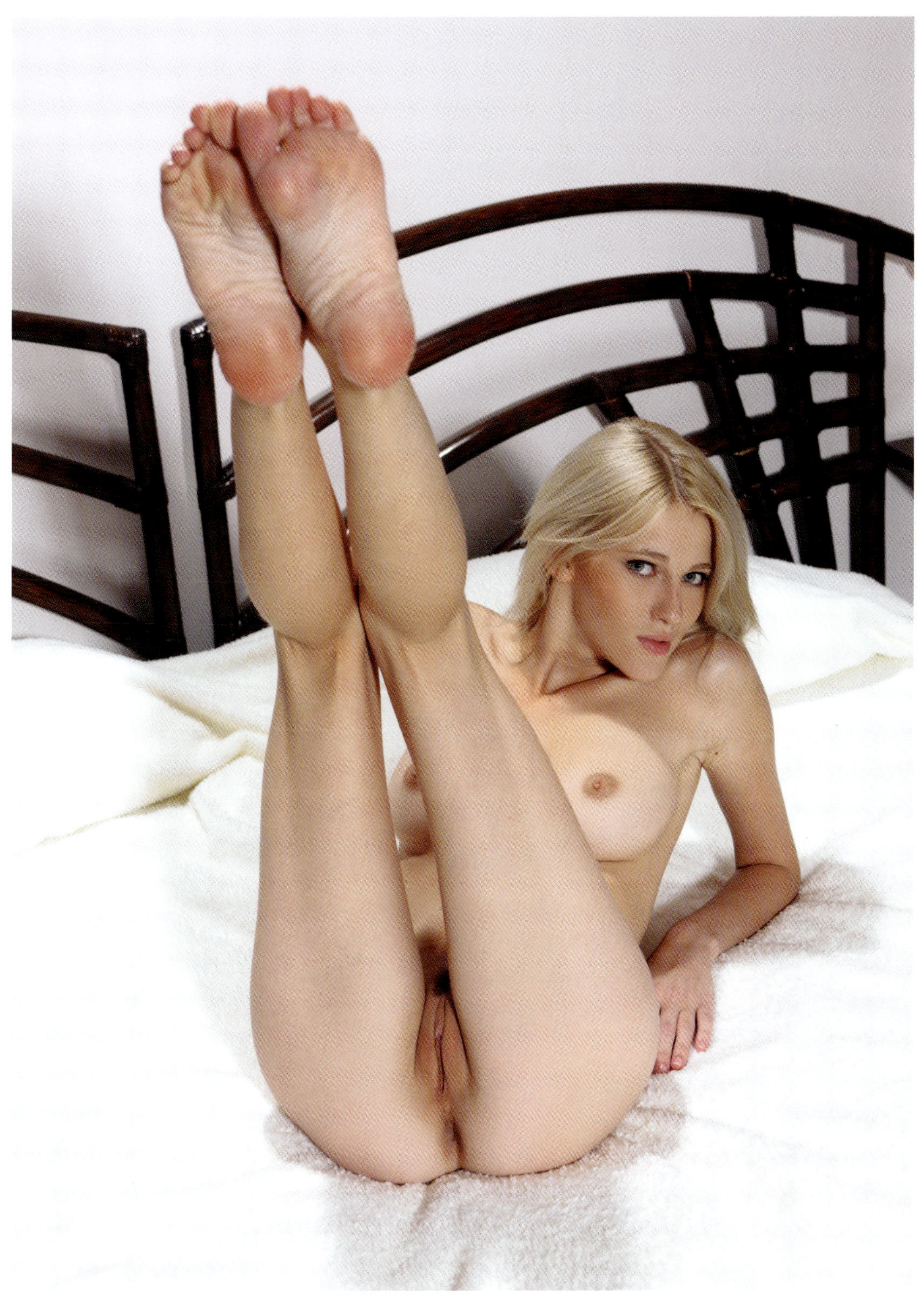

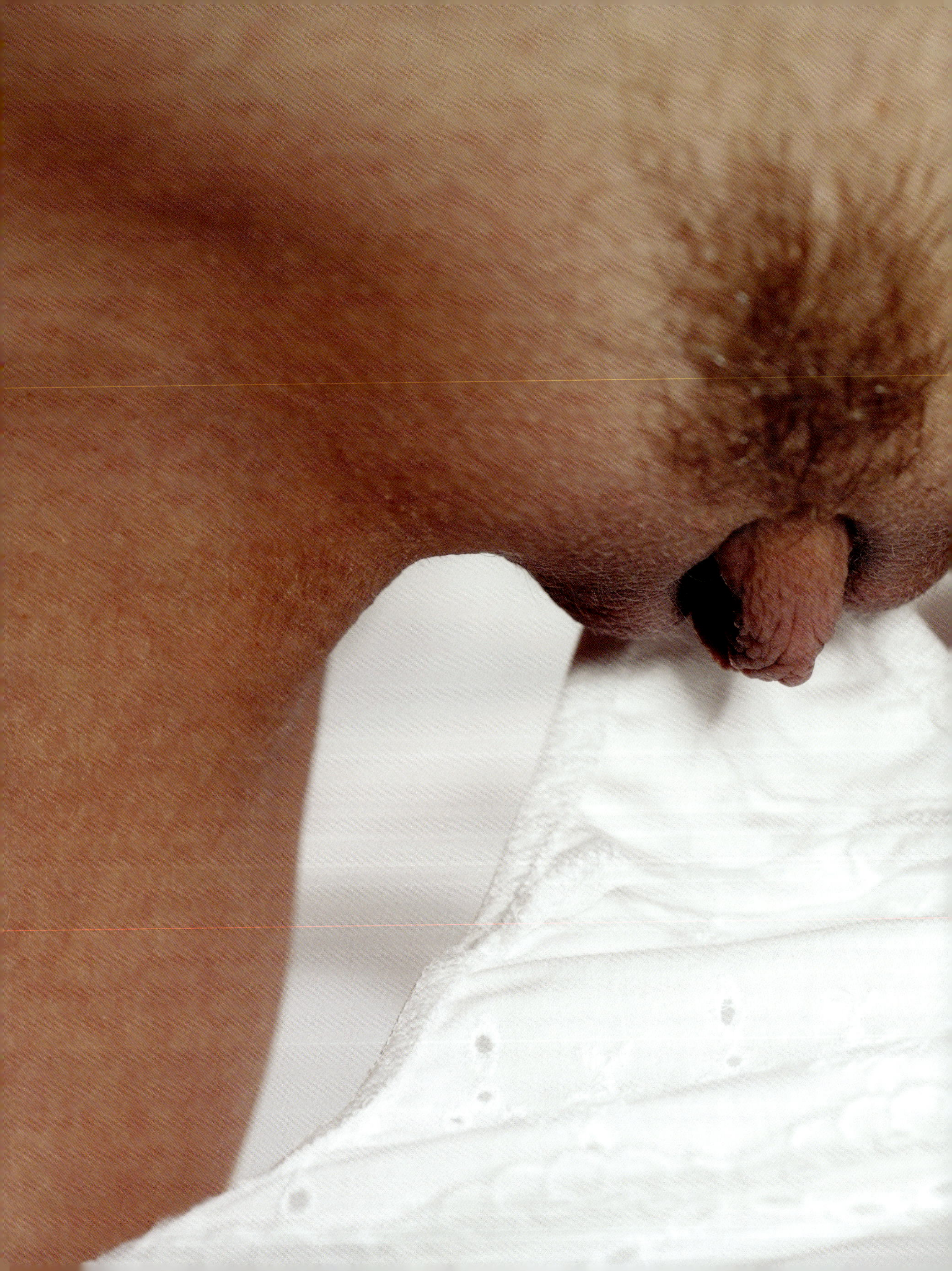

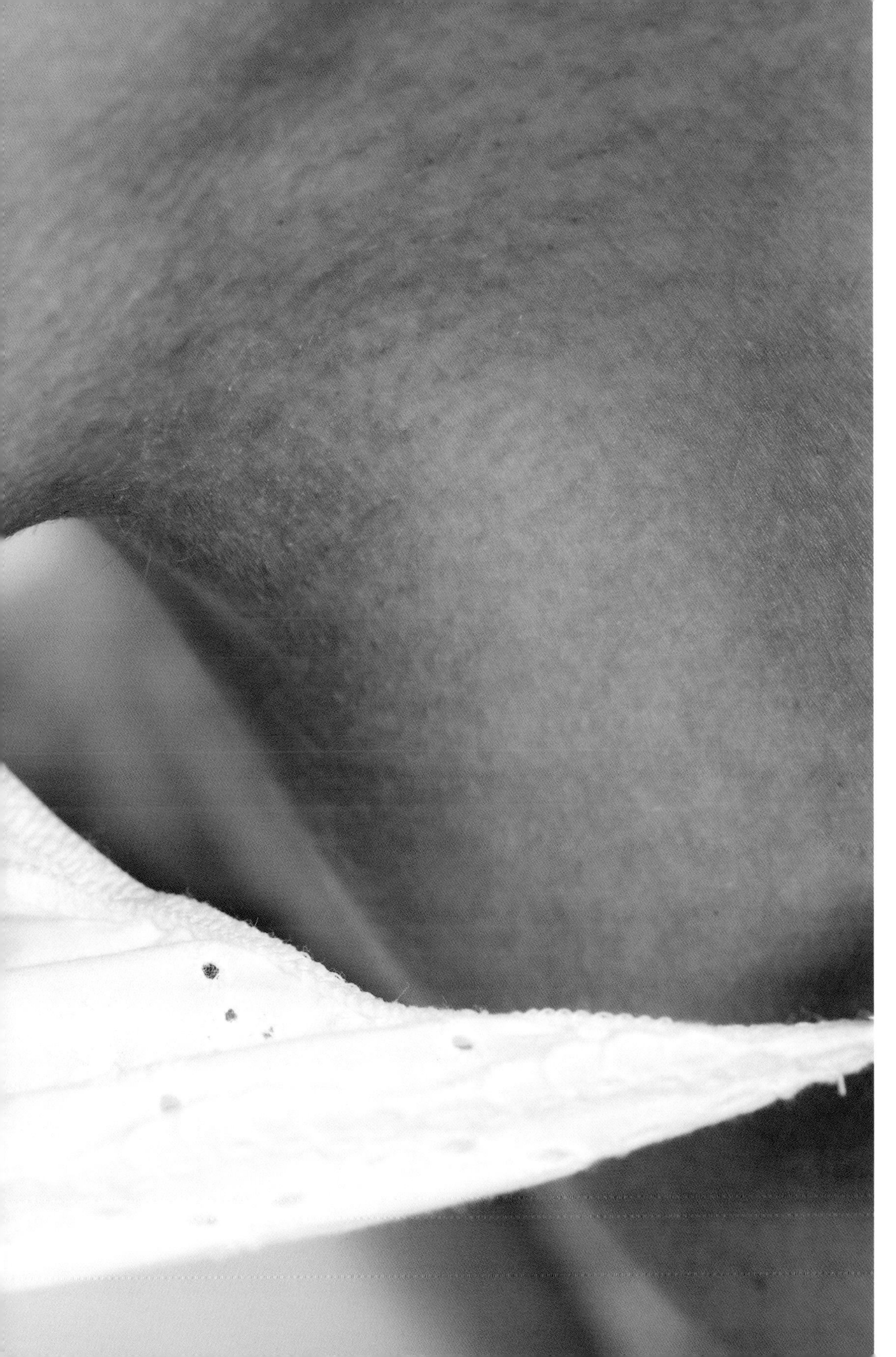

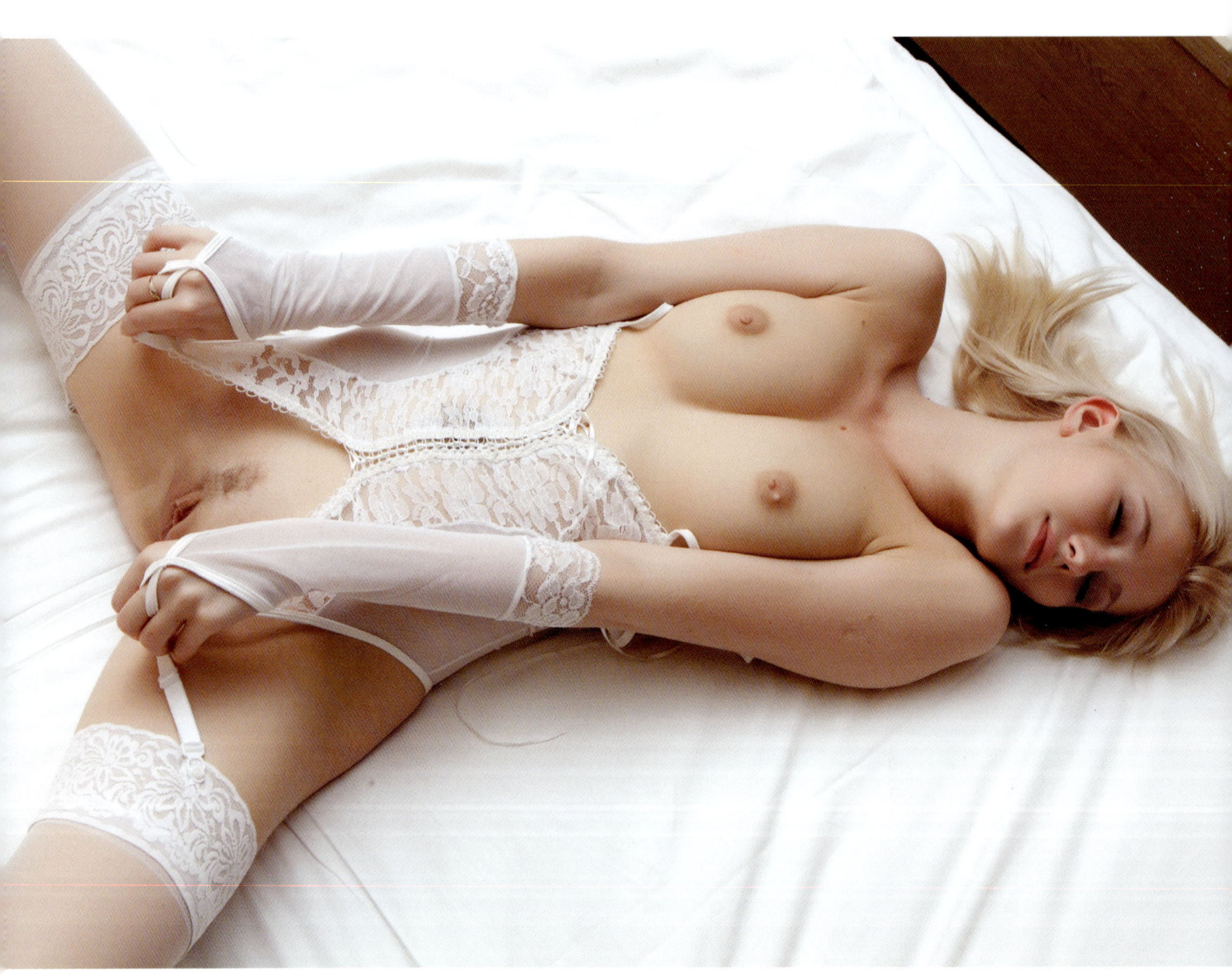

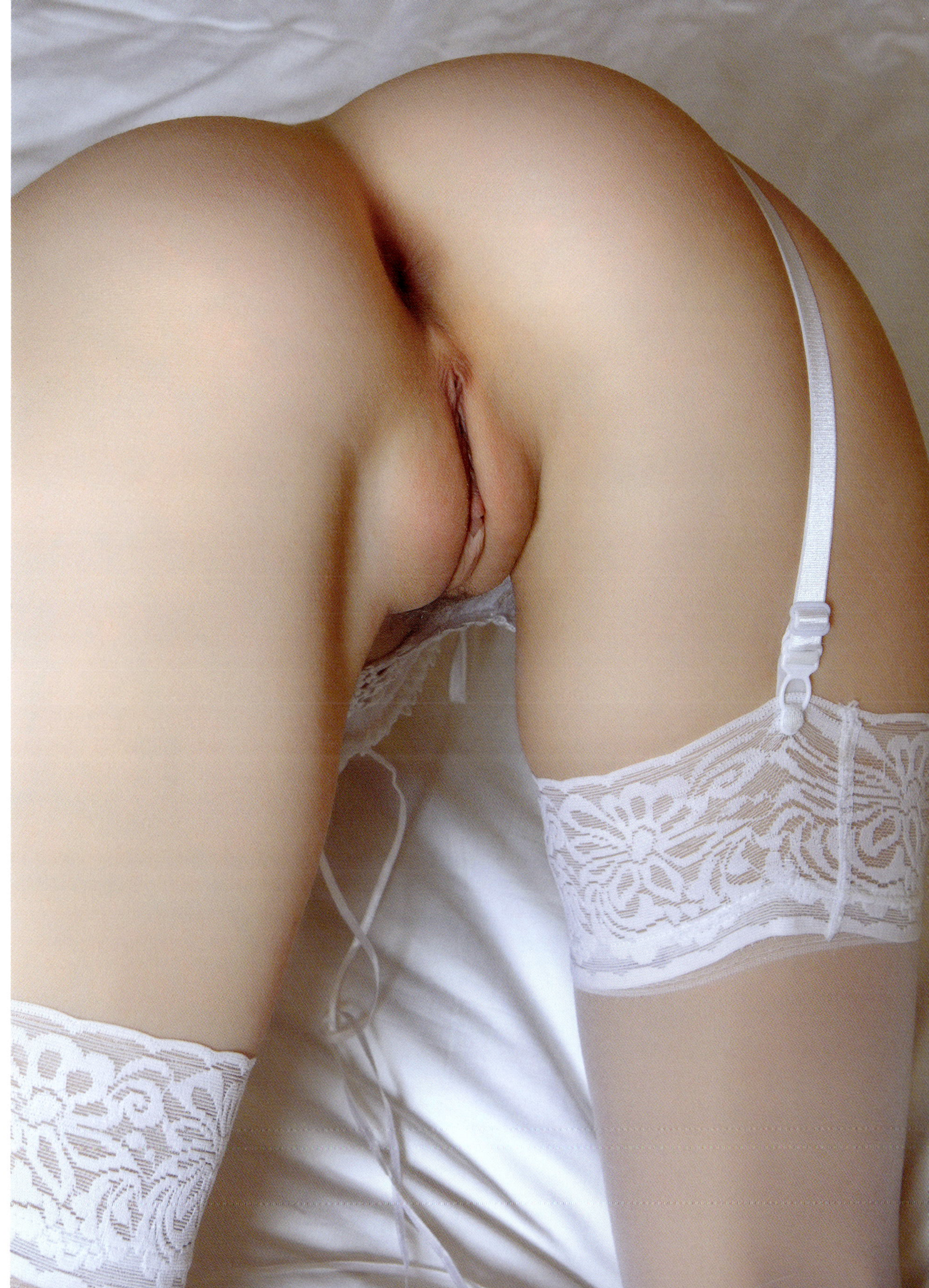

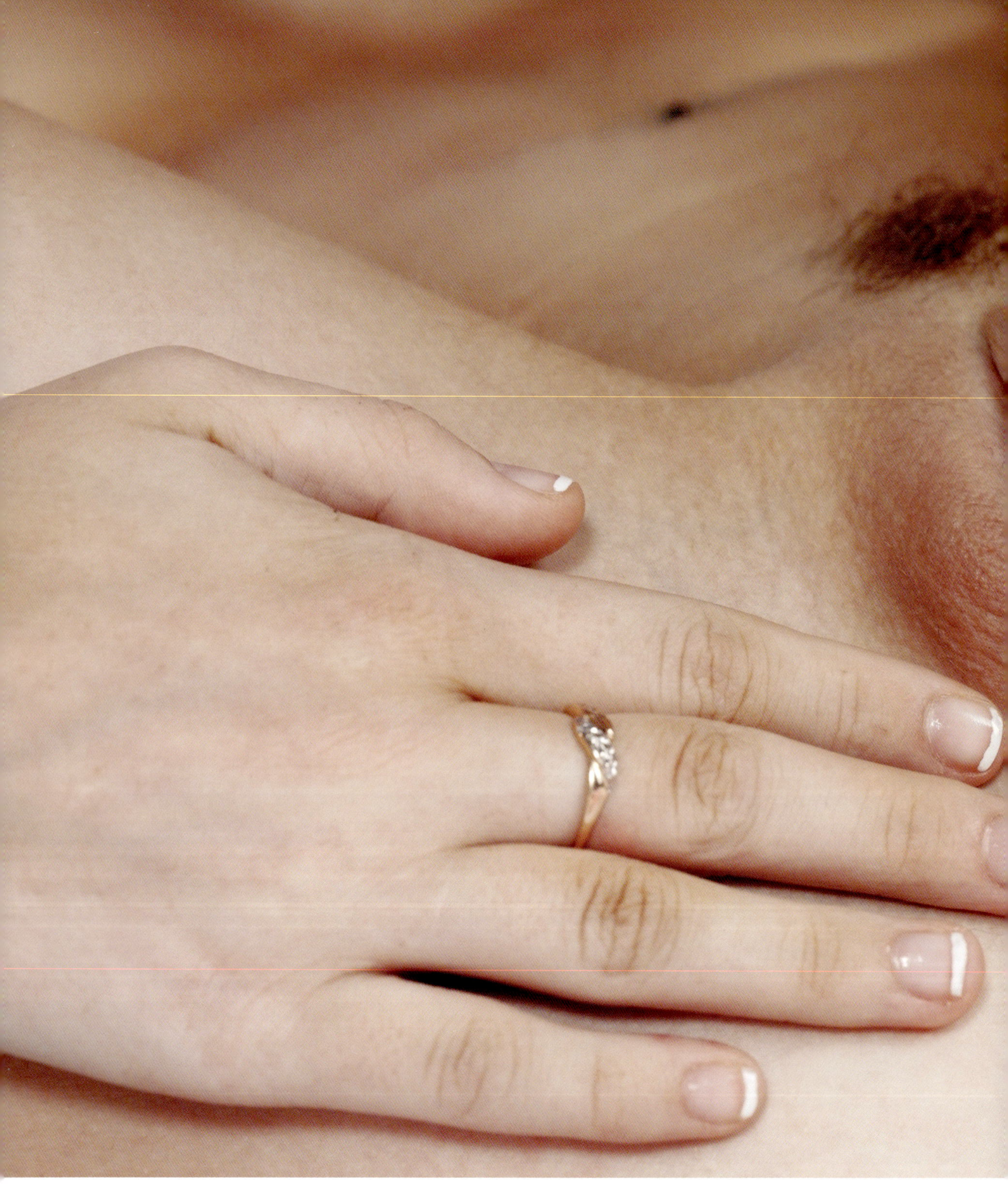

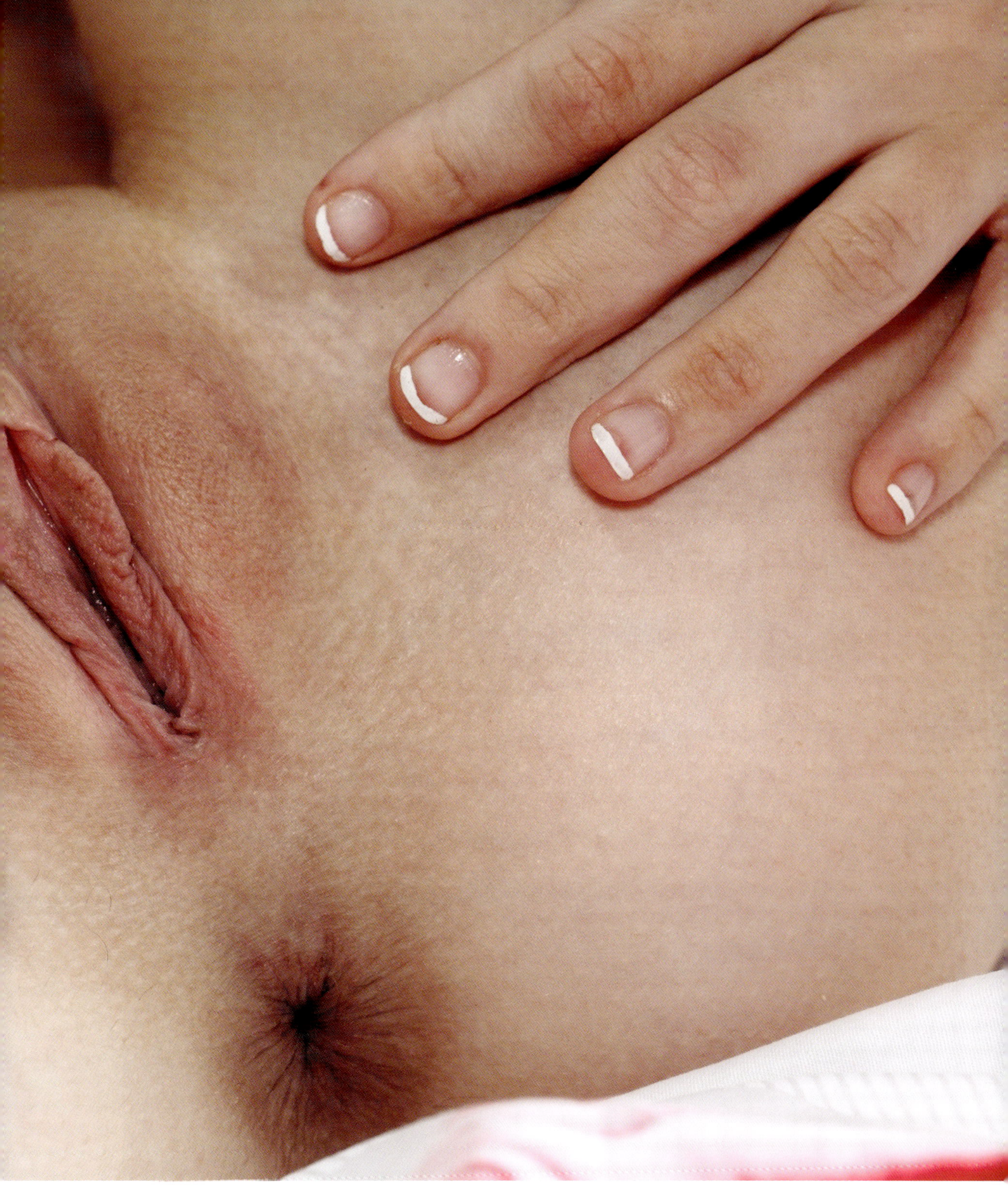

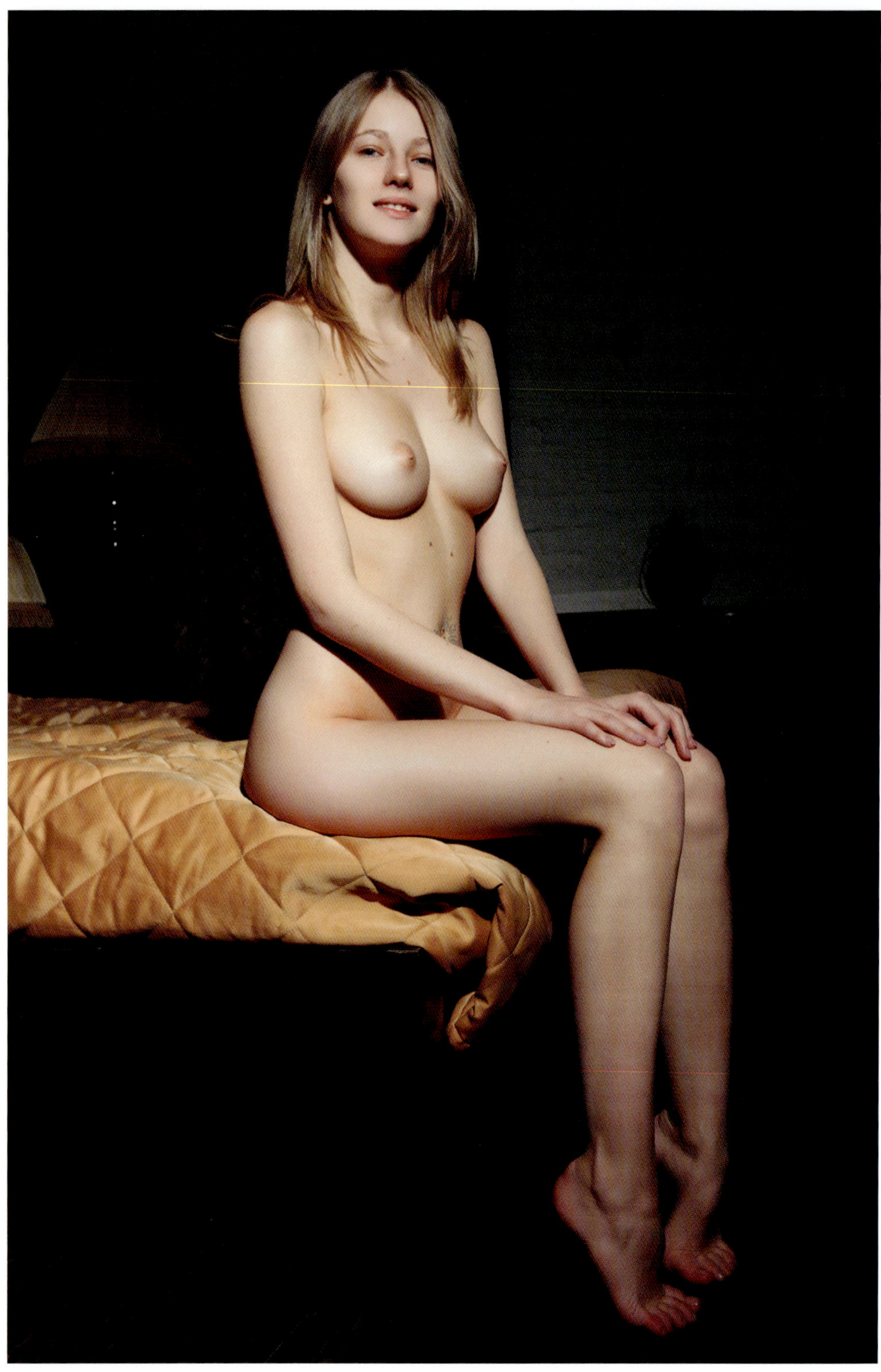

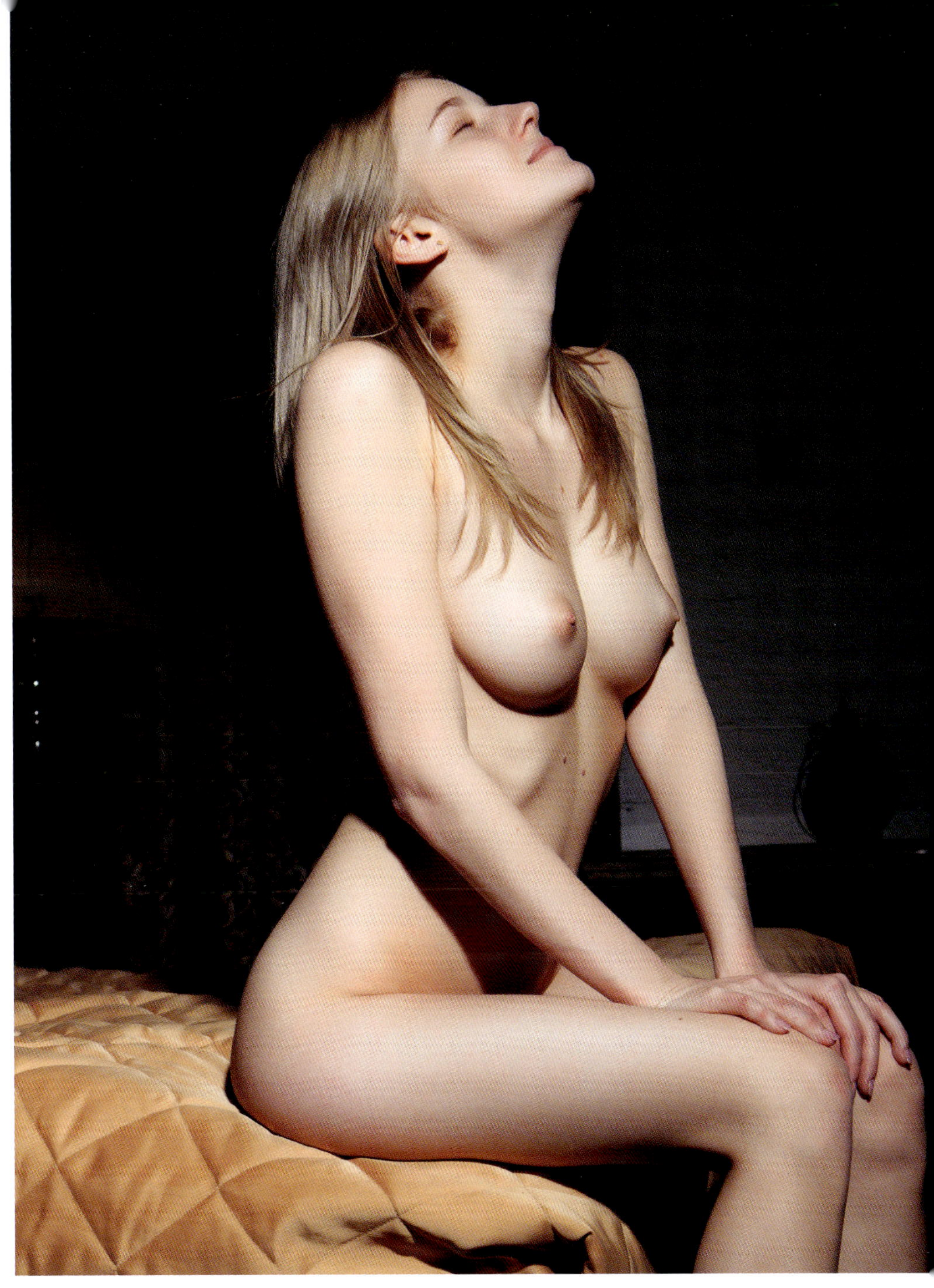

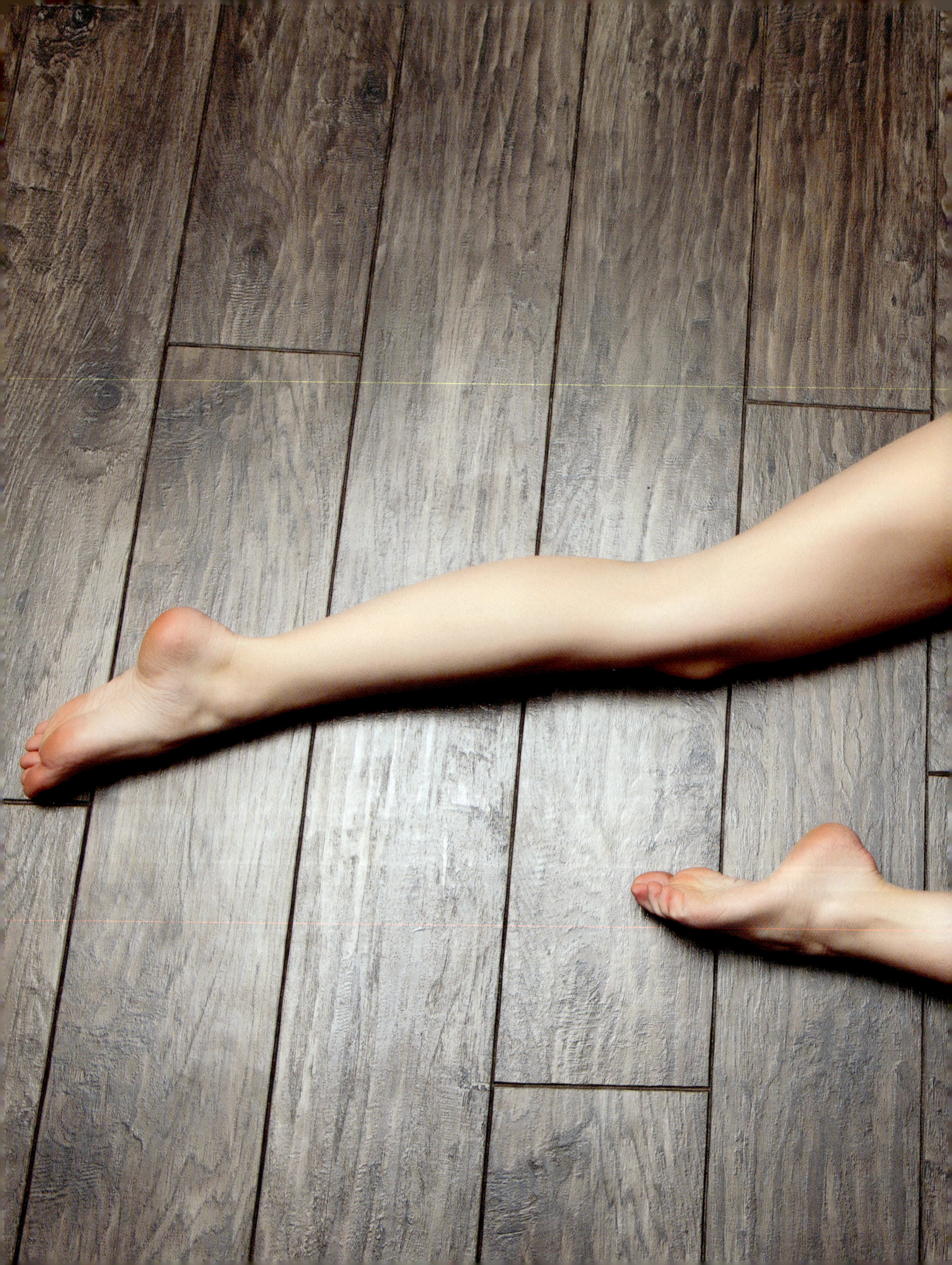

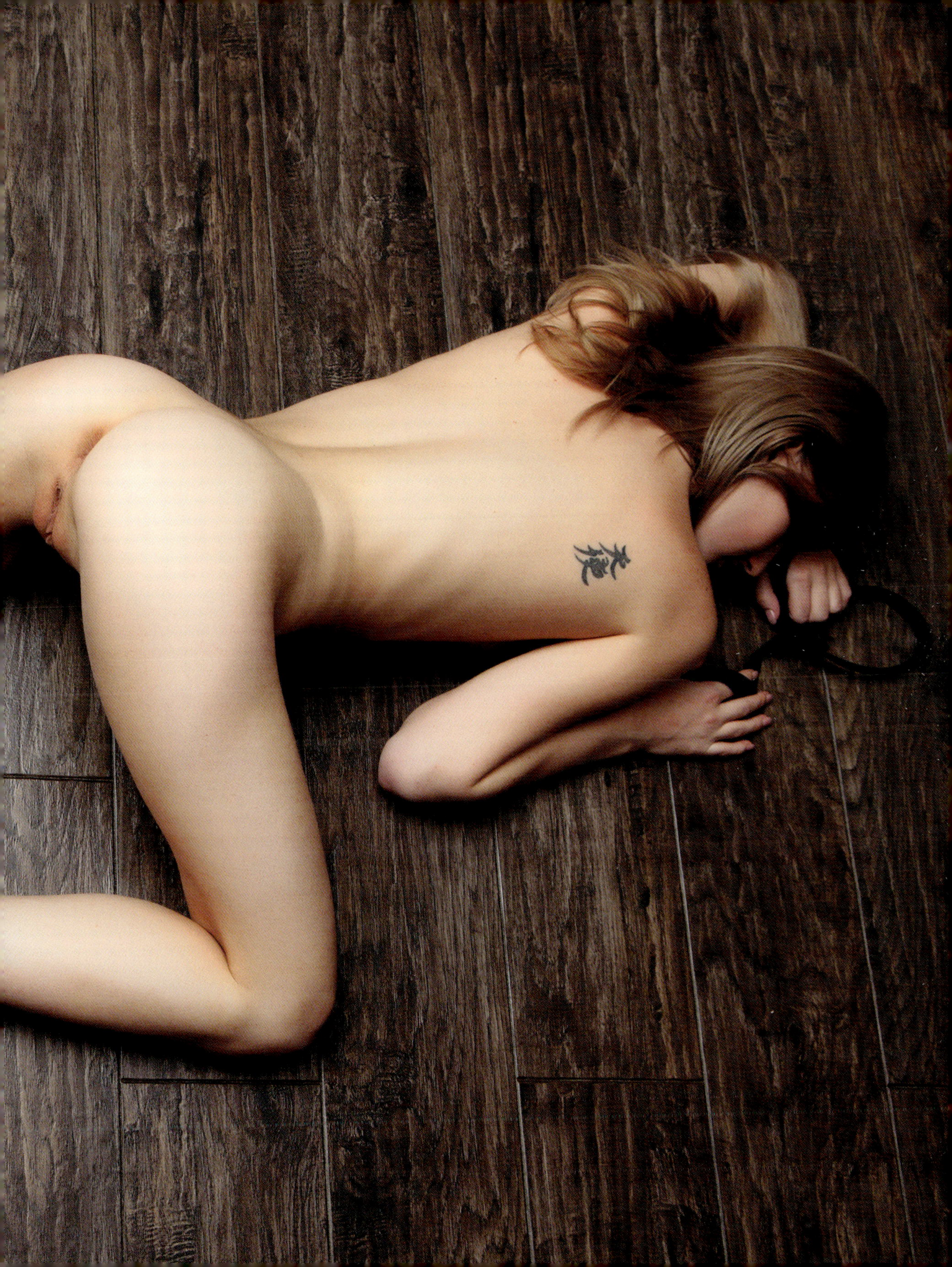

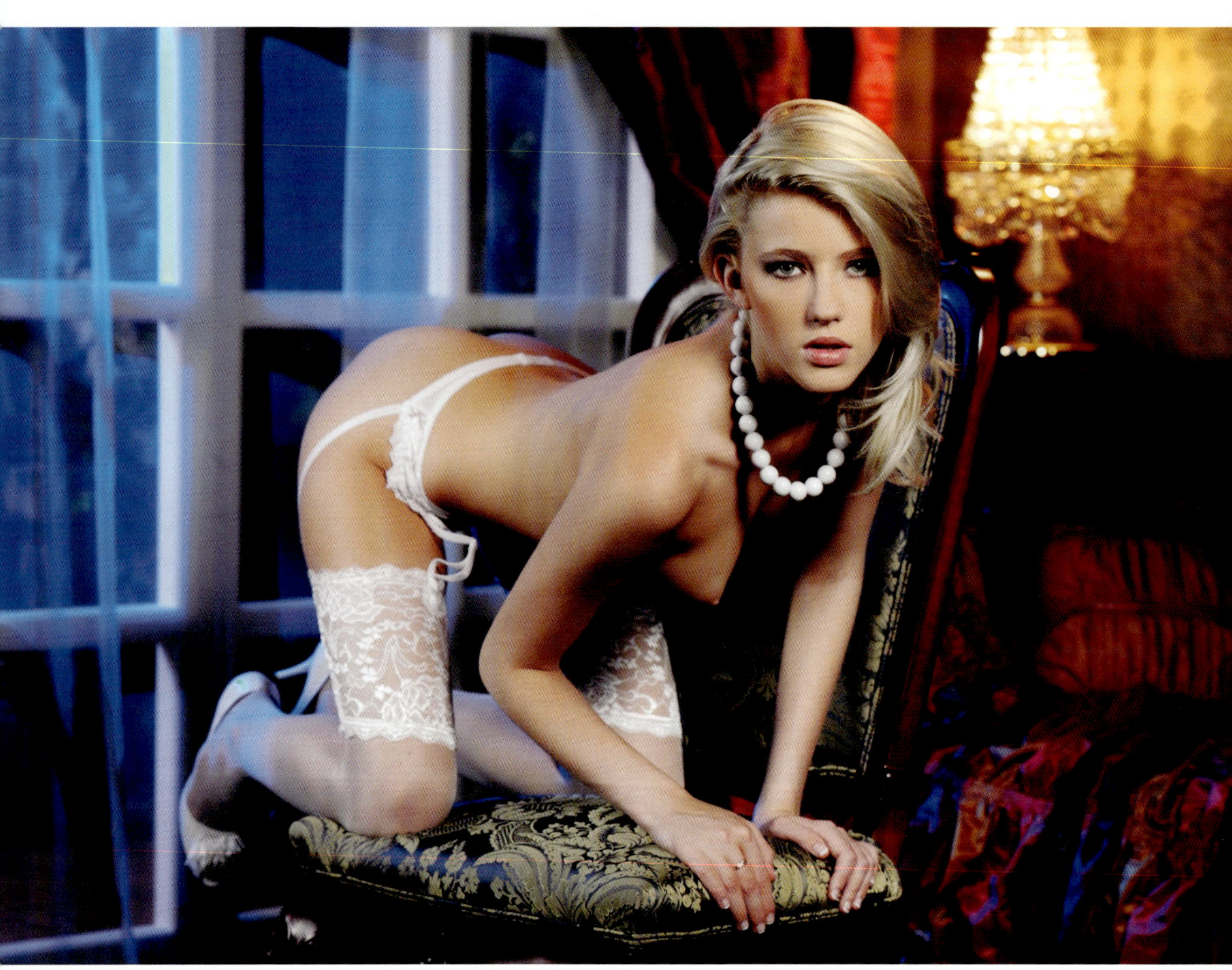

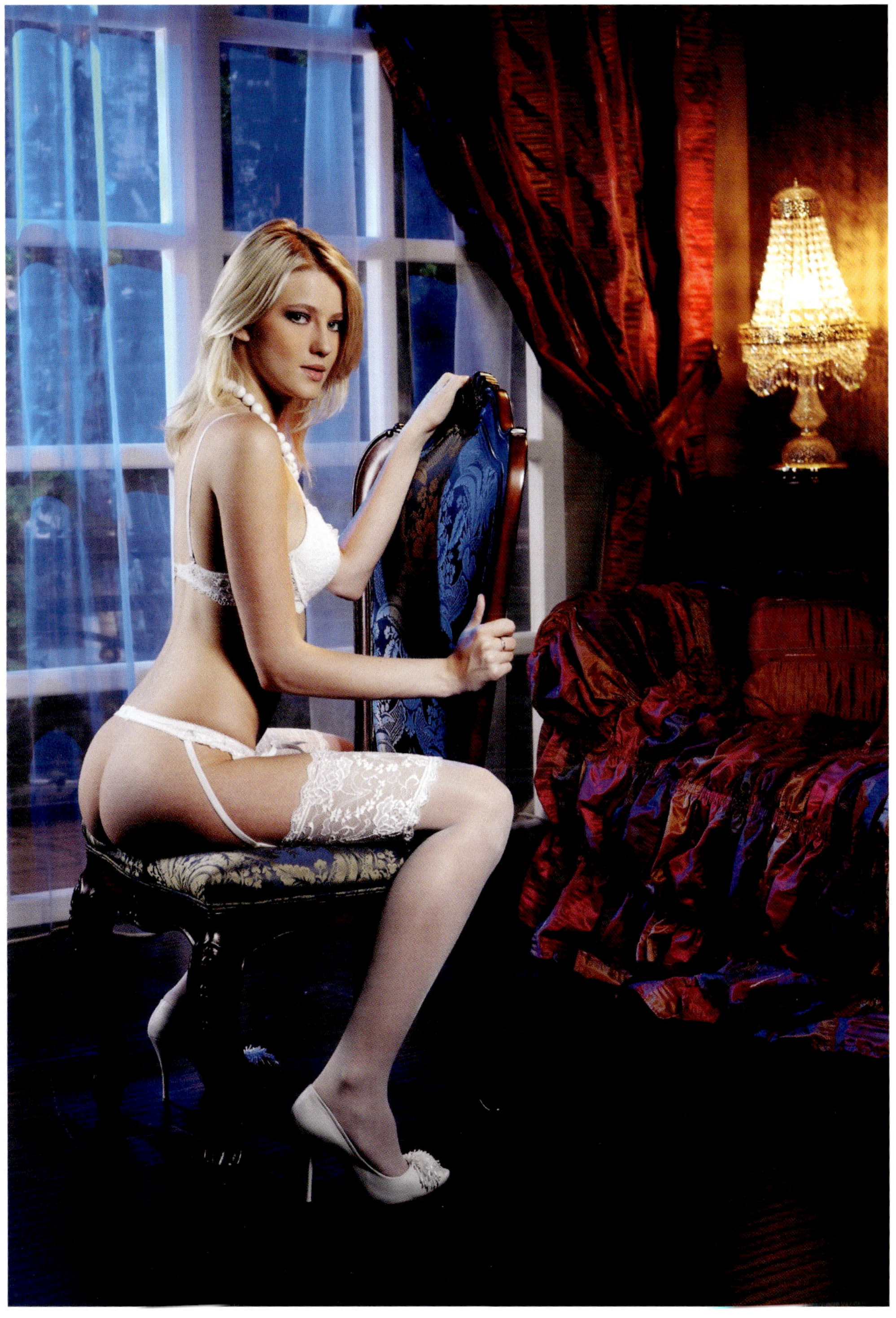

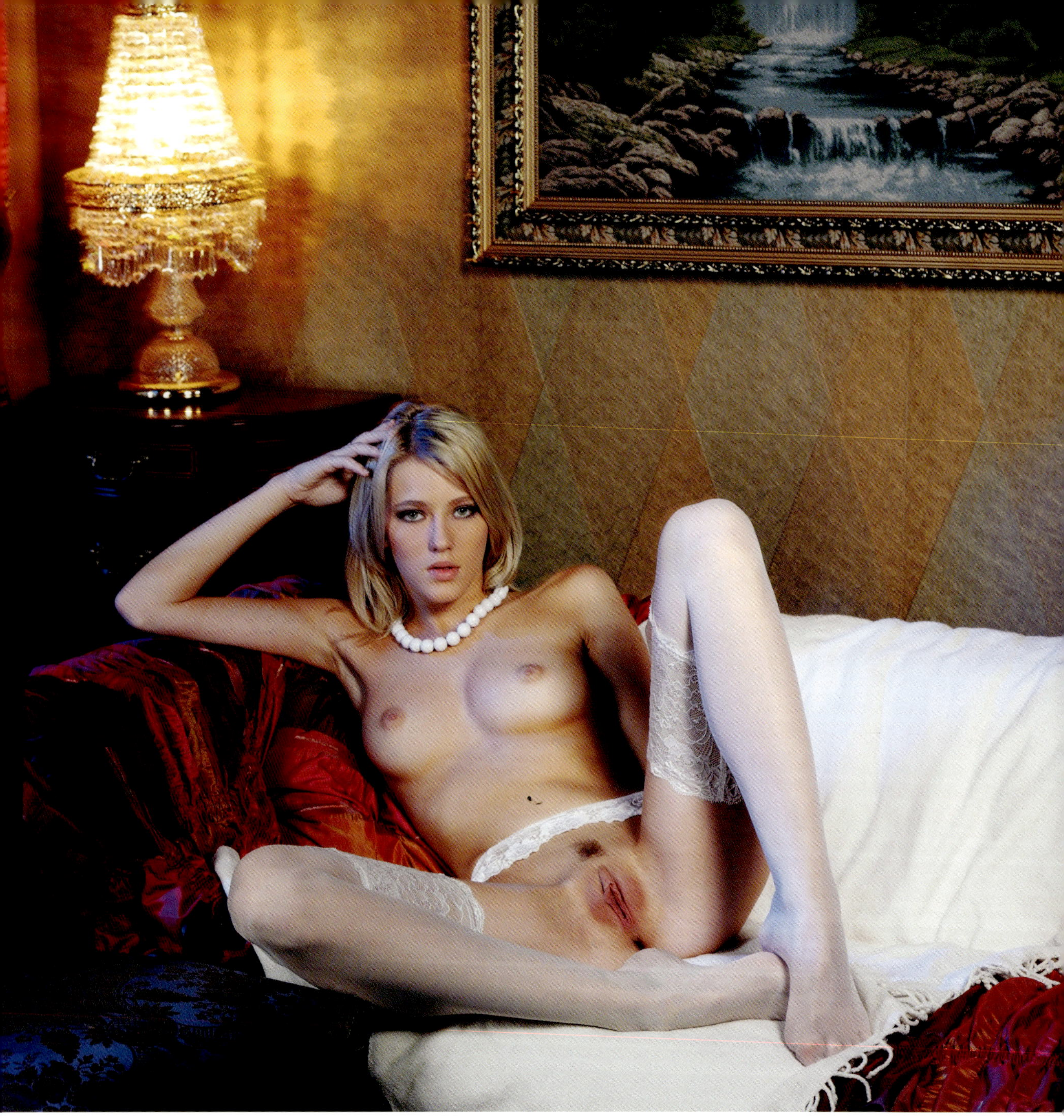

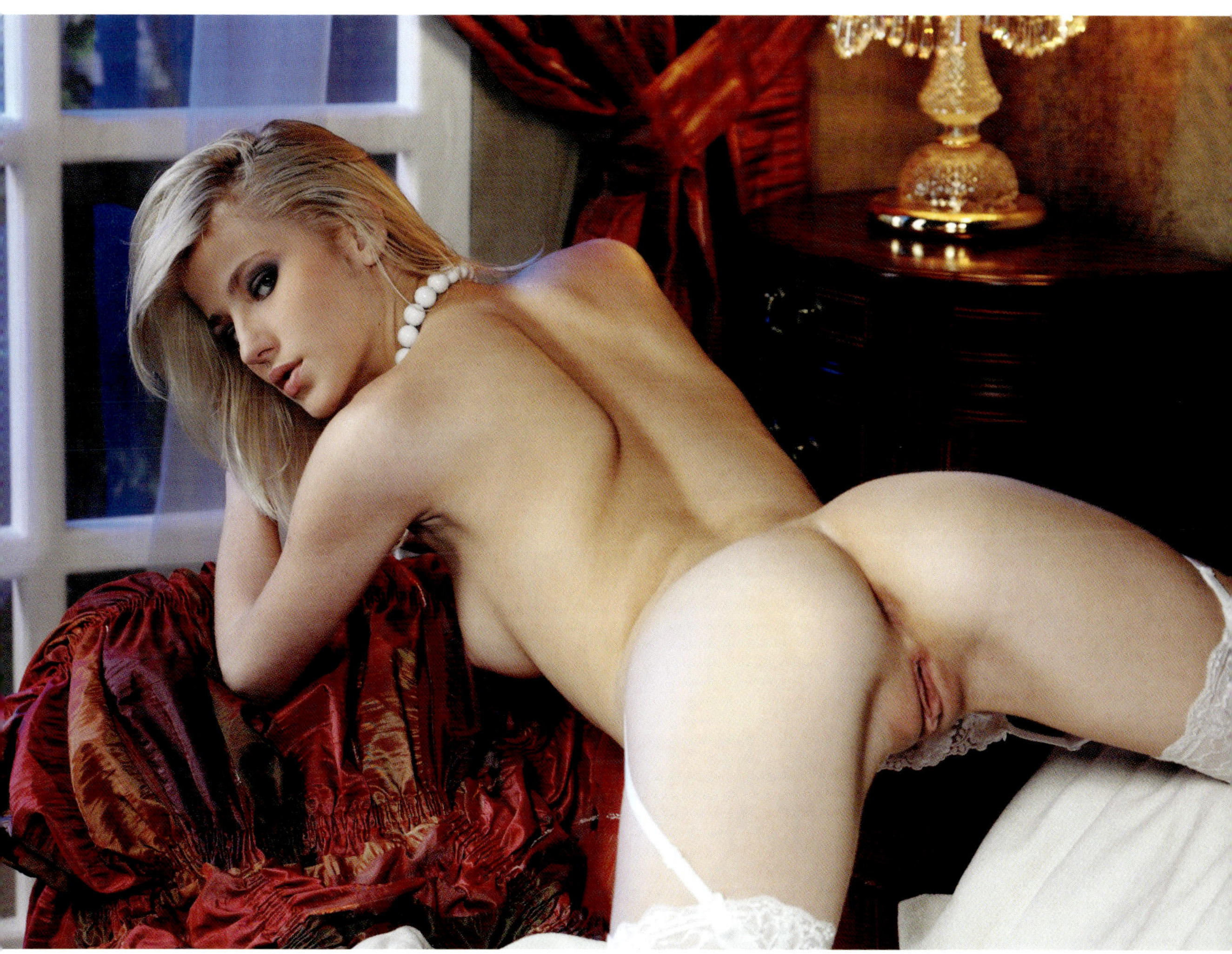

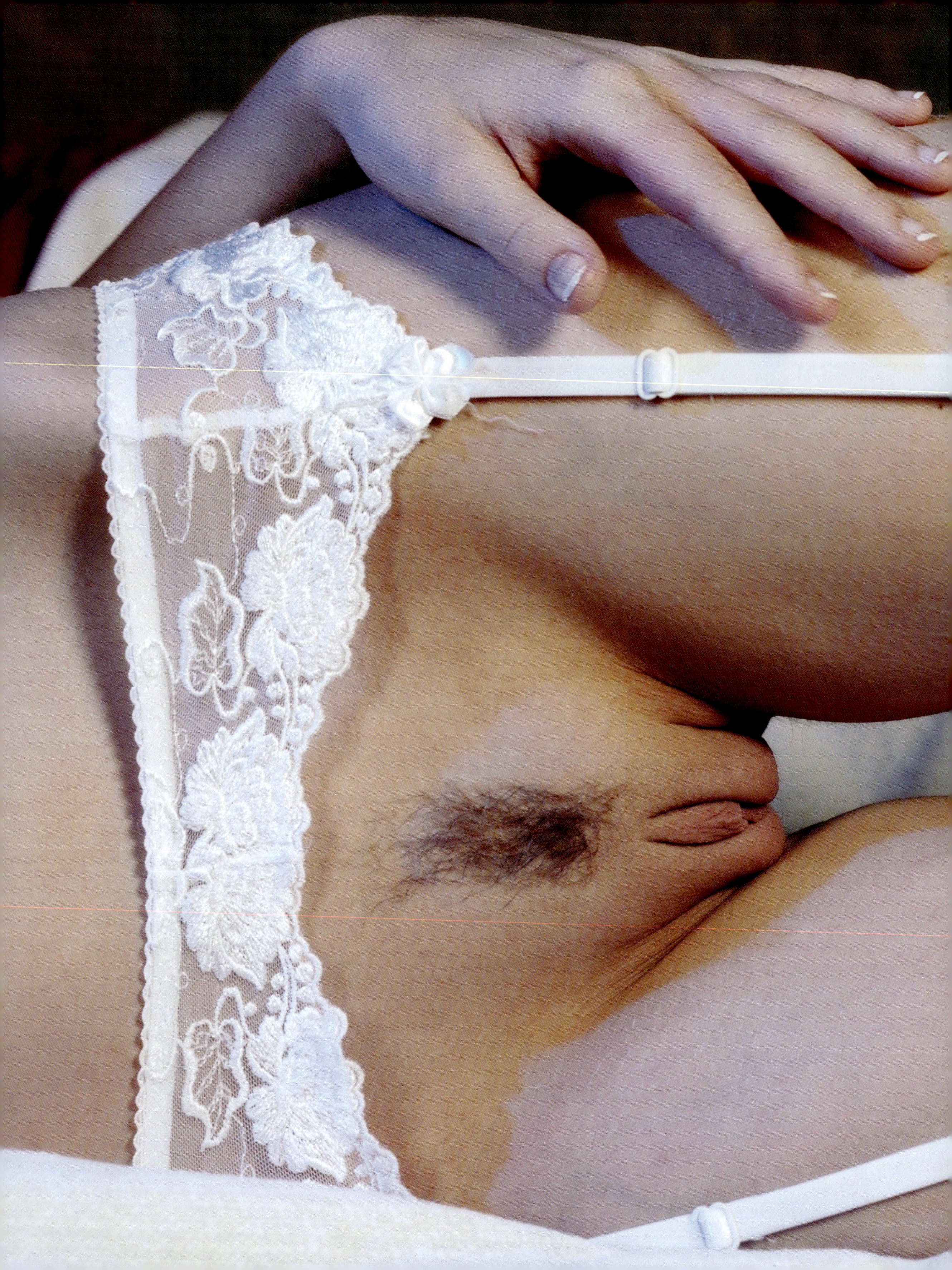

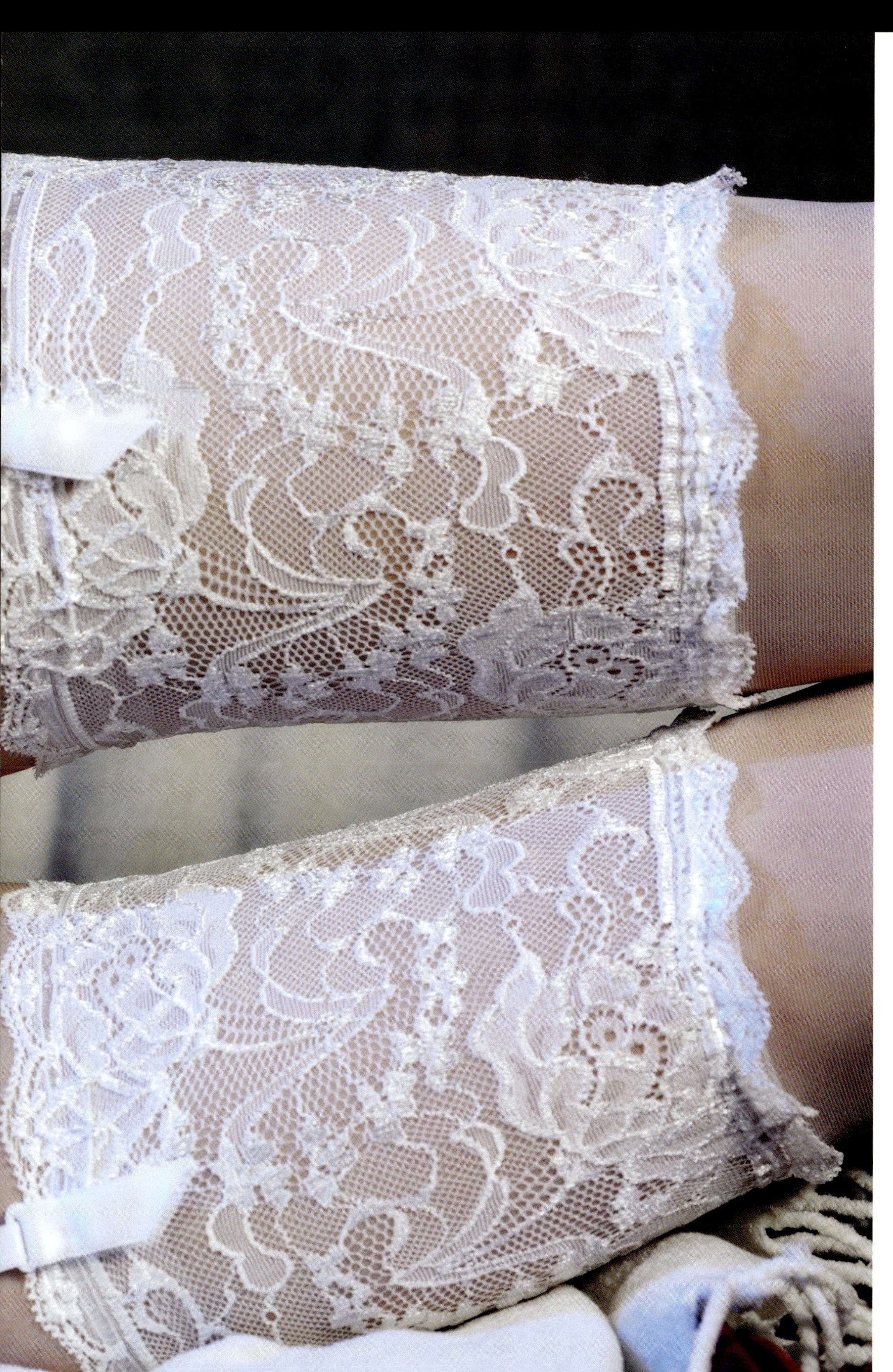

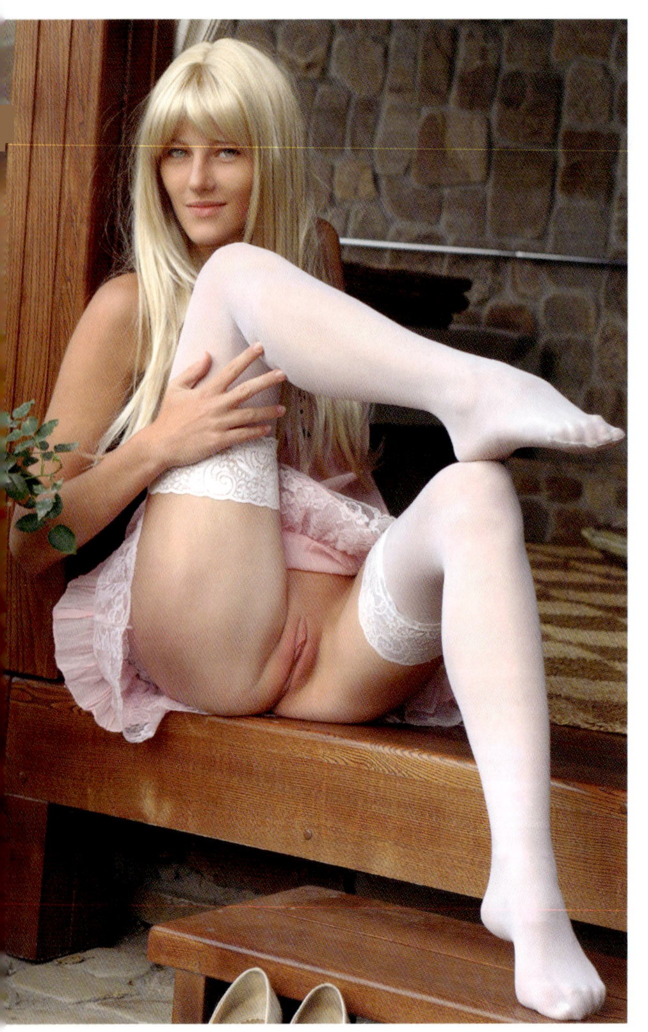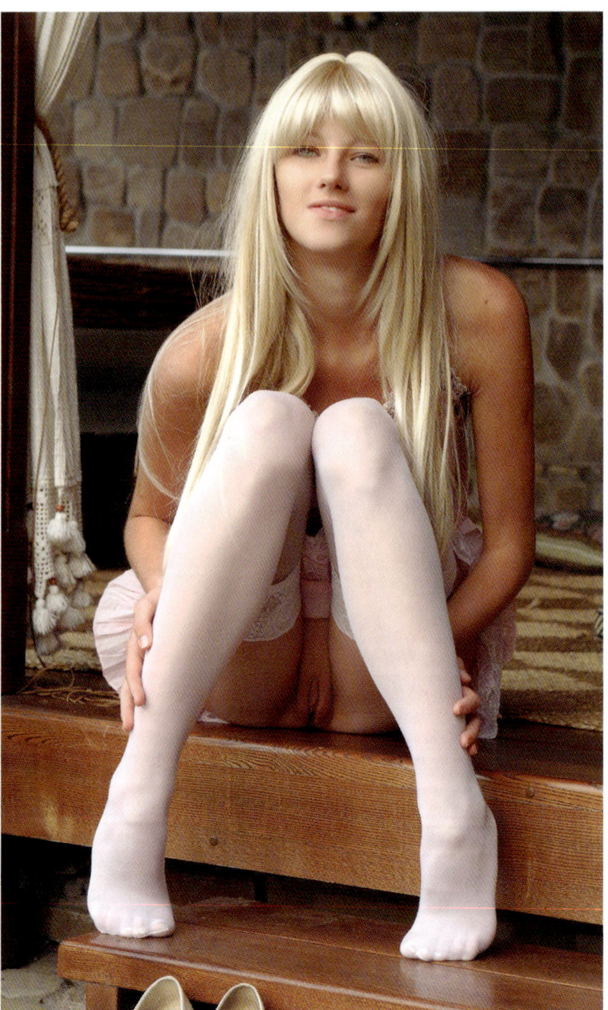

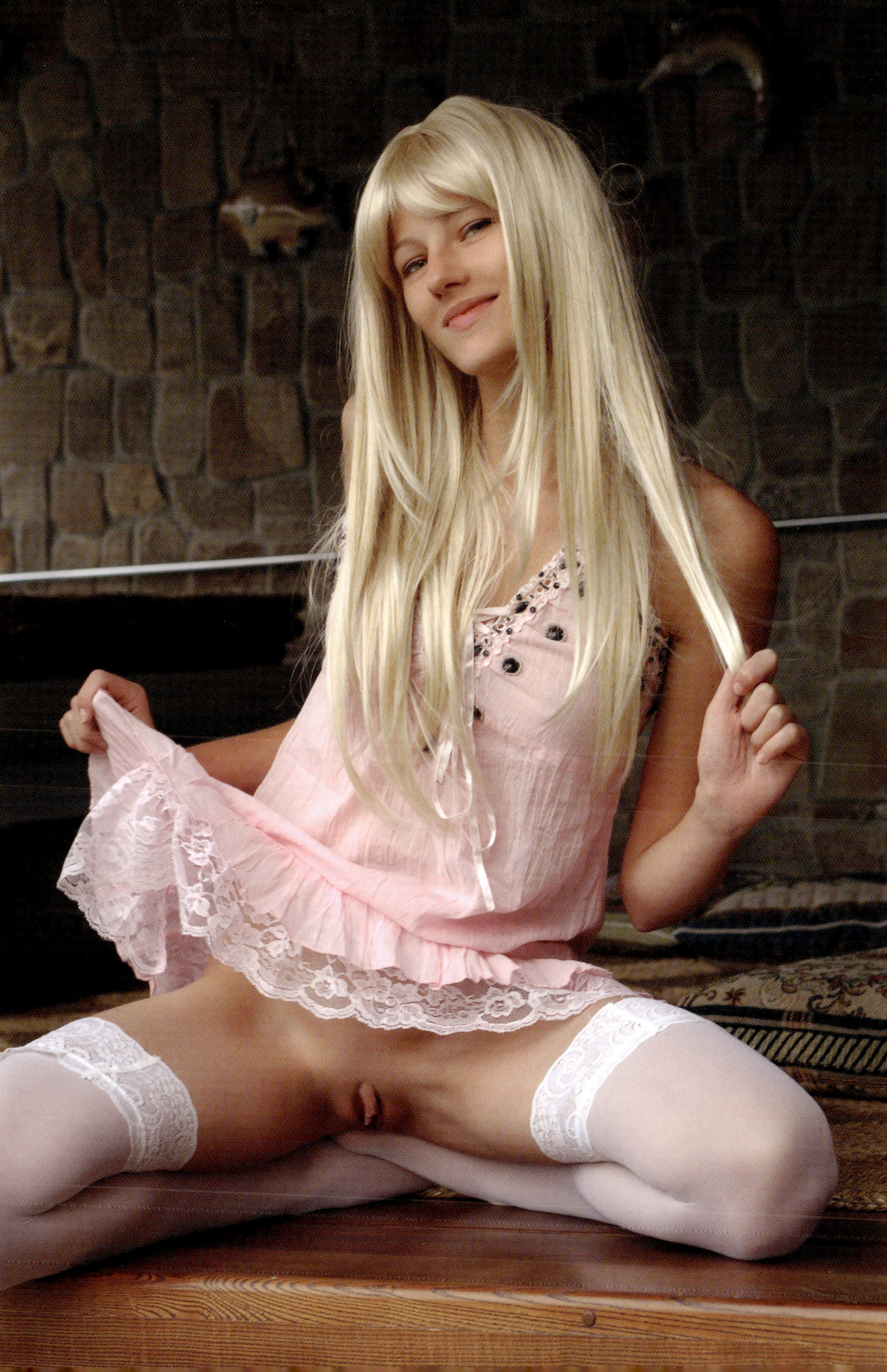

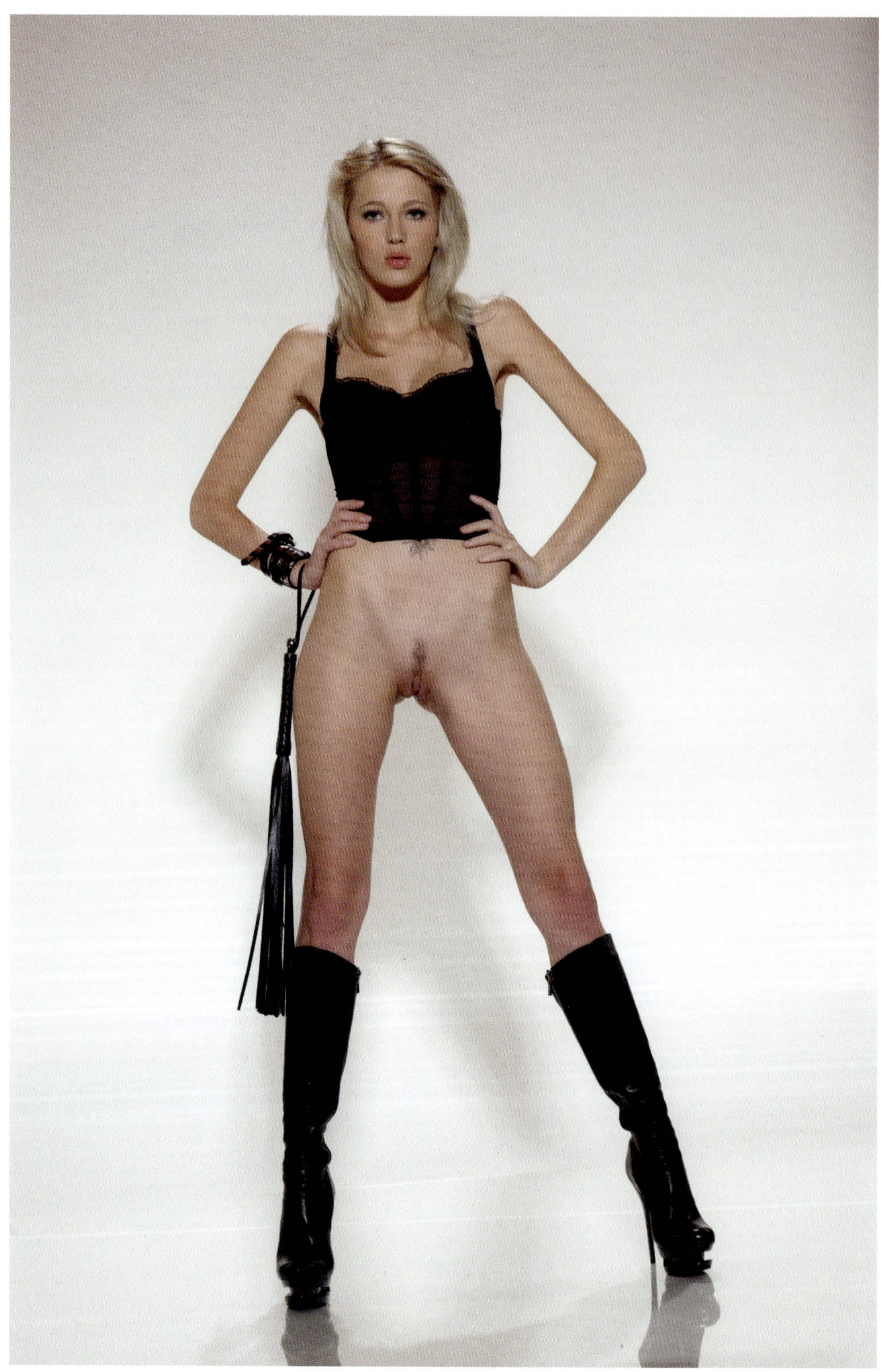

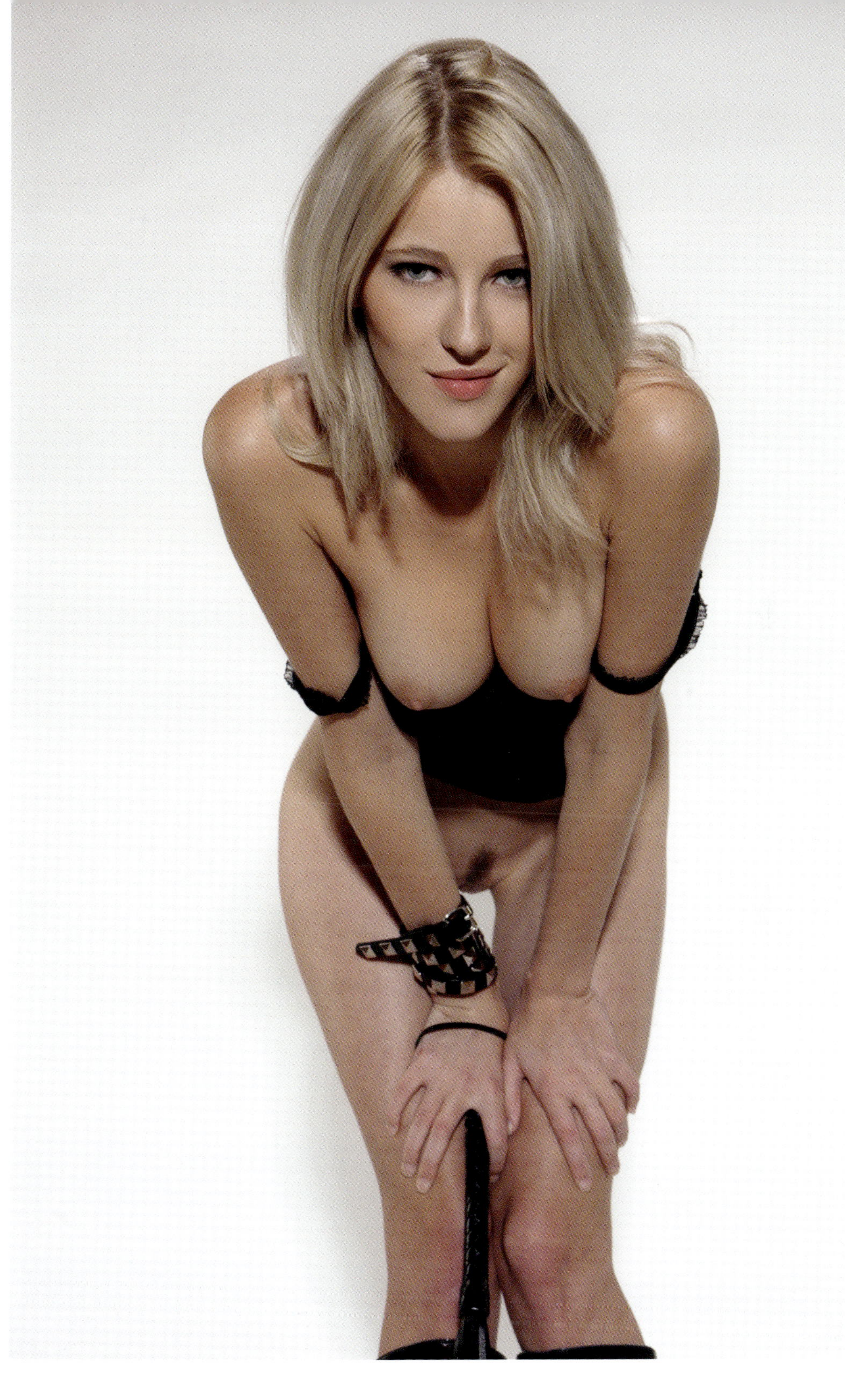

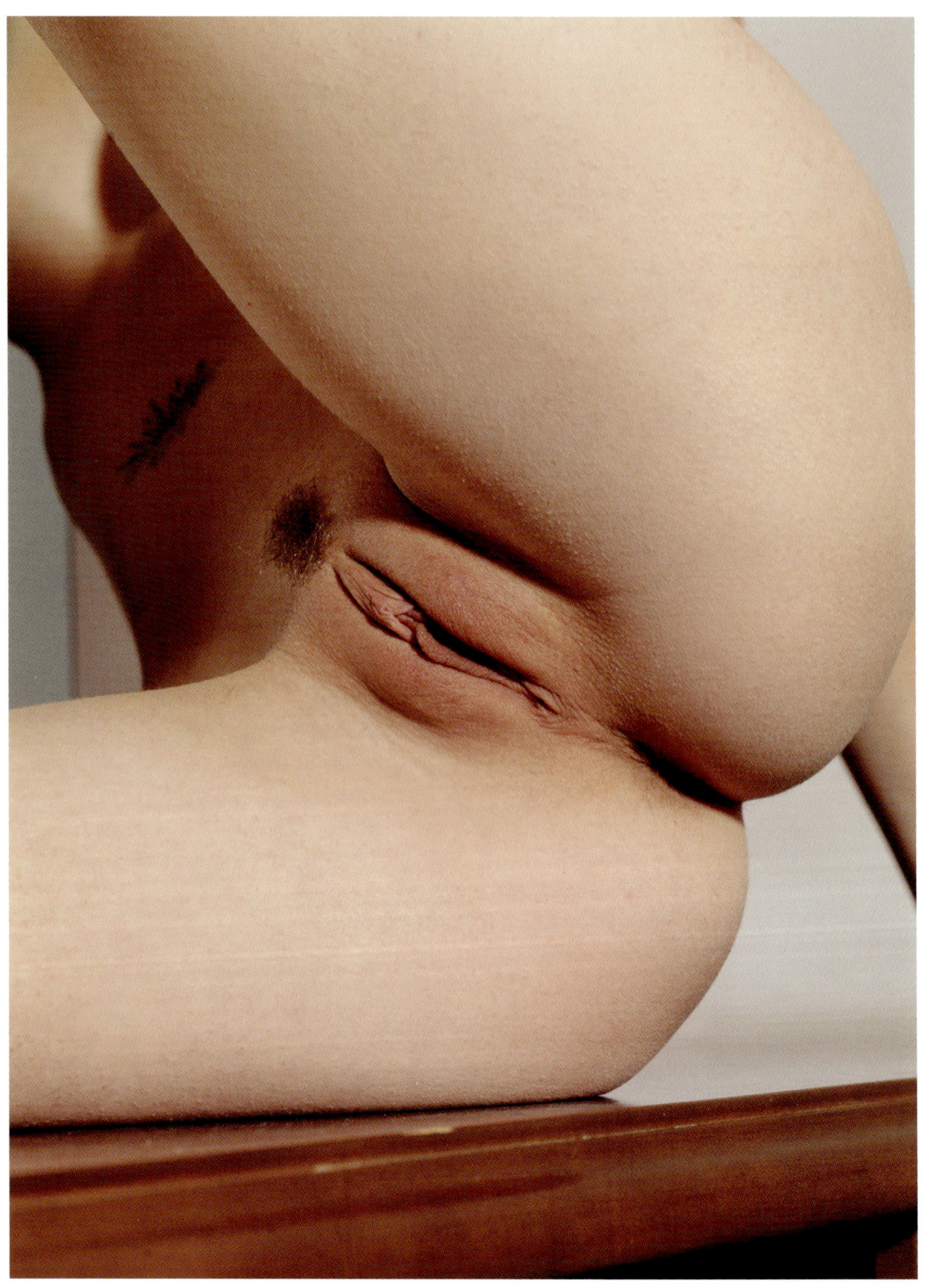

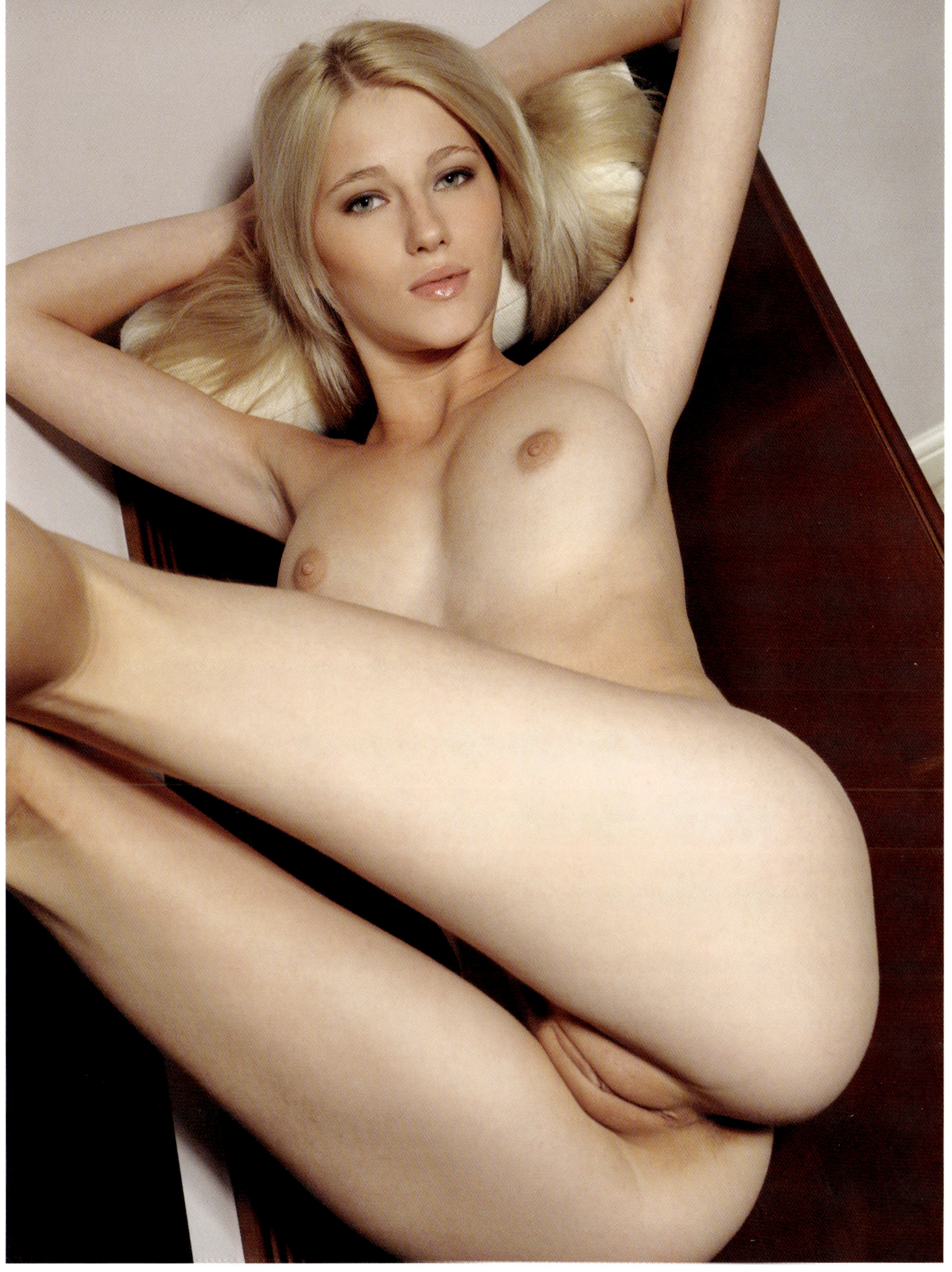

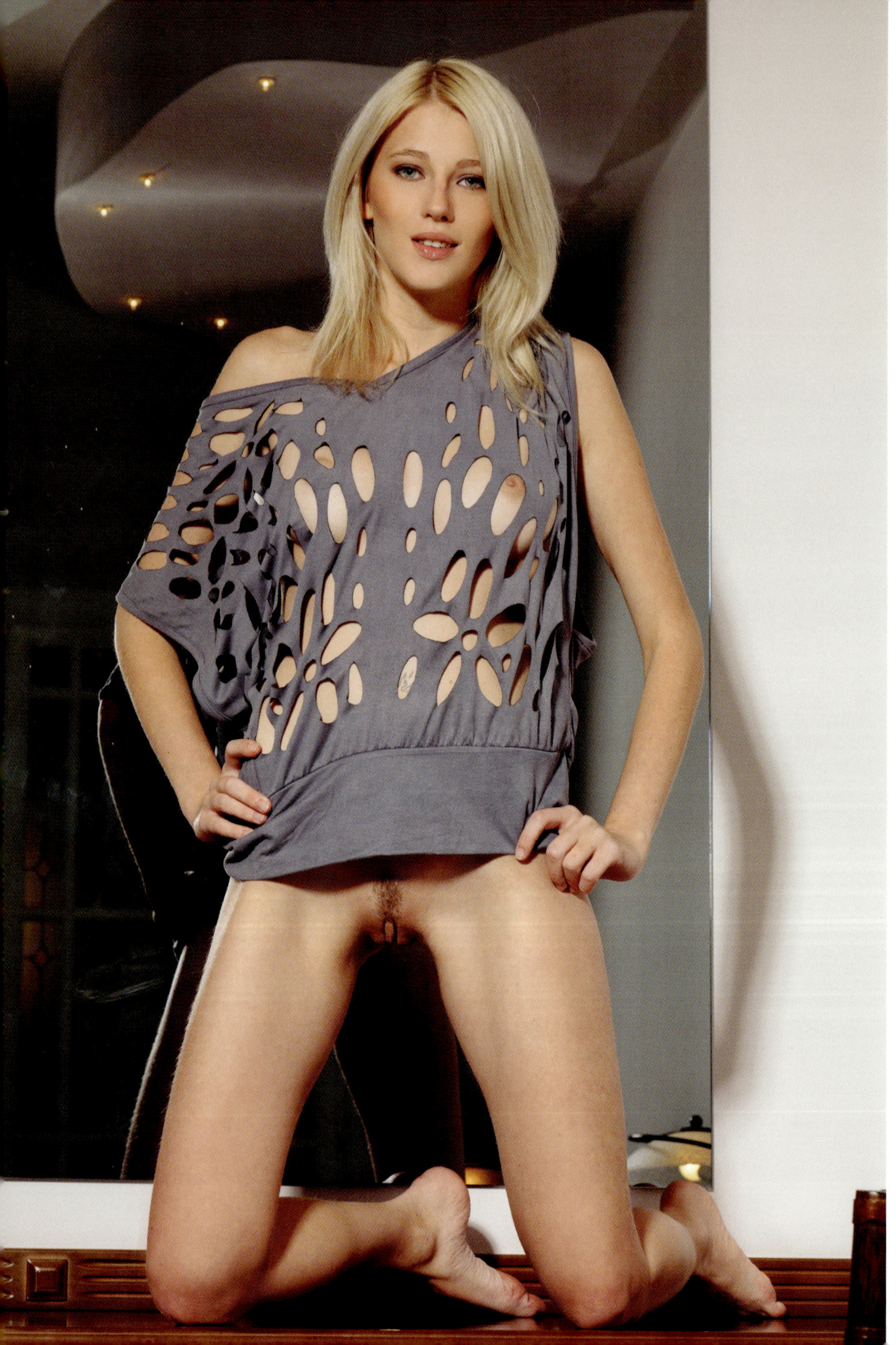

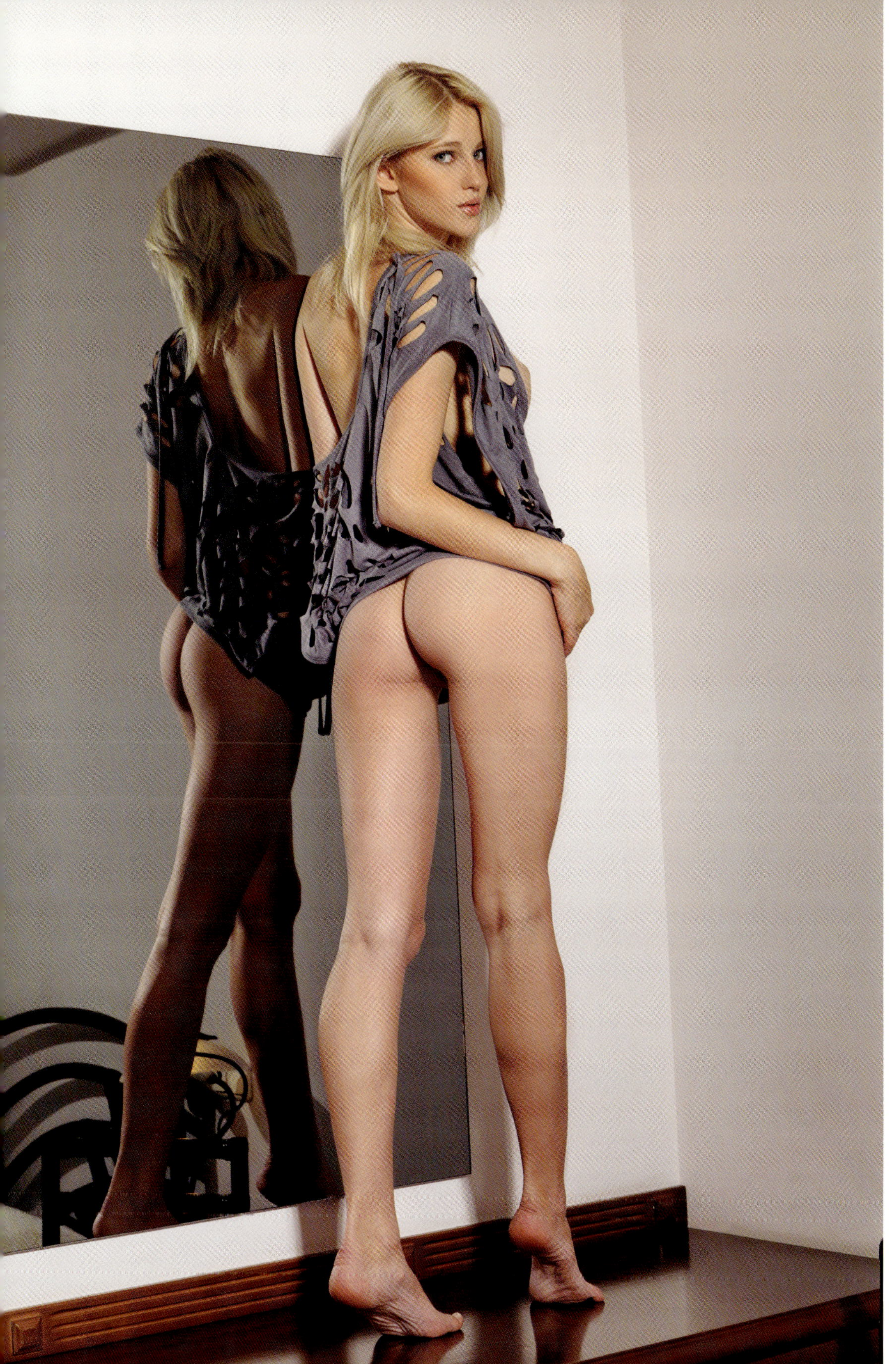

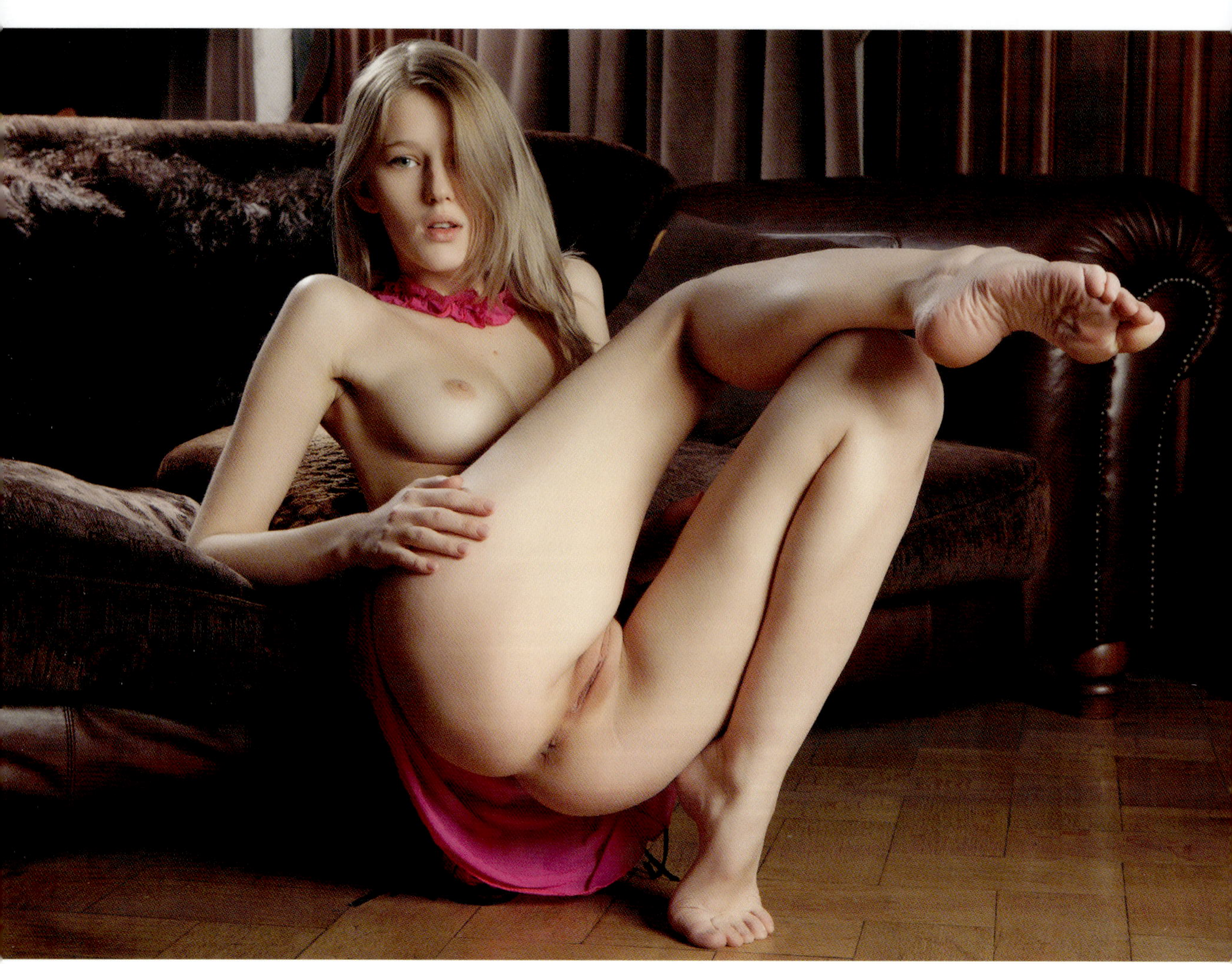

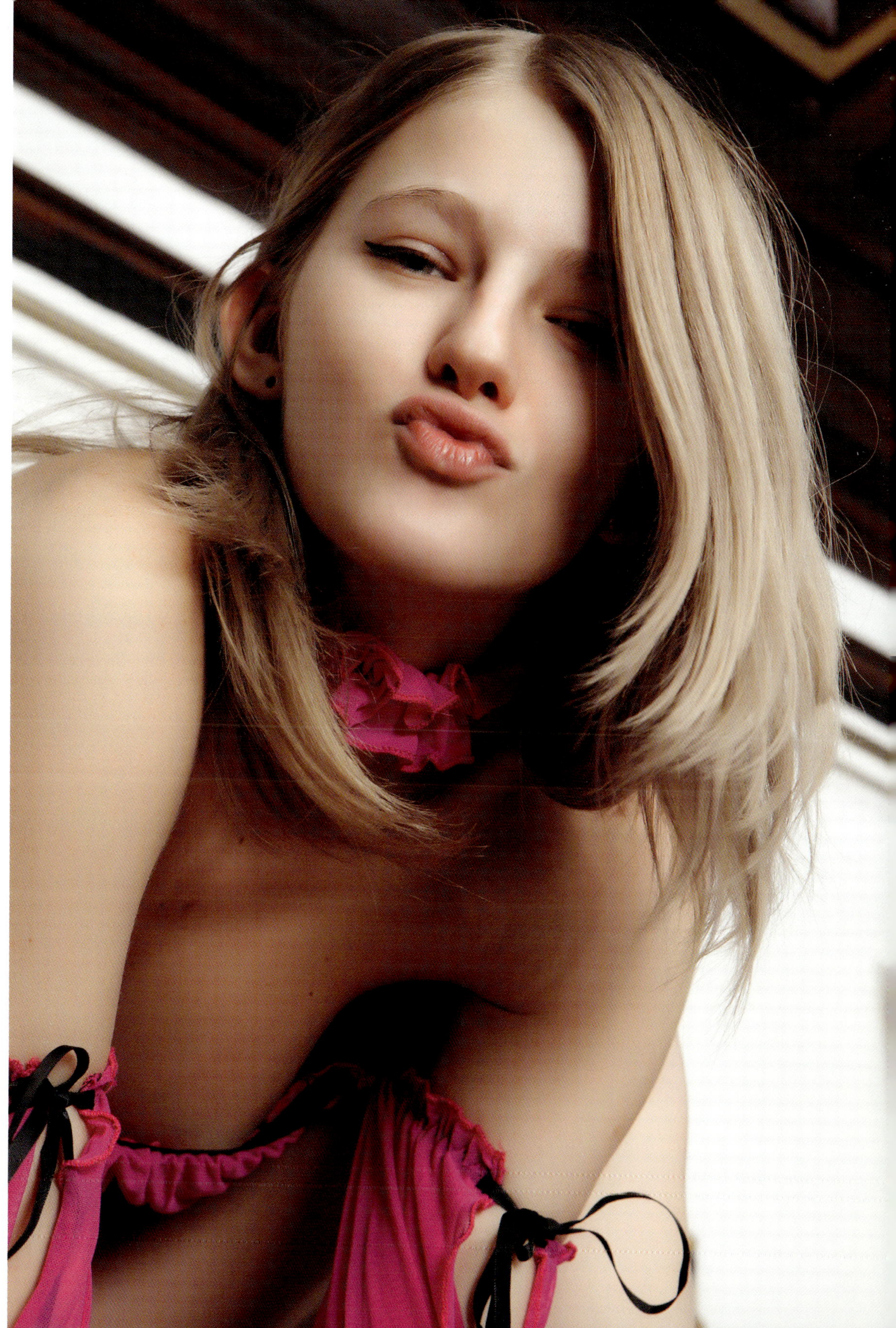

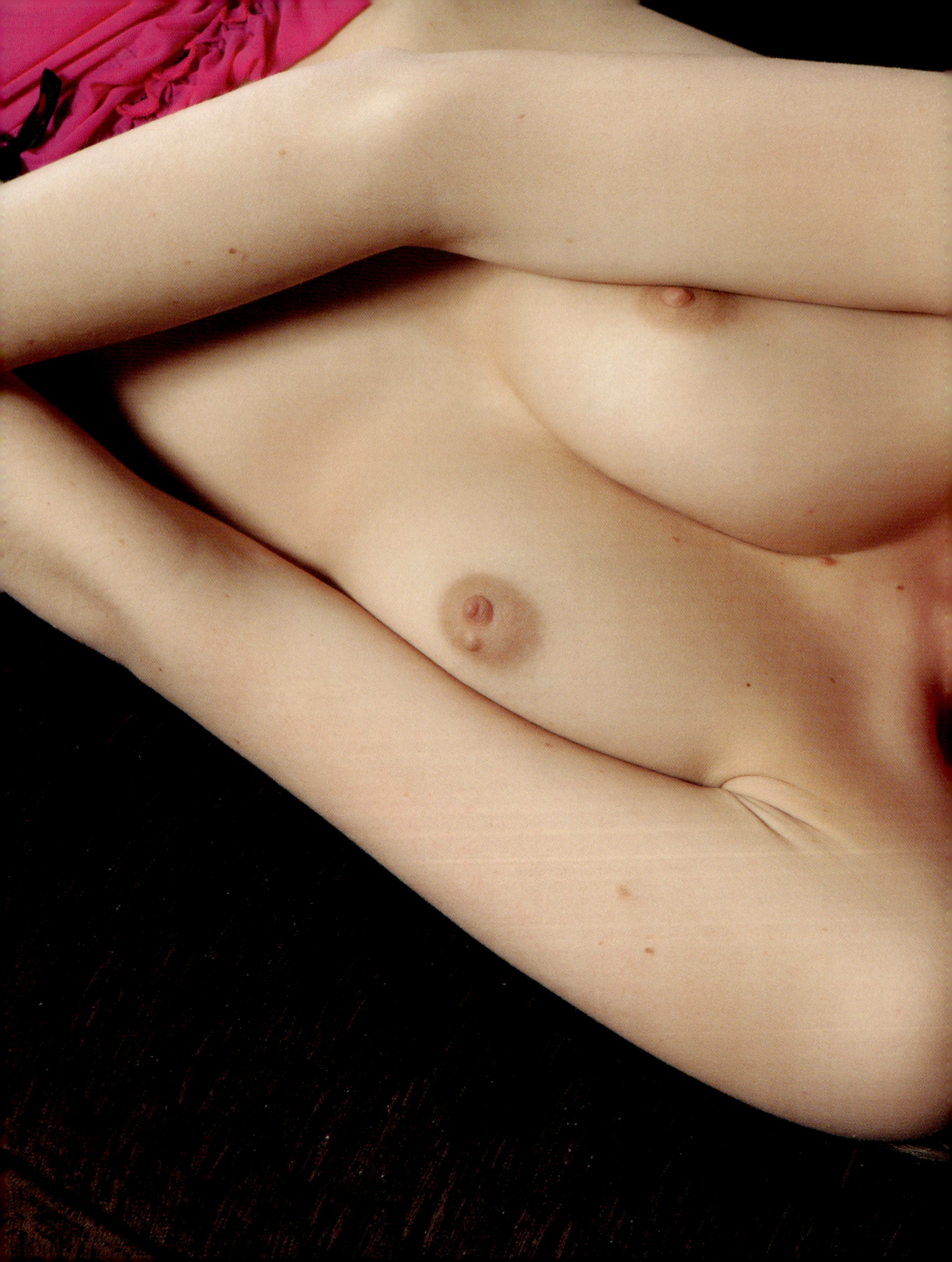

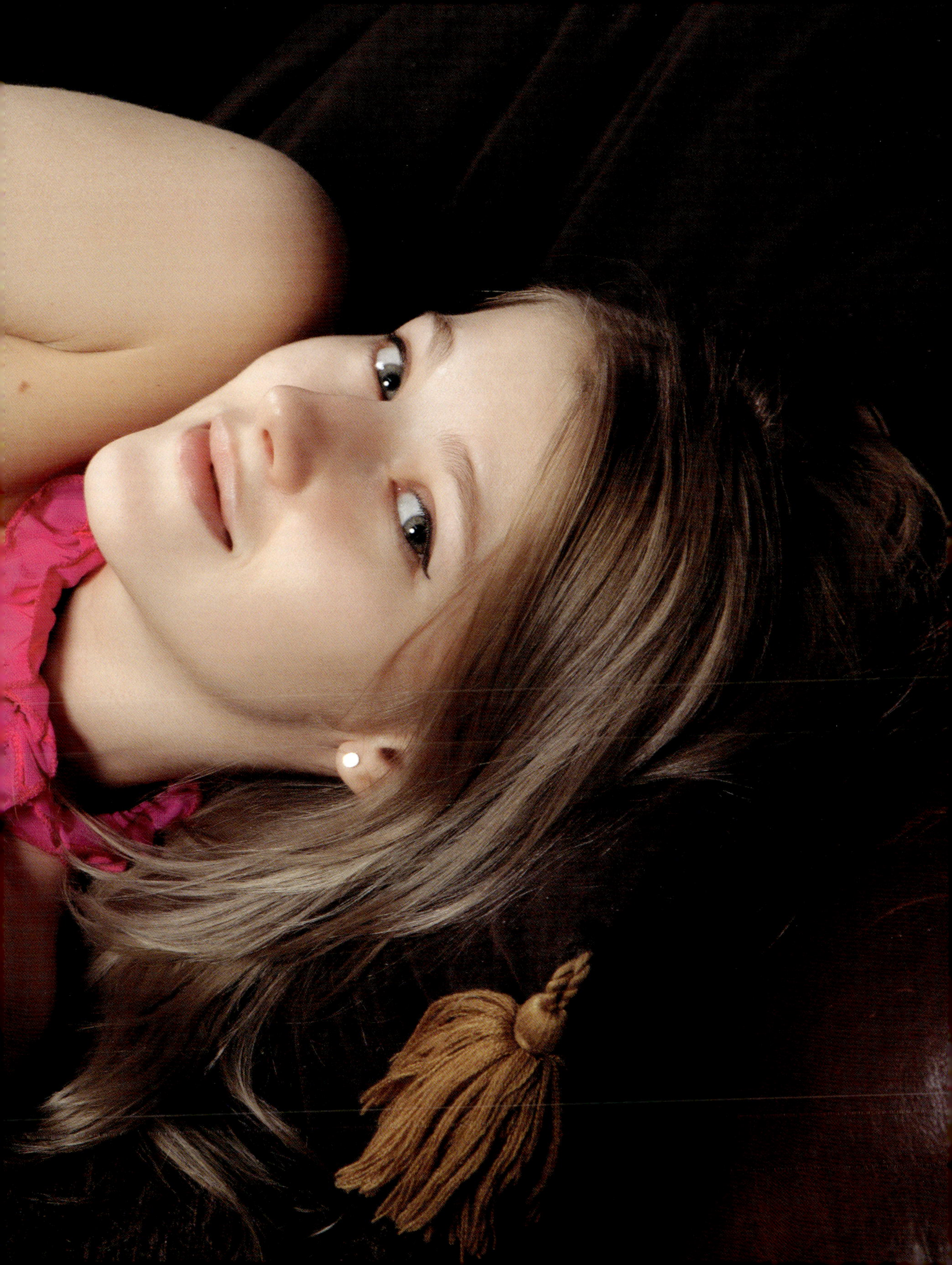

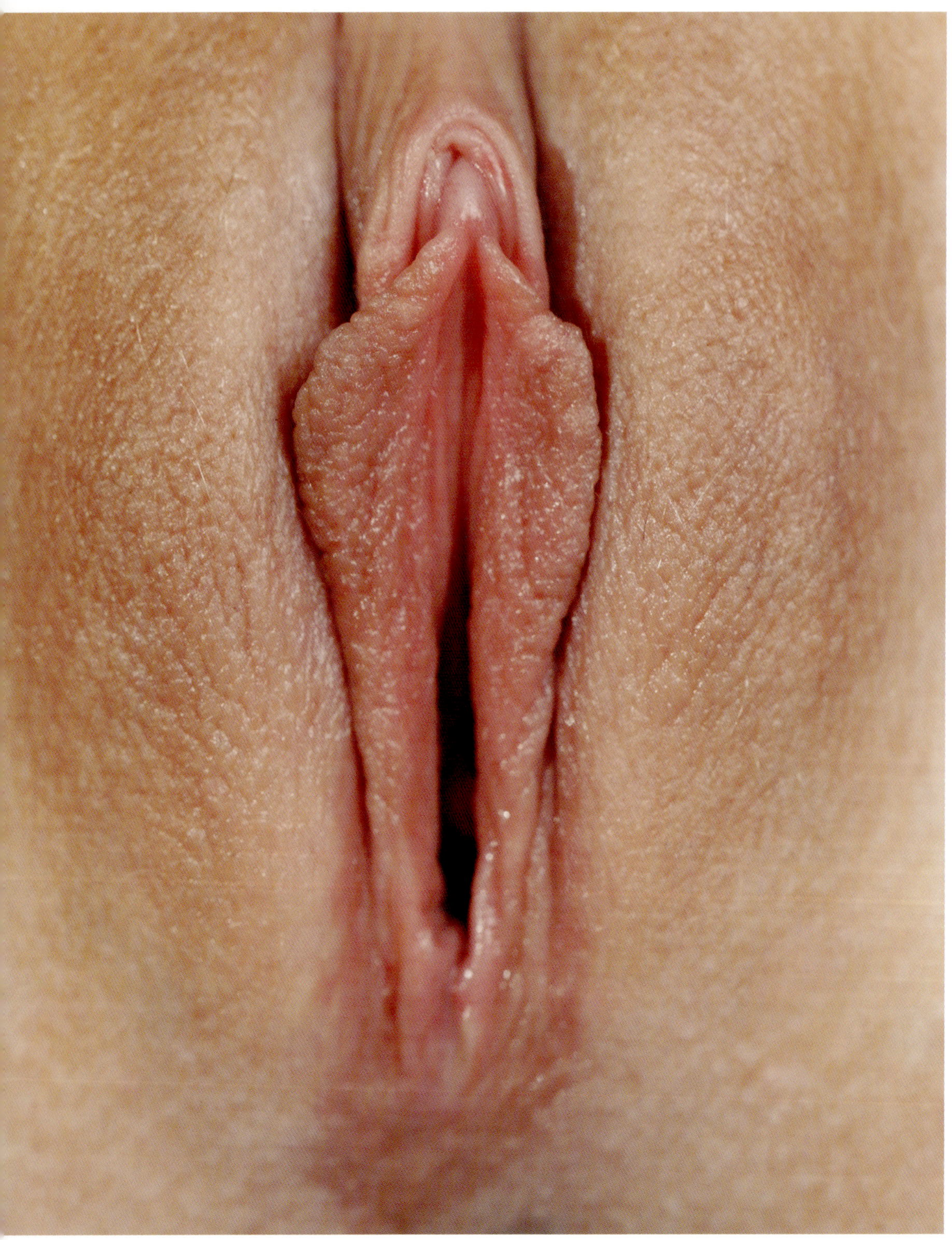

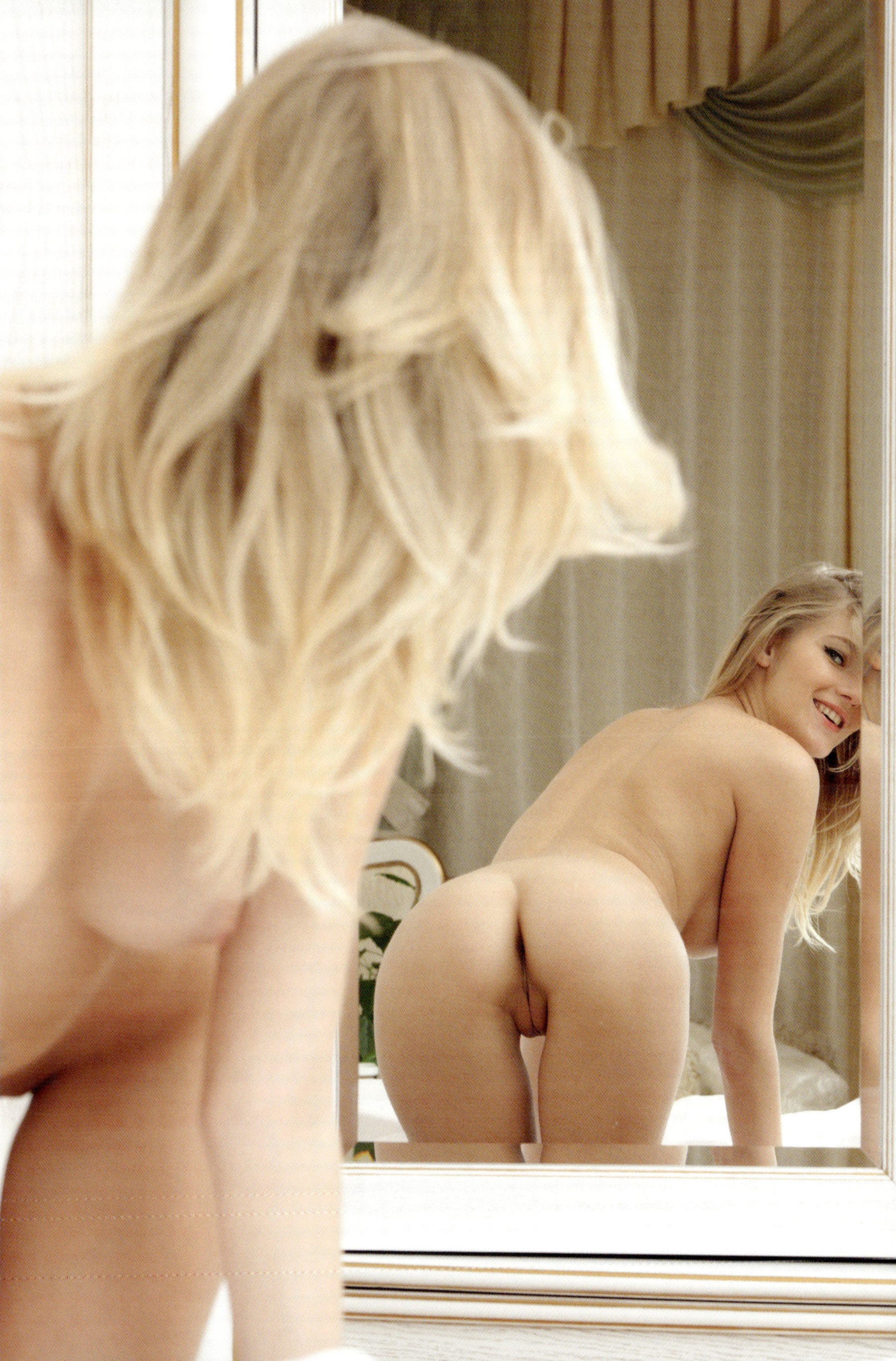

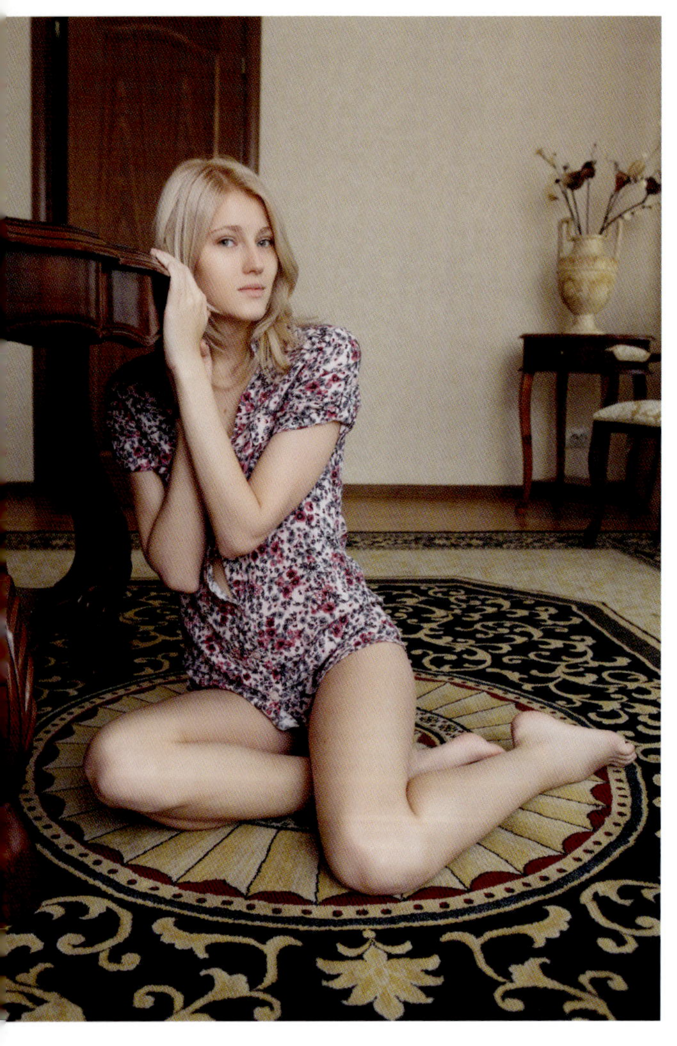

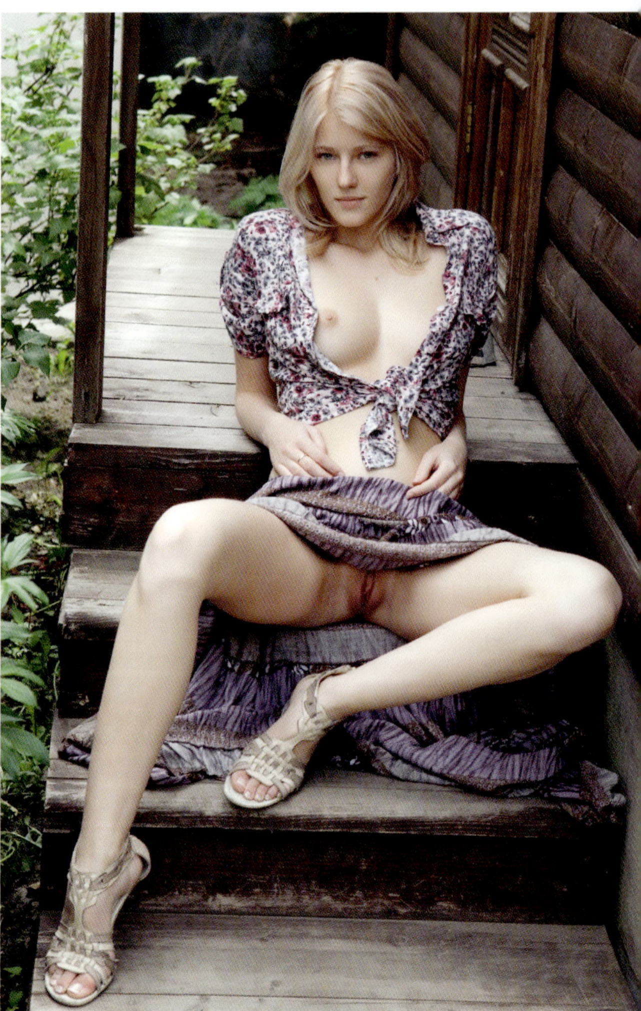

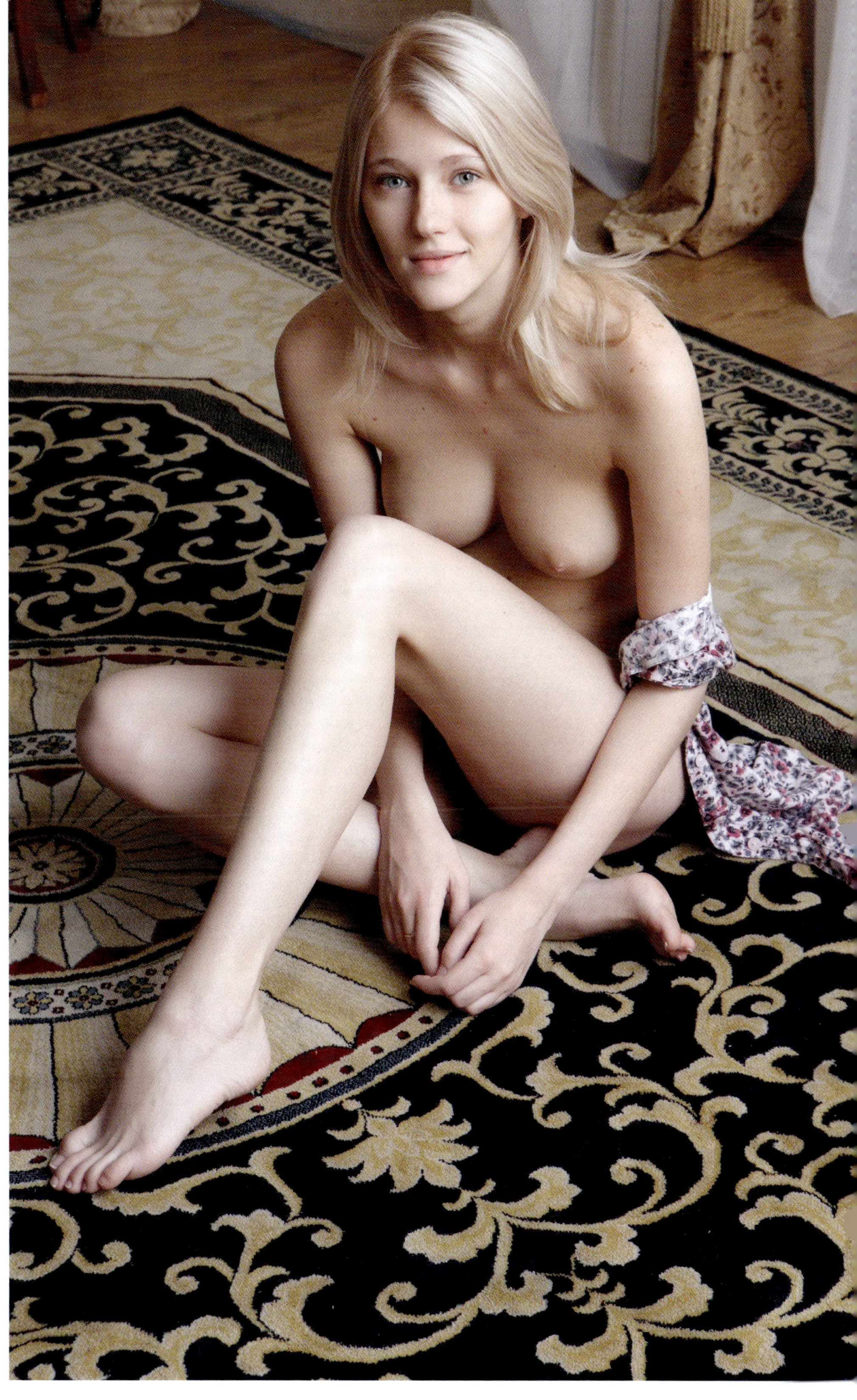

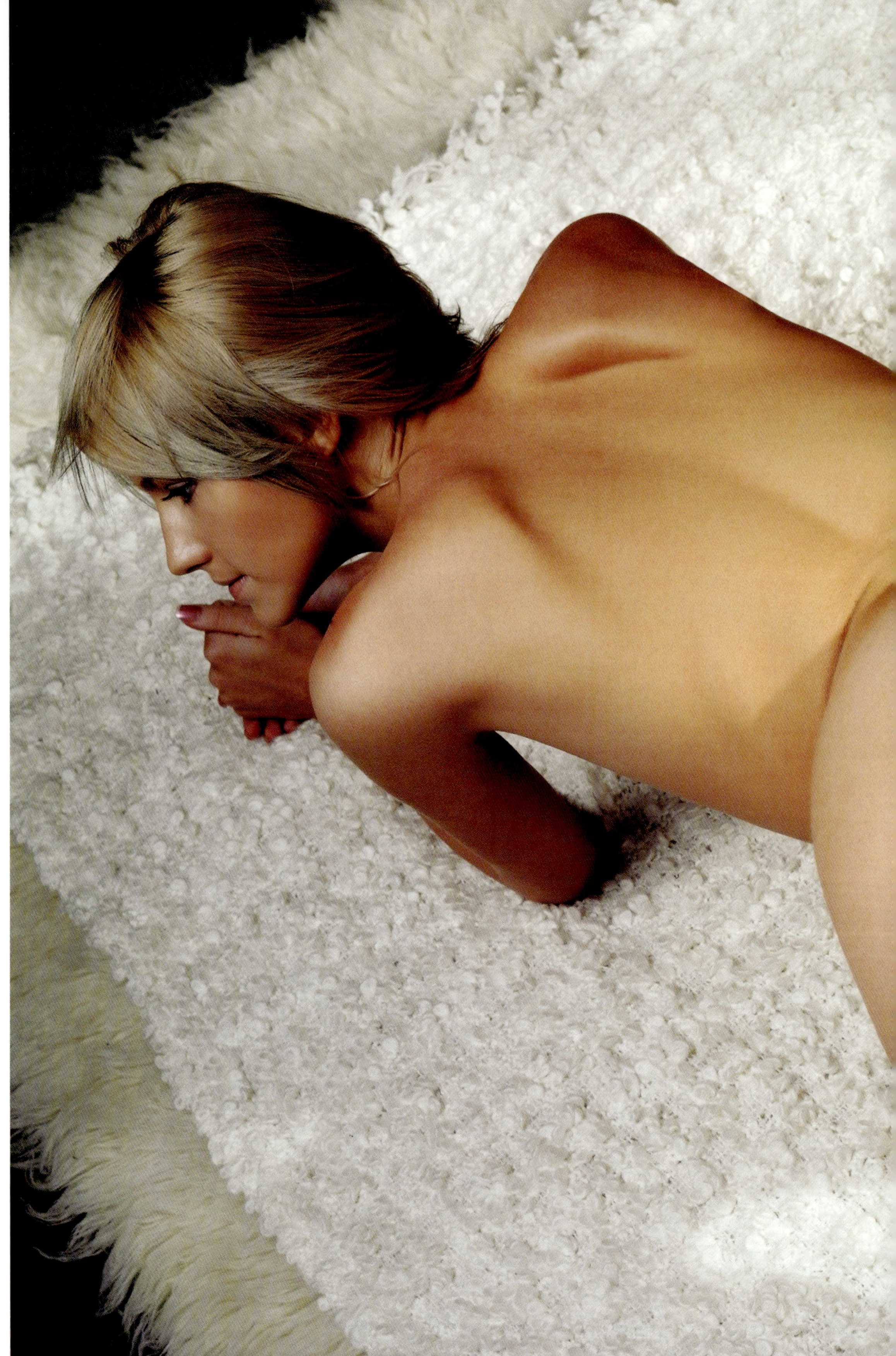

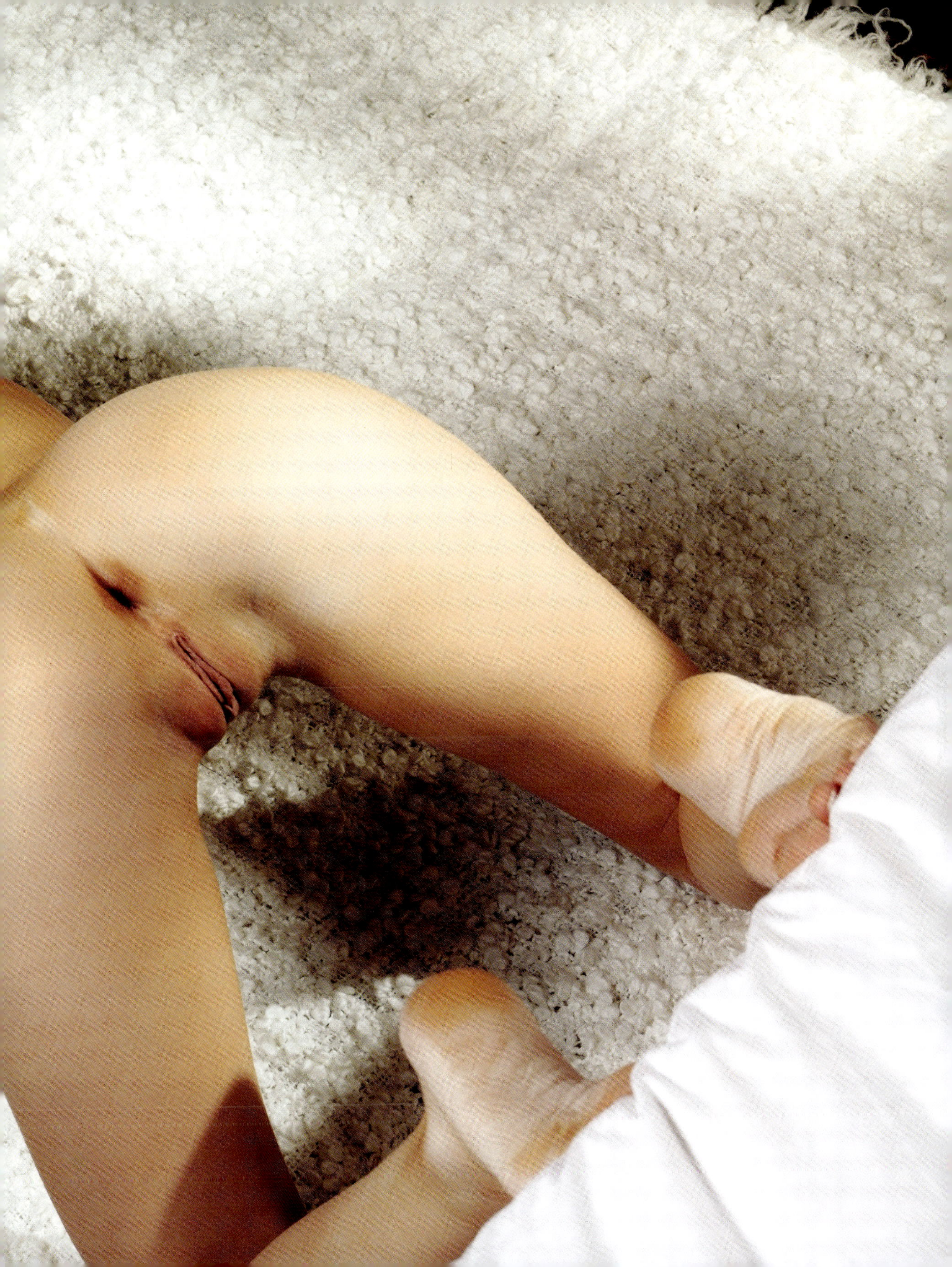

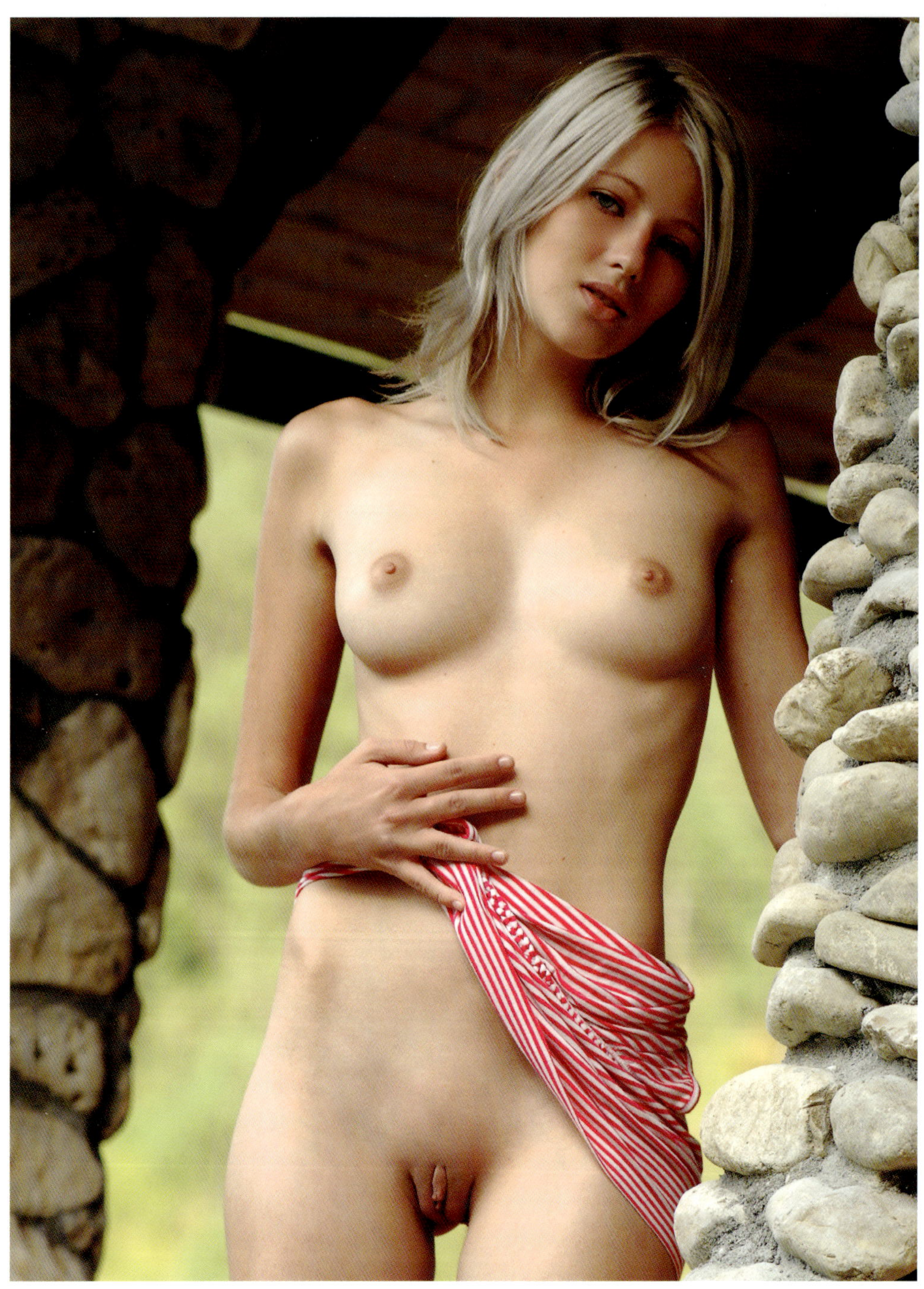

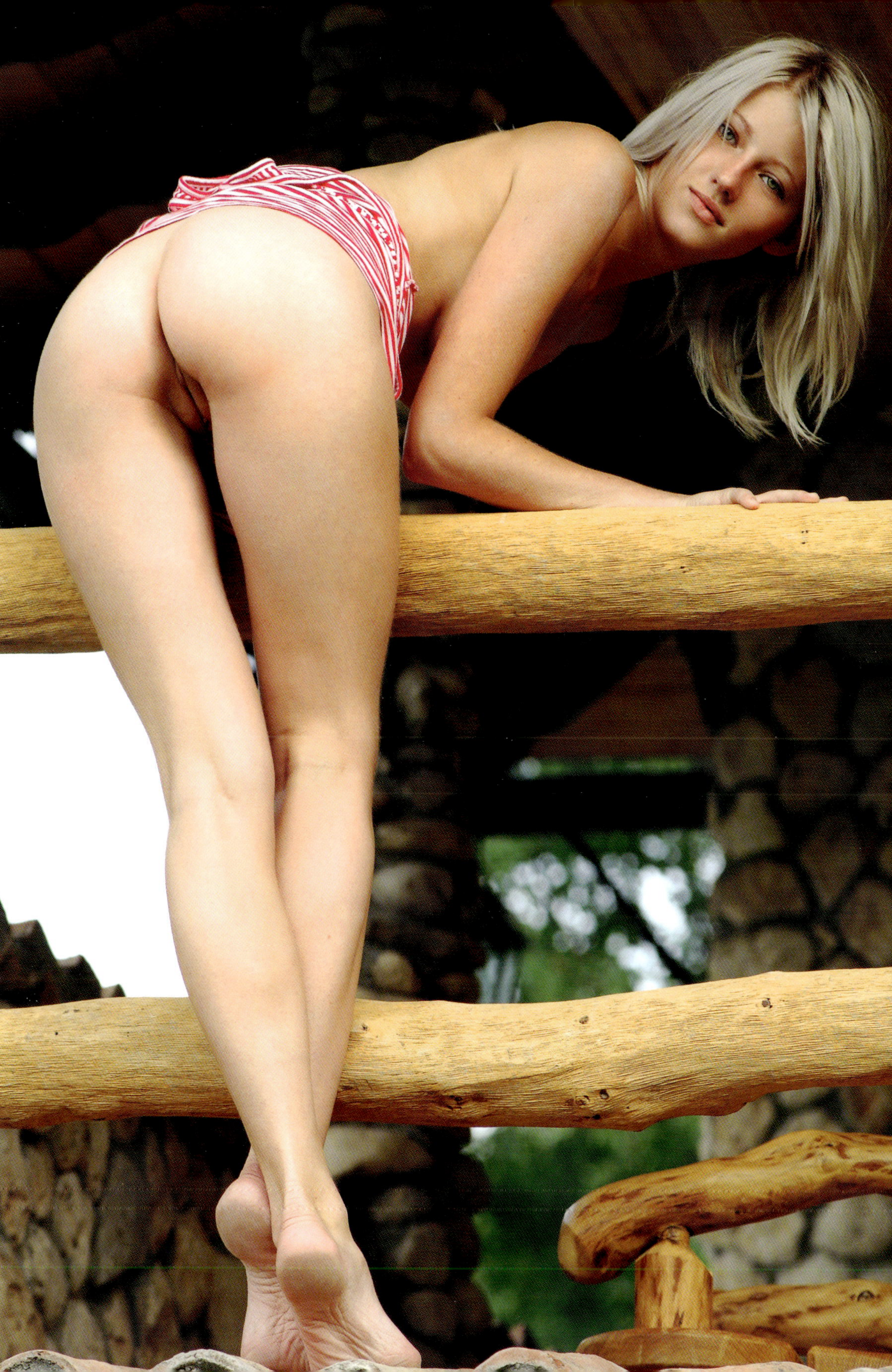

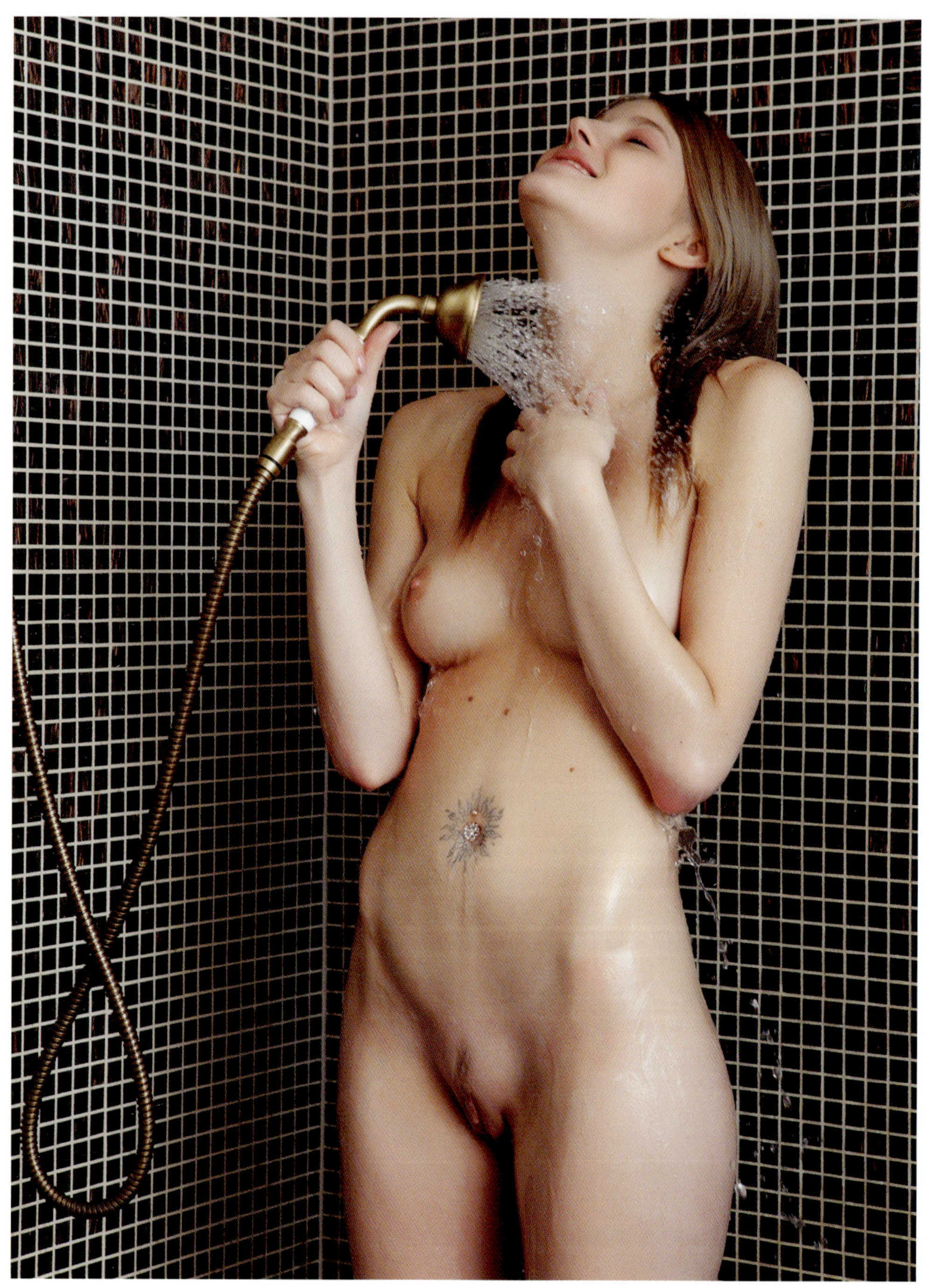

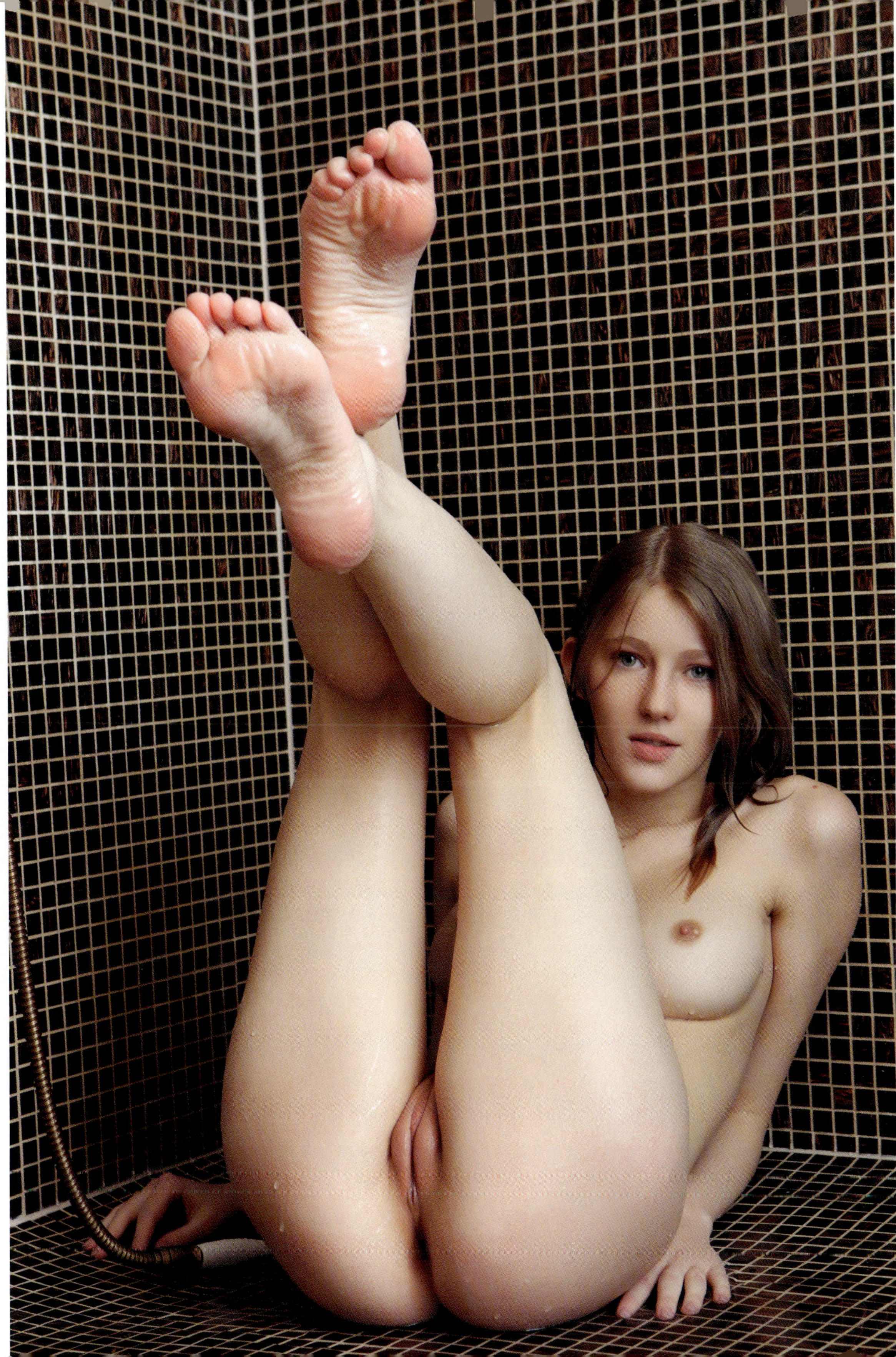

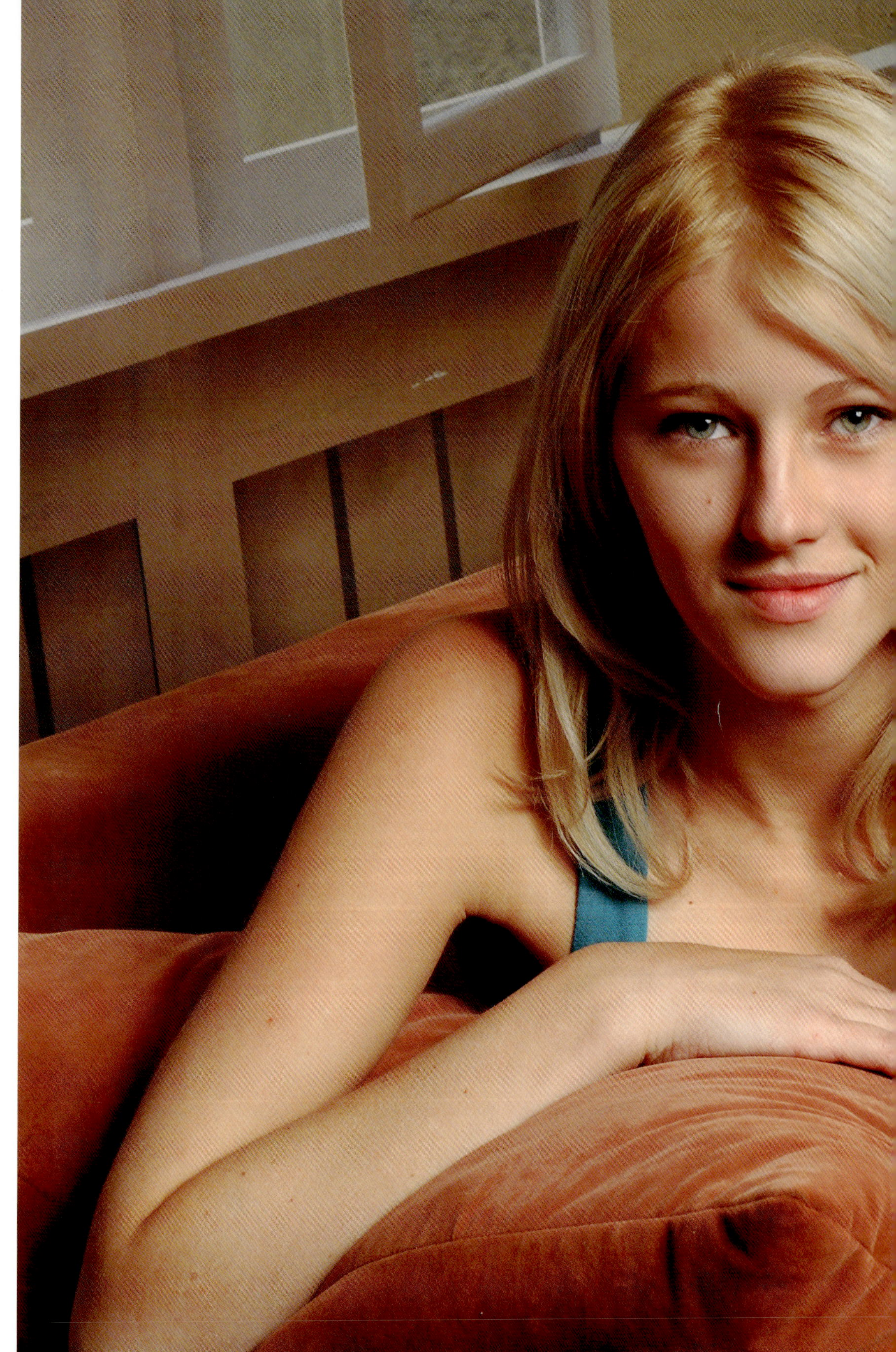

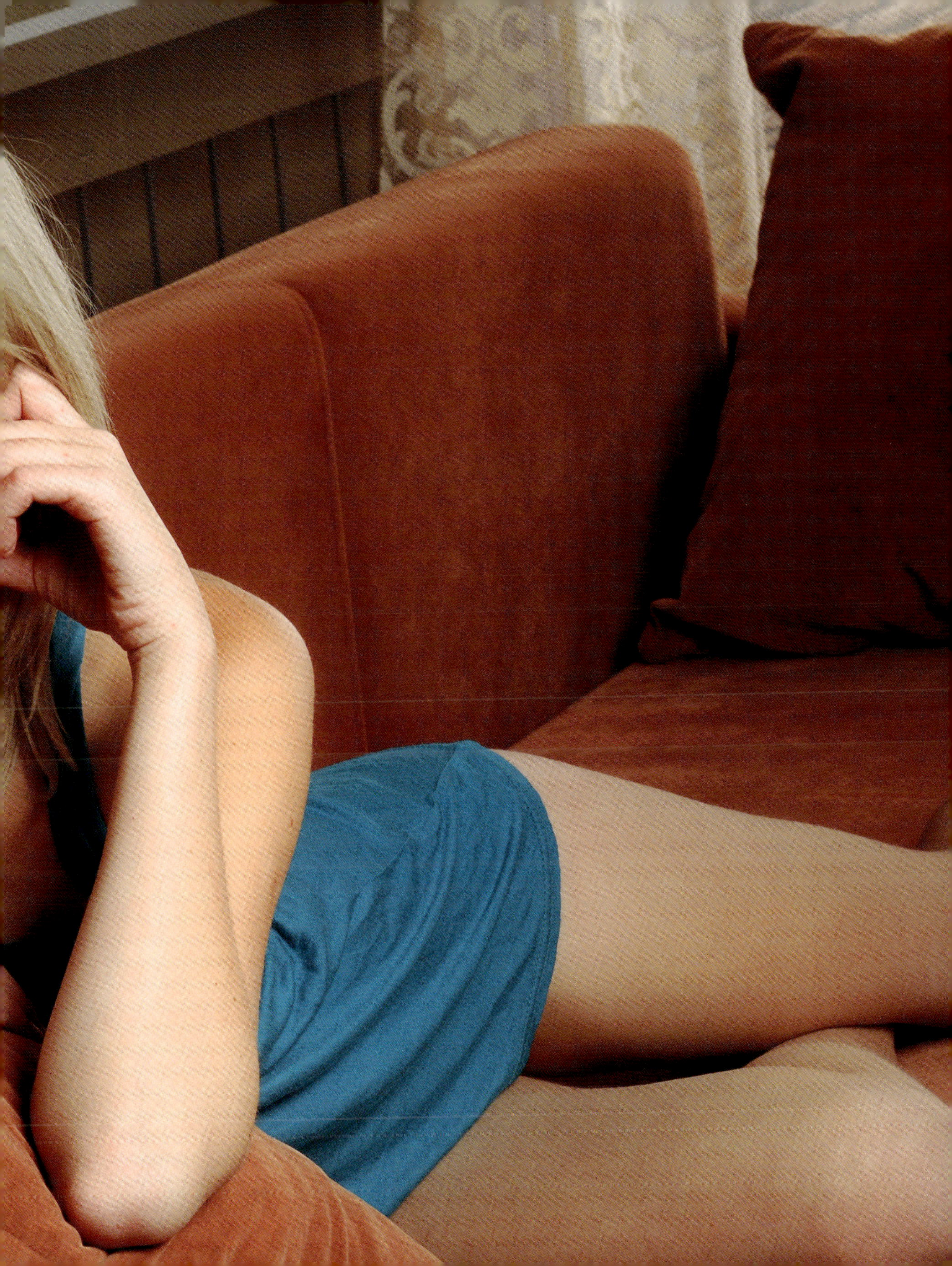

COLLECT THEM ALL: OUR MOST BEAUTIFUL

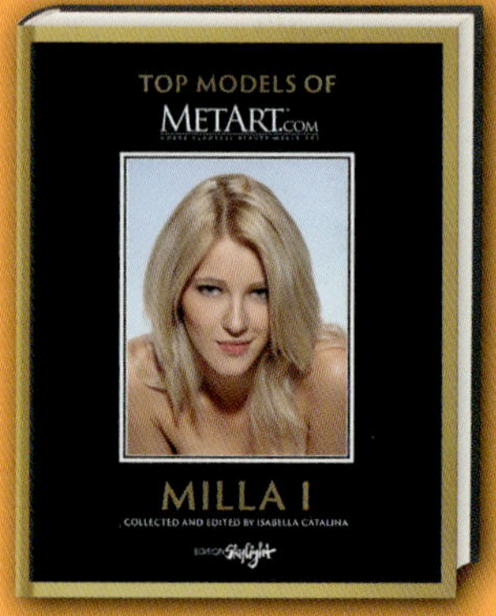

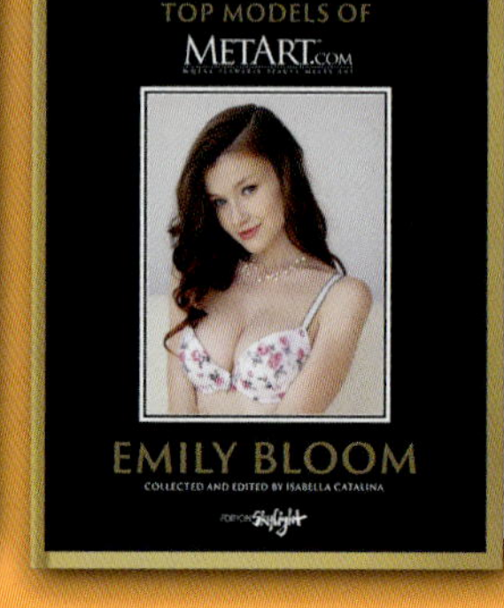

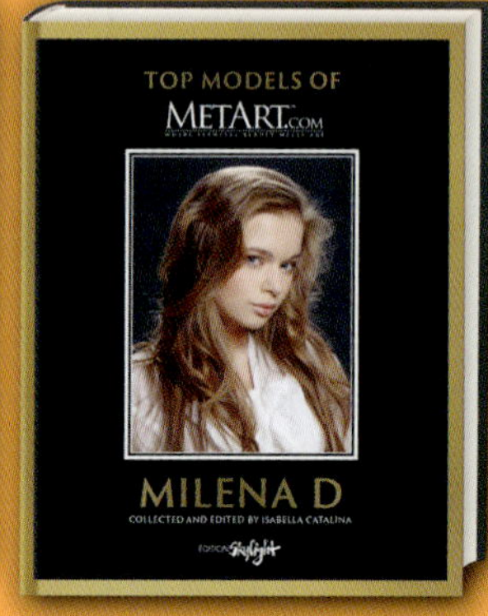

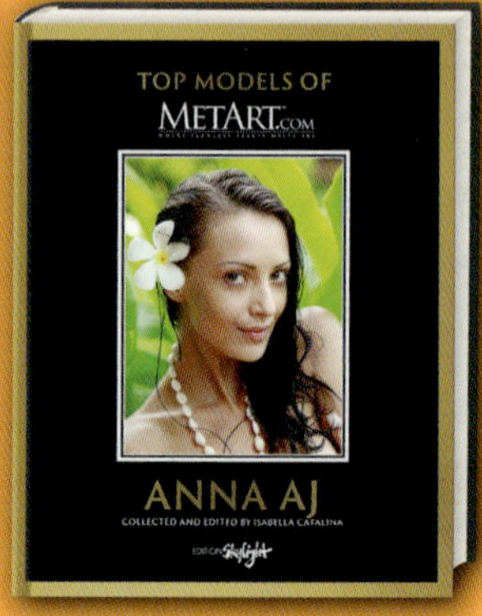

ISBN 978-3-03766-703-3   ISBN 978-3-03766-704-0   ISBN 978-3-03766-696-8   ISBN 978-3-03766-695-1

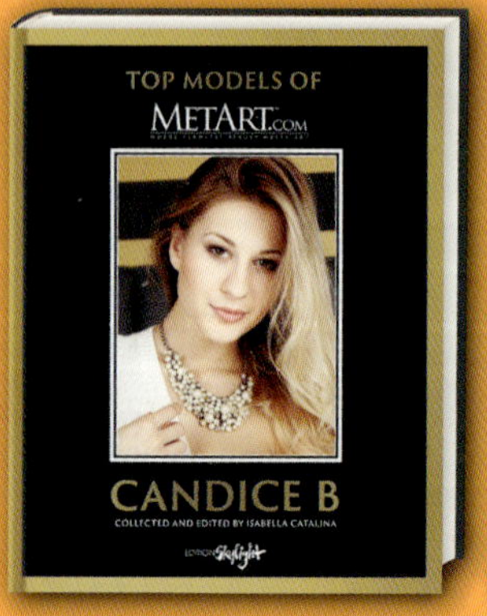

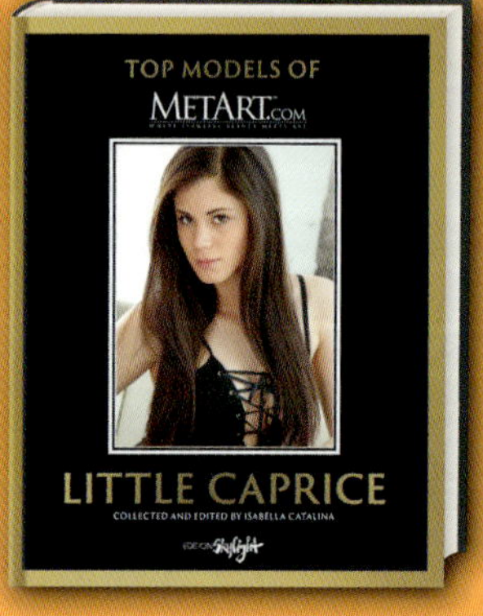

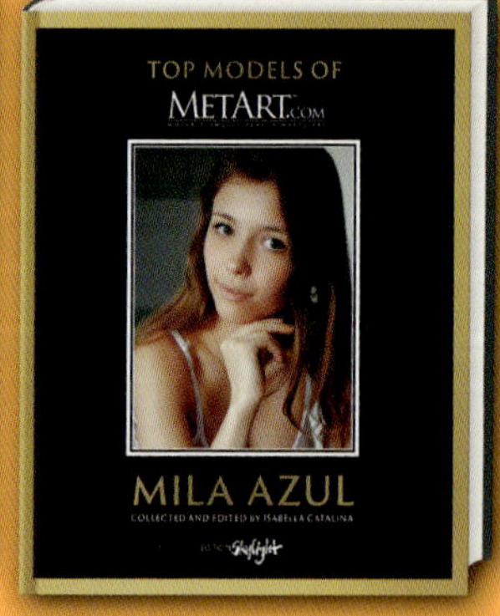

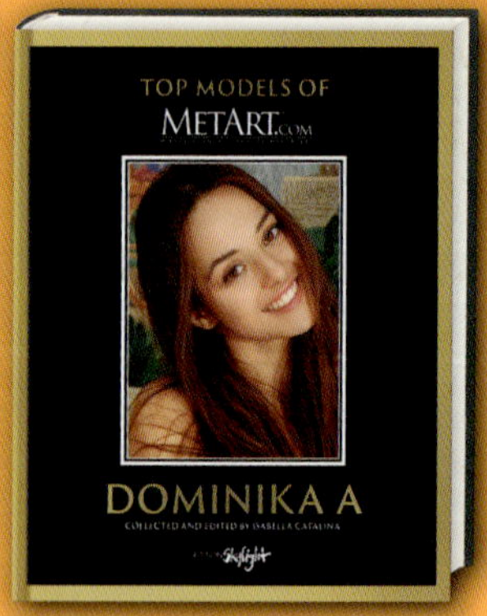

ISBN 978-3-03766-660-9   ISBN 978-3-03766-659-3   ISBN 978-3-03766-680-7   ISBN 978-3-03766-679-1

WWW.EDITION-SKYLIGHT.COM